BASEBALL
and the American Dream

OTHER BOOKS BY JOSEPH DURSO

Casey: The Life and Legend of Charles Dillon Stengel

The Days of Mr. McGraw

Amazing: The Miracle of the Mets

The All-American Dollar

Yankee Stadium: Fifty Years of Drama

Screwball

The Sports Factory

My Luke and I

Whitey and Mickey

Madison Square Garden: 100 Years of History

BASEBALL

and the American Dream

By
JOSEPH
DURSO

PUBLISHED BY **The Sporting News**

Published in the United States by THE SPORTING NEWS Publishing Co., 1212 North Lindbergh Boulevard, St. Louis, Missouri 63132.

Library of Congress Catalog Card Number: 86-70337

ISBN: 0-89204-220-6
10 9 8 7 6 5 4 3 2 1

First Edition

TABLE OF CONTENTS

This is proudly dedicated
to Anthony—
A great athlete, coach, teacher and brother.

Foreword

This is not exactly a history of baseball, and it is absolutely not an encyclopedia of baseball. It is a story—the story of the corner of American life occupied by baseball for the last century and a half.

It is about the people and the passions of a game that grew with the country, enlivened the national mood, stirred the national imagination and dramatized the national spirit. It did this because baseball came from the parks and yards of America and quickly became the game of America, the team game, the town game, your city against mine.

It followed the railroad south and the frontier west, and the jetliner from coast to coast and beyond. It traveled with the armies on both sides in the Civil War, barreled through the Gay Nineties into the new century, roared through the Twenties, starved through the Depression, suffered in the world wars and then, along with everybody else, soared into the era of television, space technology and the computer.

Baseball reflected these stages of the national life better than any other game and most other businesses. You didn't have to be gigantic to play it, brilliant to understand it or rich to follow it. You could visualize Babe Ruth and remember Henry Aaron, love the designated hitter or leave it, trade Tom Seaver for Nolan Ryan in bubblegum cards and, best of all, you could imitate Pete Rose's batting crouch as he chased Ty Cobb down the corridors of history.

Baseball reflected the language of America, and spiced it, too. Presidents, politicians, executives, generals and parents touched all the bases regularly so that nobody would be out in left field or caught off base in the greater pursuits of life. If you did it right, you hit a grand-slam home run; if not, you struck out. Your teacher might throw you a curveball on a test; or, for a change of pace, might just skip the quiz altogether, in which case you could take a seventh-inning stretch and contemplate the joys of life in the big leagues.

Baseball reflected the focus of American life, and what could be more visible than William Howard Taft in handlebar mustache and derby hat leaving the White House in 1910, showing up at the ball park and cheerfully flinging out the first ball, showing off the old Yale form and touching off a new presidential custom.

Every President from Taft to Calvin Coolidge saw Walter Johnson of the Washington Senators pitch at least one opening game. And Coolidge's vice president, Charles G. Dawes, saw the great Johnson pitch 15 innings in the 1926 opener (and win the game, 1-0). Woodrow Wilson once was the manager of the baseball team at Princeton, and Herbert Hoover at Stanford, and Warren G. Harding once owned a minor league team at Marion, O.

Franklin Roosevelt made it eight times on opening day, and Dwight D.

Eisenhower, who used to play the outfield at West Point, threw out the first ball seven times. Harry S. Truman, another seven-time "starter," was the first lefthander. Lyndon B. Johnson the hungriest (four hot dogs at the 1965 opener) and John F. Kennedy the cheeriest. He usually appeared hatless and coatless, fired fastballs from the presidential box and, after the Senators won the 1962 opener, told Manager Mickey Vernon: "I'm leaving you in first place. You take it from here."

That's identity and continuity and high visibility, and baseball has had all three. Its place on the public stage has been fixed, so to speak, just as its dimensions have been pretty much fixed. Bases 90 feet apart, three outs to an inning, nine innings to a game. The ball still has 108 stitches, it measures between 9 and 9¼ inches across two seams and weighs from 5 ounces to 5¼, and it's had the same measurements since 1872.

Revolutionary change has swept over the business of baseball in recent years, but that hasn't changed the place of the game on the public stage, either. It stays "the national pastime," and it plays out the tradition of "the American dream" in public view for all the world to see and to share—in Tennyson's words: to strive, to seek, to find, and not to yield.

★   ★   ★

The people who contributed to this story are too numerous to credit properly. But special acknowledgement must be made to Richard Waters, the president of The Sporting News and the chief executive muse of this book. Also, to Dick Kaegel, who was the editor of The Sporting News and of this project when it began; and Tom Barnidge, the present editor, and Lowell Reidenbaugh, the historian, whose passions are baseball and the Civil War.

Larry Halstead, the president of the Baseball Blue Book and a keeper of the archives in St. Petersburg, Fla., opened his own archives back to the days of Henry Chadwick, who was the first to tell the story of baseball.

Gene Kirby, who once shared a broadcasting booth with Dizzy Dean, helped to recreate the days of barnstorming teams and broadcasting. He has been an executive with three major league teams and is now a writer, broadcaster and commentator, but revels most in his rank as the world's leading scholar of Dean, pitcher and grammarian.

And special thanks to Joseph B. Stevens Jr., the chairman, chief executive officer and chief spirit of Harry M. Stevens Inc., and to Homer Rose Jr., senior vice president and historian of the company. They are grandsons of "Score-Card Harry," one of the stars of this story. They fed me insight and memories as nobly as Joe Stevens' family has been feeding the baseball multitudes for the last hundred years.

Joseph Durso

Base-ball dates its origin from the old English game of rounders, to which, however, it now bears as much resemblance as chess to draughts or "chequers."

—*DeWitt's Base Ball Guide, 1877.*

The main idea is to win.

—*John J. McGraw.*

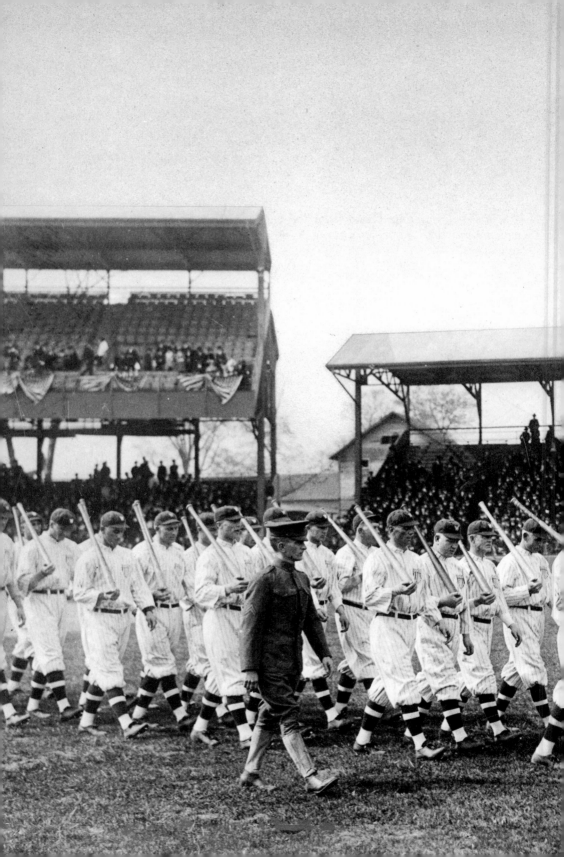

OVERLEAF: *Marching across the Griffith Stadium field in 1917, the Washington Senators put on a show of national support for the U.S. war effort. Leading the march was Franklin D. Roosevelt, then-Assistant Secretary of the Navy, who kept marching on.*

The age of Victoria

1

In 1862, Union Civil War prisoners in Salisbury, N.C., revived something they had left behind—base ball, the "town game."

CHAPTER 1

In 1876, Ulysses S. Grant was President, Victoria was Queen, Phineas Taylor Barnum was ringmaster, Alexander Graham Bell was on the line for the first time, John Joseph McGraw was 3 years old, Billy the Kid was 17 and not long for this world and George Armstrong Custer was gathering his Seventh Cavalry and his personal demons for a thrust into the valley of the Little Bighorn, where he would hurl 210 soldiers against 2,000 Sioux and Cheyenne warriors with the triumphant shout and soaring overstatement: "Hurrah, boys, we've got them."

It was only 11 summers after Appomattox, and 100 years after the Declaration of Independence. And commissions of planners and artists were at work orchestrating the celebration of the Centennial of the United States, which was caught somewhere between the Frontier and the Machine Age.

A few years earlier, Gen. Philip H. Sheridan calculated that 100 million bison were roaming the plains of Kansas and the Indian Territory. Now, they were being shot down so fast that only 1,091 would be counted 15 years later.

It was a time when waves of immigration would soon rocket the population of the United States from 50 million souls to 75 million in one generation. A time when cities were beginning to replace towns in the East, and towns were replacing the wilderness in the West. A time when life was being transformed by the typewriter, reinforced concrete, the Westinghouse air brake, celluloid and barbed wire—all of which made the scene in the decade after the Civil War.

In one revolutionary decade, cable cars were installed for the first time on the steep streets of San Francisco in 1873, Bell's telephone was unveiled three years later, and then came Mergenthaler's linotype and Parsons' steam turbine. Edison started lighting the cities in the 1880s, Daimler produced his high-speed internal combustion engine in 1886, Eastman his hand camera in 1888 and Otis his electric elevator a year later. And when Thomas B. Reed, the Speaker of the House of Representatives and 300-pound sage from Maine, was asked what was the greatest problem facing the American people at the time, he replied: "How to dodge a bicycle."

In Manhattan, brush-arc lamps were replacing the gas lights, cable cars were chasing the stage coaches off Broadway and the Third Avenue Elevated was rocking the sidewalks of New York with rattling trains overhead that coughed clouds of black smoke onto the cobblestone streets below.

Manhattan was still largely an island where horses pulled carriages by summer and sleds by winter, where people in tall hats pedaled bicycles with tall wheels, where boating people rowed or sculled along the rivers past low buildings. But it also was an island where the flat skyline began to gain dramatic peaks, where buildings began to climb higher than the five floors of the Equitable headquarters. By 1870, the Tribune Building reached an altitude of 285 feet. Eighteen years later, the Tower Building soared to 13 floors. And, by the turn of the century, thanks to Otis and his new elevator, the Park Row Business Building rose incredibly 29 stories above the streets of downtown New York.

For better, for worse, it was a time of whirling change, and not everyone believed it was better. Baltimore, for example, was known for good reason as Mob Town. And in later years, H.L. Mencken looked back on the old hometown and proclaimed: "Baltimore, by 1890, was fast degenerating, and so was civilization."

He may have been right, although Baltimore was still a Southern city with chickens in backyards, Civil War veterans on front stoops, high-tariff Republicans, Gladstonian collars, policemen in helmets and cigar-store Indians. It was world-famous for the roughness of its cobblestones, the quality of its crab cakes and the terseness of its Baltimore Sunpaper, which reported on page 1 with remarkable restraint one day in 1888: "Berlin, March 9—William I is dead aged 91."

But Baltimore, like New York and other cities and towns this side of the frontier, found that life was being revolutionized by invention, mechanized by industry and urbanized by both. It was an age of passion as well as prudence, and the Age of Victoria was not nearly so Victorian as later generations imagined. It was an age of growth and transition, from the East to the West in one sense, but from the farm to the city in another sense. But mostly, it was an age when the Republic was growing up and filling out, and turning the energy and emotion of its Civil War summers into new areas, new enterprises and new ways of life.

For a city like Baltimore, "fast degenerating" though it may have been, it was a time when the public could take its heroes and villians seriously and vent its passions violently, though not the way it did a few years earlier during the War Between the States. Mob Town was still a tough town, but not as tough as it had been when the Massachusetts regiment heading south had to fight its way through the streets. Or when the Confederates heading north had to fight and run to keep from being tarred and feathered.

Now, in the generation after the troops had left the cobblestone streets, Baltimore could devote its mind and its money to the better life, and it did. It was a town of famous churches, like the Watch Your Step Baptist Temple. Also, a town of famous saloons, like the one Jake Kilrain opened on Baltimore Street after losing to John L. Sullivan in 1889, and that was distinction enough for any saloon in any city. And it was a town that turned out: When the celebrated black fighter Joe Gans died, they had to hold his funeral in three phases in three churches to accommodate the waves of mourners.

But if the art of dying marked a society as firmly as the art of living, New York was not undone by Joe Gans and the torrent of worship that he prompted in Baltimore. And, if Baltimore turned out for a hero, Manhattan could turn out just as grandly for a villain. It was becoming part of the new life in the big city.

The star, in this case, was the Wall Street financier and finagler Jim Fisk. And, when he died of two well-aimed gunshot slugs, New York was able to forgive if not to forget his sins against the community: His body lay in state in the foyer of the Grand Opera House, while the mourners and the curious filed past and the Ninth Regiment Band rendered the dirges.

Now, that was a pretty handsome sendoff, even in the temper of the times, because Fisk and his partner Jay Gould had aroused storms of public indignation over their scandalous manipulating of the Erie Railroad and other money-making properties. But, also in the temper of the times, Jim Fisk did not pay the price for *that*. He paid it for Mrs. Helen Josephine Mansfield Salor, the comely divorcee from Boston who reigned as Jim Fisk's "hostess" in a brownstone behind the Grand Opera House on 23rd Street, between Eighth and Ninth avenues.

The "other man" was Edward S. Stokes, the equally free-spending member of a prominent New York family, who was allied with Fisk in some questionable business deals, but who was outraged at Fisk's success with Josie Mansfield.

Their paths crossed on the afternoon of January 6, 1872, on the long flight of stairs that Fisk was taking to the second floor of the Grand Central Hotel. He glanced up and saw Ned Stokes blocking his path with a pistol. Stokes fired twice at hand-shaking range, and Fisk toppled down the stairs.

As he lay dying in a room of the hotel, Fisk took the final salute and received the personal condolences of his allies Jay Gould and William Marcy Tweed, the "Boss," the man who came closest to owning New York. And, after the funeral, Harper's Weekly ran a cartoon by Thomas Nast that depicted Gould and Tweed mourning at the grave, with Gould intoning: "All the sins of the Erie lie buried here."

Not quite. There was no greater public sinner, and no riper example of the excesses of society in transition, than the "Boss," along with "Slippery Dick" and the "Forty Thieves." When it came to ripping off the city's cash, they were giants in their own time: Tweed, the chief of Tammany Hall, the Democratic organization of New York County; "Slippery Dick" Connolly, formally Richard B. Connolly, the city controller, and the "Forty Thieves," the obliging members of the City Council.

Cuspidors for the City Council chamber were sold for $190 apiece. Police jobs and transfers went for anywhere from $300 to $15,000 (captain, midtown). Tweed, a onetime cabinetmaker, stocked the city's armories with phantom chairs and phantom services, and billed for millions. He billed the city $170,729 for chairs alone, and $432,264 for carpentry; and, as the *pièce de résistance*, $2,870,000 for plastering a new county courthouse.

The Boss in due time was booked, and convicted, in his lavishly unplastered county courthouse. The toll was 12 months in jail, which he served, plus a fine of just $12,500, of which he paid $250, with legal fees of $500,000 for the whips who had arranged for him to beat the rap. But two years later, he was arrested again, and this time was escorted to the Ludlow Street Jail, which he also had built and billed for.

The dramatic changes in Tweed's public standing were occasioned by some relentless newspaper work by George Jones, the editor of The New York Times, and by Nast, who drew his first "Tammany Tiger" cartoon for Harper's Weekly on November 11, 1871. They found, and reported, that Tweed was raking it in with both hands.

When Tweed was finally hauled off to his Ludlow Street cell, The Times reported the Boss' downfall in two stories on page 1 on Thursday, March 9, 1876. One was a background piece titled "History of The Ring Fraud," and it related 20 years of thievery that "steadily and stealthily" had hornswoggled the city. The other piece was the news story, headed simply: "A Verdict Against Tweed."

"The proceedings in the suit against Tweed," it said, skipping his first name, "came to an end, as far as the jury trial was concerned, yesterday with the rendering of a verdict in favor of the people for $4,719,910.35, with interest amounting to $1,817,177.03, making altogether the sum of $6,537,087.38, or about two-thirds of the amount sued for. The announcement made that Judge Westbrook would charge the jury yesterday had the effect of drawing a large crowd together."

The crowd turned out for the Boss, as it had turned out for different reasons and different moods for Jim Fisk and Joe Gans. And, Tweed did the jail scene in high style, too, emerging in the evening with the warden and turnkey, who accompanied him in a carriage to his Madison Avenue mansion so that he might dine in the customary splendor. He took advantage of their good nature one evening, slipped away and finished the trip in Spain. However, he was identified there by a Nast cartoon, was brought back on a Navy cruiser and died in April 1878.

Civilization may have been degenerating by then, or soon thereafter, as Mencken suggested later, but at least it was degenerating with gusto. It also was showing a distinct turn toward the pastimes and pursuits that the city life made possible, and that the new industrial life probably made necessary.

When Charles Dickens first visited the United States in 1842, he found it to be a crude and clamorous place where people "ate piles of indigestible matter." But, by the time Dickens returned 25 years later, things had improved. At a dinner in honor of the renowned English author, Delmonico's offered these items of interest, to say nothing of elegance, on its menu:

Among the *hors d'oeuvres chauds: timbales à la Dickens*. Among the *poissons: saumon à la Victoria*, or *bass à l'italienne* with *pommes de terre Nelson*. Among the *relevés: agneau farci à la Walter Scott*. Among the *entrées: petits pois à l'anglaise* and *côtelettes de grouses à la Fenimore Cooper*. The decorations included such creations as *Temple de la Littérature, Les Armes Brittaniques, Pavillon International, Colonne Triomphale* and, for the local horsey set, *The Stars and Stripes*.

New York was now a seaport of nearly a million persons, and it was beginning to bloom as the center of the urban life that was transforming America, and of the after-hours life that was enlivening America.

By 1876, Central Park was basically laid out, with its lakes and reservoirs and carriage drives, and its half-million plants and trees. Farther downtown, the city's public life developed along the north-and-south avenues skirting Madison Square. To the south, down Broadway, the "Ladies' Mile" of fashion was anchored by ornate new department stores like A.T. Stewart & Co., Arnold Constable, James McCreery & Co. and Lord & Taylor. Great restaurants, hotels and clubs lined the streets, and became the targets of the night life that spilled out of the theaters and, beginning in 1879, the new Madison Square Garden.

Down near City Hall, the politicians and judges gathered at the Astor House, with its celebrated rotunda restaurant. Nearby were French's Hotel, Nash and Crooks, Lovejoys, and the United States, at Pearl and Fulton streets. The Cosmopolitan, on Chambers, stood conveniently close to the boats for Boston. At Canal and Centre streets, there was Earle's Hotel; at Prince and Broadway, the brownstone Metropolitan. At Waverly Place, the St. Nicholas; at Eighth Street, the Sinclair House; and, at 11th and Broadway, the St. Denis, neatly situated on the southern flank of the "Ladies' Mile" of stores and shops.

At Union Square, the Morton House became an oasis for the actors who lived and worked in the area. The Clarendon still remembered that its earlier guests had included Thackeray and the Prince of Wales, and the Westminster boasted a guest list headed by Charles Dickens himself. At Fifth Avenue and Eighth Street stood the Brevoort; at 23rd Street, in the heart of what was then the restaurant and theater row, the Fifth Avenue Hotel, which also served as the headquarters for the Republican Party in New York. It had a recess in the lobby that came to be known as the Amen Corner, presumably because the party faithful flocked there to say "amen" to the party policy.

The farther north you traveled, the farther you were likely to travel up the social ladder. Two bedrooms and a parlor ran $30 a day at the Fifth Avenue Hotel, and more to the north. At Fifth and 26th, across Madison Square from Gilmore's Garden and its successor, Madison Square Garden, the Brunswick Hotel was where the crowd headed after watching the springtime and autumn parades of the Coaching Club. Across the street: Delmonico's, not far from the twin marble palaces, the Albemarle and the

Hoffman House, the latter with its world-renowned bar embellished with murals of nude beauties painted by the Parisian artist Adolphe William Bouguereau.

President Grover Cleveland in later years liked to stay at the Victoria Hotel whenever he visited New York. But a block or so to the east, and extending to the north, several less elegant hotels catered to the acting and sporting types. The Oriental drew the theater crowd. The Gedney House became home to Tom Sharkey and Charlie Mitchell, the prize fighters. And the Vanderbilt, at 42nd and Lexington, became the headquarters for the one and only John L. Sullivan.

Men's social clubs were sprouting around town, too, and they reflected the fact that society was growing more stratified. It also was growing a little peculiar, as Cleveland Amory noted many years later in "Who Killed Society?":

"The Union League, a Republican club dating from 1863, was formed in answer to the fact that a Confederate Secretary of State was allowed to resign from the Union Club when, according to Union leaders, he should have been expelled. The Manhattan, originally a Democratic club, was formed a year later in answer to the answer.

"The Knickerbocker (1871) was formed because its members felt the Union was taking too many out-of-towners and wanted a club limited to men of Knickerbocker ancestry. The Metropolitan (1891) was formed because the elder J.P. Morgan could not get a friend of his into the Union, and thereupon, in the Morgan manner, built his own club.

"The Brook (1903) was formed because two young Union Clubbers had been expelled for having attempted, unsuccessfully, upon the bald head of the Union's most revered patriarch, to poach an egg."

"The Century," Amory reported, "was formed in the belief that the Union was slighting intellectual eminence. 'There's a club down on 43rd Street,' said one Union Clubber, 'that chooses its members mentally. Now, isn't that a hell of a way to run a club?' "

It probably was. But then, there was no explaining the behavior of a lot of people in those days of discovery. When P.T. Barnum imported the Swedish singer Jenny Lind to New York, he did it with so much fanfare that 20,000 people thronged the pier to witness the arrival of the 30-year-old blond nightingale. A few of them even fell off the pier in the crush. Then, when Miss Lind made her debut at Castle Garden on the Battery, she was greeted by a crowd of 6,000 persons who had paid as much as $25 for a ticket on the black market.

"It is amazing how people spend their money," said James Fenimore Cooper, marveling at the tide of the arts sweeping into town. "Twenty or thirty dollars to hear Jenny Lind are paid by those who live from hand to mouth. I cannot consent to pay thirty dollars for a concert, and they are welcome to their ecstasies."

Cooper would have been astounded at how people paid their money to see Lola Montez, who advanced from the corps de ballet of a Paris theater into high favor with the King of Bavaria, Ludwig I, an elderly patron of the arts, who gave her the title of Countess of Lansfield. He also gave her a voice in the affairs of state, until he was forced to abdicate. Lola, also forced to abdicate, didn't waste time wringing her hands in Bavaria. She joined the rush of culture to New York, filled the Broadway Theater as a dancer at twice the regular price for tickets, later played the lead in a Broadway play titled "Lola Montez in Bavaria," and finally became a lecturer on the subjects of beauty, love and European politics, which touched all the bases of her remarkable career.

On the same stage of the Broadway Theater where Lola had danced, the great tragedian Edwin Forrest handled 18 roles, from Macbeth and Hamlet to Othello and Richard III. He also carried on a running feud with the English actor William Charles Macready, and it escalated so ferociously that gangs of toughs descended on the Astor Place Opera House to drive Macready from the stage. In the riot that followed, the Seventh Regiment opened fire on the mob, killing 22 persons and injuring many more.

Forrest wasn't quite finished. He then accused his wife of infidelity, and sued her for divorce. Next, he turned on his old friend Nathaniel P. Willis, editor of Home Journal magazine, and even horsewhipped him in Washington Square. And, to clinch the point, he then got into the habit of taking curtain calls on stage and punctuating them with speeches denouncing both his wife and Willis.

★   ★   ★

On February 2, 1876, surrounded by the thespians, international divas, heavyweight champions and other culture stars of the day, a small group of men gathered in the Grand Central Hotel on Broadway.

It was Wednesday, and a stormy sort of winter's day with gales whipping New York and other cities along the Eastern Seaboard. The New York Times reported on page 1, under the heading "Synopsis and Probabilities," that the weather was packing a kick:

"A very low barometer is now central over the Middle Atlantic States, having advanced eastward over Illinois, and stormy weather is prevailing from the lower lakes to the Atlantic coast. The Cumberland and Ohio rivers have continued falling. The Mississippi River has risen nine inches at Cairo, and three inches at Memphis, and fallen seven inches at Vicksburg and 18 inches at St. Louis."

The national debt, which occasioned page 1 mention in those days, was reported from Washington as no great debt at all: "The balance in the Treasury is now $69,465,085 in coin and $10,343,051 in currency." The bottom line, the dispatch said, was that there had been "marked improvement" in reducing the debt in the last year.

But then, this was an election year, as frequent reports from around the country made clear. In Michigan and Pennsylvania, the Republican state committees were holding meetings to organize state conventions to elect delegates to the National Convention in Cincinnati. And a story from Detroit put things into partisan perspective this way:

"It was also ordered that this (state) convention should elect the next State Central Committee, and then all invite the participation of all who view with apprehension the possibility of the restoration of Democratic ascendancy, no matter what their recent political affiliation may have been."

Whatever their recent political affiliation may have been, some people were more concerned on that winter's day with finding a job or a place to live. In Victorian language and cadence, one job-seeker placed this classified ad in The Times: "An American lady of refinement and capability desires a responsible position in a gentleman's family; can take entire charge of a household; best of references given."

Another put it this way, with appropriate notice given of her religious bearing: "Chambermaid and seamstress: by a Protestant young woman; thoroughly experienced as chambermaid and a first-class seamstress; cuts and fits, operates on Wheeler and Wilson machines, and can furnish references that will bear the strictest investigation."

The Stuyvesant House hotel, on Broadway at 98th Street, advertised "all modern improvements" in its rooms, at $4 a day, *with board*. And, if that weren't enough of an inducement, the hotel described itself as being situated "near theaters and depots," which may have been a bit of an exaggeration at Broadway and 98th.

Overseas on that February day, things were boiling in Turkestan, and a dispatch from London told why:

"The Times Berlin special this morning contains the following: The St. Petersburg MIR says that the Russian authorities in Turkestan, finding their 40,000 men insufficient to suppress the rebellion, have asked for the immediate dispatch of 5,000 reinforcements to Tashkent. According to the latest advice from Khokand, the insurgents have been joined by Kashgar soldiers calling themselves deserters from Yakoob Beg's army, while the Ameer of Bokhara has gone to Sharlabhk, where he is collecting troops. His presence there has excited armed rebellion in the neighboring Russian territory of Zarofshan."

But Sharlabhk and Zarofshan seemed a long distance away from New York on February 2, 1876, and they *were* a long distance away when the small meeting was called to order in the Grand Central Hotel.

The meeting was called by William Ambrose Hulbert, a businessman from Chicago, and he had a proposition to offer in this Centennial year of the United States. Hulbert wanted to bring some order out of some chaos in one corner of the land: professional baseball.

William Ambrose Hulbert of Chicago wanted to bring some order out of the chaos of professional baseball, and he did in 1876 when he organized the National League.

Hulbert was not only a businessman but a fan, and it grieved him on both counts to be witnessing the decline of the sport after only five summers of organized play in the National Association of Professional Base Ball Players. The association sprang from a similar meeting held at Collier's Cafe on Broadway at 13th Street on March 17, 1871. It cost $10 to get into the league, and $10 was duly put up by representatives of teams called the Boston Red Stockings, the Chicago White Stockings, the Cleveland Forest Citys, the Fort Wayne Kekiongas, the New York Mutuals, the Philadelphia Athletics, the Rockford Forest Citys, the Troy Haymakers and the Washington Olympics.

A 10th team was represented at the meeting, the Brooklyn Eckfords, but they suspected the Association was a bad risk, so they decided not to risk the $10. When the Fort Wayne franchise folded in August, the owners of the Brooklyn club coughed up the $10 and joined on the second bounce. But they may have been right the first time.

The National Association lost money and public interest every year, and deteriorated into heavy gambling, rowdyism, drunkenness on the field and even bribery to throw games. The fans seemed fervent for the idea, but not for the integrity of the league.

That was when William Ambrose Hulbert decided to do something about it. He enlisted Albert Goodwill Spalding, the star pitcher from Boston, and took the first steps toward creating his own league. He placed four franchises in the West: Chicago, St. Louis, Cincinnati and Louisville. Then he obtained the power of attorney from those clubs, and headed to the East to line up four more clubs for geographical balance: New York, Boston, Philadelphia, Hartford.

Those cities met Hulbert's basic need: a population of not less than 75,000. So, armed with plans for a schedule of 70 games apiece, he gathered the four Eastern teams at the Grand Central Hotel, where Ned Stokes had pulled the trigger on Jim Fisk on a winter's day four years earlier.

The point of it all, Hulbert told them, was simple. You play 10 games against every other team, for a total of 70. And the team that wins the most games wins the championship and the emblem of victory that goes with it, a flag that should cost not less than $100.

You know, the team that wins the most games wins the pennant.

The big league

2

In New York town, the baseball pioneers were the Knickerbockers and Alexander Joy Cartwright (second row, center), the team's organizer. The young surveyor drew up the game's dimensions, putting the bases 90 feet apart, nine men to a side and three outs to an inning.

CHAPTER 2

In the generation after George Washington rode to the hounds in Virginia and the great stallion Messenger arrived by ship from England, the sporting life of the new American states spread with their frontier. In the Old World, the philosopher Thomas Hobbes reasoned, life was "nasty, brutish and short." In the New World, as the migrations widened into the middle colonies and the South, much of the puritanical strictness of New England began to yield to the settlers' need for some leisure in a life that they hoped would grow less nasty, brutish and short.

In New England, it took the form of wrestling, running and jumping. In the new cities down the Atlantic Coast: horse racing, bowls, ice skating, cockfighting and cricket. In the countryside to the South: boxing matches, the breeding of blooded horses and the raising of gamecocks. And in the West, where the frontier marked the edge of the white man's society, the Sioux and the Wichita tribes played field hockey in symbolic contests between the evil of winter and the revival of spring.

Spring was the time when everybody threw off "the evil of winter," clearing the land and planting the fields, and organizing life in the towns. It was, as Swinburne noted, the time when "winter's ruins and rains" had ended:

> And time remembered is grief forgotten
> And frosts are slain and flowers begotten
> And in green underwood and cover
> Blossom by blossom, the spring begins.

In the early decades of the 19th Century, one of the most enduring signs of spring, and one of the most enduring imports from the Old World, was the outpouring of young men to the fields and to the town common with the symbols of the season: ball and stick. They were there to play *base ball*, spelled in two words and derived from cricket, rounders, one old cat and other games that had been played with stick and ball for centuries in English schoolyards.

In the Colonies, it began as town ball, a sort of mass-participation sport played by the villagers during town meetings in New England. There was no limit to the number of people on each side, so at times it grew into a swirling crowd until it seemed the whole town became embroiled. By the middle of the 1830s, some order was applied: The players were limited to 11 or 12 to a side, and Robin Carver was printing woodcuts of boys playing the game on the Boston Common. Then Alexander J. Cartwright, a surveyor in New York, reduced even that lineup to nine to a side, and began to fix the geometry of the sport.

Cartwright also began playing ball with his friends on open land near Madison Avenue and 27th Street in Manhattan. They were playing a game that was still a pastime for the well-to-do young men who had the leisure time to spend in pleasant pursuit, at a time when more and more of their neighbors were being drawn into the rigors of the dawn-to-dark life of the Industrial Revolution. They called themselves the Knickerbocker Club, and they played the first base-ball match on record on June 19, 1846, on the Elysian Fields just across the Hudson River in New Jersey.

They were trounced for their trouble by a rival club, the New York Nine, by the unseemly score of 23-1, with Cartwright serving as the umpire. Even in that role, though, he made history by fining one of the players six cents for "cussing." But, by then, he had already made history by drawing up a set of rules that lasted: the bases 90 feet apart in the shape of a diamond, unchangeable batting orders, three outs to a side.

Three years later, the Knickerbockers added some style to their sport: long blue woolen trousers, white flannel shirts and straw hats. But, by then, Cartwright was off blazing new frontiers for himself. He bought a covered wagon, joined the Gold Rush of the Forty-niners and eventually wound up in Hawaii, an imposing figure with white hair and a long beard when he died in 1892, which was two years after a child named Charles Dillon Stengel was born in Kansas City.

But, if Cartwright established baseball's geometry and dimensions, the man who popularized the sport was the writer Henry Chadwick, born in 1824 in Exeter, England, and transplanted, like his game, to America. He arrived in 1837, and was growing up even as baseball was growing up. And, by the time he was building his career as a sportswriter, the game was building its role as a kind of national pastime.

Chadwick worked on the staffs of The New York Times, the Brooklyn Eagle and the New York Clipper, where he was cast as "base-ball editor," and where he began in 1869 to compose early baseball annuals or *guides*. So, he was firmly fixed at age 51 as the principal voice of baseball when William Ambrose Hulbert gathered his small group of franchise-seekers in the Grand Central Hotel on February 2, 1876, and created the National League of Professional Baseball Clubs.

Hulbert called the meeting with a fine mixture of malice and nobility. As the master of the Chicago club in the National Association, he was fed up with the domination of the league by the Boston Red Stockings, who won four straight pennants and compiled a 71-8 record as the 1875 champions. He also was fed up with the deterioration of behavior on the field and off the field, and with the one sure consequence of it: bad business.

He made his move during the season of 1875 when he lured the renowned Albert Spalding from the Boston club, where he reigned as the league's leading pitcher. Hulbert's aim was simple enough: "I'll take control of the game away from the Easterners." Or, as he phrased it to the Illinois-born Spalding: "You've no business playing in Boston. You're a Western boy and belong right here. If you'll come to Chicago, we'll give those Easterners the fight of their lives. You can be captain and manager at $4,000 a year."

Spalding not only accepted, but arrived with reinforcements: Ross Barnes, Cal McVey and Deacon White, who formed the "Big Four" of the Red Stockings along with Spalding. And, when Hulbert also signed Adrian (Cap) Anson of the Philadelphia club, the most accomplished hitter of his time, Hulbert's coup was complete.

Well, not quite complete; but, at least, poised and waiting. Hulbert was smart enough to realize that he now was a pirate among thieves, and he assumed that "the Easterners" would retaliate by suspending his new stars and aiming some sort of counterpunch at him as a renegade within the National Association. So, he next decided to beat them to the punch.

"Mr. Hulbert and myself were in a serious discussion on what we should do," Spalding wrote years later. "For a few moments I noticed that he was engrossed in deep thought, when suddenly he arose from his chair and said, 'Spalding, I have a new scheme. Let us anticipate the Eastern cusses and organize a new association before the March meeting, and then we shall see who will do the expelling.'"

And that was when Hulbert scurried around to the four Western teams and won their consent to bolt. He also won the power of attorney to act for them, and used it when he then summoned the four Eastern clubs to meet with him in New York. He pulled it off one month before "the March meeting" of the National Association, and it was the *coup de grâce*.

The goal, his constitution said, was "to encourage, foster and elevate the game of base ball." Or, in simpler words: No drinking or gambling on the ball grounds.

It was a league that had a purpose, a schedule and a geographical balance, as well as a constitution; or, at least, the draft of a constitution, and that was promptly voted at the meeting. It also had a president before they left the hotel room, but it was not William Ambrose Hulbert. He felt that baseball needed a new tone of respectability following the rowdiness of the National Association and the public's aversion to it. He also deduced that the new respectability should be embodied in a figure of unimpeachable quality, someone who in the next century would be described as a "class act," and he went beyond that point to another: The front man for the new league should be an Easterner, for all the virture and influence such a person might command.

Hulbert, in fact, was thinking on a high level, and he particularly was thinking of restoring the game to a high level after its five years in the no man's land of the National Association. And he even had a candidate: Morgan Gardner Bulkeley of Connecticut, representing the Hartford team at the meeting. He was 38 years old, and already a public figure of some substance en route to a significant career as mayor of Hartford, governor of

Connecticut and even United States senator. Bulkeley advised the other franchise owners that baseball was only a pastime for him, and that he would serve for only one year, at best.

But that was good enough for Hulbert and his allies, and so they cast the votes and elected Morgan Bulkeley the first president of the National League.

This was an interesting choice, and a strategic step, because it wrapped a mantle of public spirit and public service around a sport that had lost faith with the American people. Now, by Jove, there was a proper Yankee running the show, and his credentials were absolutely impeccable.

He was born in East Haddam, Conn., the son of the spectacularly named Eliphalet Adams Bulkeley, a lawyer and state legislator and, in 1850, the founder of the Aetna Life Insurance Co. In 1846, the family moved to Hartford, where young Morgan worked as an office sweeper at Aetna for $1 a week. His father, a Yale man, intended that he should go to Yale, but a great many things intervened, and Morgan did not get his degree until 1889, when he was 51.

One of the things that intervened was the Civil War. By the time it broke out, Bulkeley had moved to Brooklyn to work in his uncle's dry goods store, where he learned merchandising and became a partner in 1859. Two years later, he enlisted in the New York National Guard as a private, and headed straight for the Virginia campaigns under Gen. George McClellan.

After the war, he returned to Brooklyn for several years until his father died, and then he pulled stakes and went home to Hartford. He took a seat on the board of directors of Aetna, organized the United States Bank in Hartford and became the chief backer of the local professional team in the National Association. So, he was the right man in the right place when the Association collapsed five years later and William Ambrose Hulbert nominated him for president of the new National League, the "big" league.

As things turned out, Bulkeley did resign after one year, as he had said that he would, and he was succeeded by Hulbert. Actually, when the second meeting of the league was called in December 1876, Bulkeley didn't even attend. But he was already spinning into a career in public office, starting in 1880 with his election as mayor of Hartford, a job he held for four terms. If it was a steppingstone, it supplied some large stones for him to step on. In 1888, he ran for governor, lost a disputed election to Luzon Morris, but was awarded the governor's chair anyway by the Connecticut Legislature.

In 1904, he made it to the United States Senate, 28 years after he had made it to the National League. And he was not exactly a paper tiger. Two years later, he rose on the floor of the Senate and announced that Aetna and other insurance companies in Connecticut would fully cover all damage caused by the San Francisco earthquake.

Bulkeley may have been a figurehead in baseball, but he was an essential one, and his one year in office set the stage for five seasons of strict control by Hulbert. And, in that first summer of 1876, it was Hulbert and his Chicago team that dominated the league on the field.

The inaugural National League game was played in Philadelphia on April 22, with Boston and the Athletics firing the first salvos; and, two days later, they staged a return match, also in Philadelphia. But, for the record, the first game in major league history was won by Boston, 6-5, with a total of 26 errors made in a nine-inning game, or as variously recorded, 18 or 20 errors. In any event, the game took 2 hours, 5 minutes to complete and was related in these words in the Philadelphia press:

"The championship season of 1876 was opened on Saturday afternoon by the Boston and Athletic, on the grounds at Twenty-fifth and Jefferson streets. As was anticipated, there was a large turn-out to witness the game, which was well worth seeing, both nines being in full force. The first inning was a blank for both clubs, although O'Rourke for the Boston, and Fisler and Meyerle for the Athletic, made clean hits, the latter's being a two-baser."

Two-basers and even three-basers followed as the opening week unfolded. Five of the league's six other teams made their debuts on April 25, with Chicago playing at Louisville, St. Louis at Cincinnati and Boston at the Mutual of Brooklyn. Two days later, Hartford made its first appearance, in a game played in Brooklyn. And, on April 29, Hartford and Boston went 10 innings in the first extra-inning game.

They played a total of 11 games in the opening week, and then maintained that rate for the rest of the season: 52 games in May, 53 in June, 46 in July, 46 in August, 42 in September and 10 in October. And, at the close of the season, nobody had quite played all 70 games contemplated, but most came close except for Philadelphia and Brooklyn, which failed to make their final Western trips and were promptly expelled by Hulbert when he succeeded Bulkeley as president.

Hulbert's coup against the National Association became an unqualified success when his White Stockings swept to the first National League pennant. They won 52 games and lost 14, finishing comfortably in front of St. Louis (45-19) and Hartford (47-21). And there was no doubt that Hulbert's imported stars had earned their keep: Ross Barnes led the league in hitting with an average of .404, with Cal McVey and Adrian Anson also among the league's top five hitters. And Albert Spalding outdid all the pitchers in the league by winning 47 games and losing 13, which meant that he had pitched in 60 of his team's 66 games.

Given his sense of strictness, Hulbert probably didn't need any more muscle after he became president of the league. But he got more from this sweeping success on the field, and he wasted no time using it in the league office. He began by exiling Philadelphia and Brooklyn, which was really the New York entry in the league, and he did it despite the obvious fact that he was dropping the two most heavily populated cities in the league. So, he played the next season with only six clubs.

He also investigated the pennant race in 1877, which Boston won by seven games over Louisville, and found that four of the Louisville players had been bribed, including Jim Devlin, the star pitcher and a close friend of Hulbert himself. His justice was swift and final: All four were banished from baseball for life. And, when another crisis arose, he reacted with the same sort of summary judgment: Cincinnati and St. Louis wanted to play Sunday baseball with admission cut in half to 25 cents and no restriction on selling beer. On all three counts, they would have violated league rules. On all three counts, Hulbert said, no way. No Sunday baseball, no 25-cent tickets and especially no beer.

★   ★   ★

"There is no game now in vogue the theory of which is more simple than that of base-ball," Henry Chadwick wrote, as he observed the launching of the National League, "and hence its attraction for the masses."

Then he carried his reasoning one step beyond, and caught the nature of the attraction: simple theory, complex performance.

"And yet," he said, "to excel in the game as a noted expert requires not only the possession of the physical attributes of endurance, agility, strength, good throwing and running and power, together with plenty of courage, luck and nerve; but also the mental powers of sound judgment, quick perception, thorough control of temper and the presence of mind to act promptly in critical emergencies."

Having made it sound more like an Olympian pursuit beyond the genius of mere men, Chadwick then returned to his thesis that it was, after all, a *game.*

"The plain theory of base-ball," he wrote, "is simply as follows: A space of ground being marked out on a level field in the form of a diamond, with equal sides, bases are placed on the four corners thereof. The contestants include nine players on each side—one side takes the field and the other goes to the bat. When the field side take their positions, the pitcher delivers the ball to the batsman, who endeavors to send it out of the reach of the fielders and far enough out on the field to enable him to run round the bases, and if he reaches the home base—his starting point—without being put out, he scores a run."

It was a simple, eloquent, even majestic description of the essence of the game, in the language of the day, in the spirit of the times. And, with the same noble cadences, as though depicting one of mankind's classic challenges, Chadwick continued:

"He is followed in rotation by the others of his side until three of the batting party are put out, when the field side come in and take their turn at the bat. This goes on until nine innings have been played to a close and then the side scoring the most runs wins the game."

That was simple and eloquent, too, and so was his portrayal of the roles in the cast:

"*The catcher:* This player's duty is to catch all balls pitched to the bat. He stands either within six feet of the home base, or about 50 feet back of it, according to the style of the pitcher's delivery, and the circumstances of the play. When the pitching is slow, he stands near to the home base. When it is swift, he retires to a distance from it; and in the case of a swift delivery, when players are running the bases, he is required to stand near the base in order to be ready to send the ball promptly to second base, so as to cut off the player running to it.

"He can put out the batsman either by catching the ball from the bat on the fly, either fair or foul, or by catching it when hit foul on the first rebound from the ground. Should the batsman strike at the ball three times without hitting it, and the catcher hold the ball either on the fly or the first bound, the batsman is out. Should he not catch the ball at all in such a case, he should endeavor to throw the ball to first base, so that it be held there before the striker reaches it, the striker being obliged in such case to run to first base.

"The catcher will find it advantageous, when facing swift pitching, to wear tough leather gloves, with the fingers cut off near the joint, as they will prevent his having his hands split and puffed up."

While the catcher was finding tough leather gloves with fingers cut off near the joint, Chadwick next turned his power of concentration on the pitcher:

"The pitcher is the most important player in the field, and on his skill and judgment depends half the battle in a match.

"His position is within the lines of a space six feet square. The rules require him to deliver the ball while standing in his position, and when in the act of delivering, or in making any preliminary motion to deliver the ball, he must have both feet within the lines of his position, and he cannot take a step outside the lines until the ball has left his hands. Should he do so, he incurs the penalty for balking.

"The pitcher should bear in mind the important fact that the true art of pitching is to deceive the eye of the batsman; that is, to send the ball to the bat in such a manner as to lead the striker to believe that it is just coming in where he wants it, while in fact it is either too high or too low, or too swift or too slow for the purpose."

And, for sheer insight, Chadwick reached heights of brilliance when he went on to say:

"He should have the pluck to face hot balls direct from the bat. Unless he can do this, he can never pitch with judgment, for he will be so impressed with the idea of avoiding being hit with the ball that he will think of little else."

To be absolutely specific, under the heading "An Illegal Delivery," he continued: "The rule governing the delivery of the ball requires that the ball shall be swung forward below the line of the hip. It will be seen that the pitcher in the above cut is delivering the ball on the line of the hip, instead of below that line, as the rule requires."

Sure enough, his exposition included drawings to illustrate the art of pitching without breaking or even bending the rules, although the line drawing that he mentioned apparently was misleading. He conceded the point, but did not suggest why the misleading cut was still included among the illustrations. But no matter; next he zeroed in on "A Fair Delivery," in these words:

"It will be seen in the above illustration what the rule means by the words, 'with the arm swinging nearly perpendicular at the side of the body.' This is the delivery of a pitch, a toss, a jerk or an underhanded throw, the ball in such case passing below the line of the hip as the hand holding it is swung forward in delivery."

Henry Chadwick made these observations and pronouncements in his chronicles of baseball, starting with his encyclopedic account of the state of the game in one of the earliest annuals printed in the sport: "DeWitt's Base Ball Guide" of 1877. It was sold by the American News Co. of 115-117-119-121 Nassau St. in lower Manhattan, and it cost 10 cents. On the front cover of the square little paperback book was a line drawing that showed a man pitching a ball underhand.

The inside front cover was given to a full-page advertisement by Peck & Snyder, Manufacturers, of 124 Nassau St. (just up the blook). They offered "new styles of base ball uniforms and outfits; base ball caps, eight corners with star in top or corded seams for $10 per dozen ($1 sample by mail); uniform flannel for $8 a dozen, and second quality flannels at $6 a dozen." Belts, advertised as "the best English worsted webbing belts," went for 60 cents apiece, or $6 the dozen. Heavy English all-worsted hose, in solid colors or stripes, went for $2.50 each, or $27 the dozen. Or, with cotton feet, only $24. Or, leggings but no feet, $21.

This was the record of the business, the story of the sport in 1876, when the National League took the field. It was, the title page announced, "a complete manual of base-ball containing full instruction in the points of the game; full statistics showing pitching, batting and fielding averages, together with the records of the various championship contests of the season, professional and amateur." And that wasn't all: "Also, special instructions for scoring and reporting the Game, the whole illustrated with cuts and diagrams showing batting, pitching and fielding positions under the new rules."

The publisher was Robert M. DeWitt of 33 Rose St. The author was Henry Chadwick, base-ball editor of the New York Clipper. And Chadwick immediately got down to basics, such as the dimensions of a ball field:

"A base-ball field should be at least 500 feet in length by 350 feet in breadth. The in-field should be level, and covered with well-rolled turf of

Albert Goodwill Spalding switched from Boston to Chicago in 1876 and pitched William Hulbert's White Stockings to the first National League pennant by winning 47 games.

fine small grass and clover. The grass should be frequently cut by machine; this will cause it to become velvety and close. Of course, the ground from the pitcher's position to that of the catcher should be bare of turf, some eight feet in width, and laid with hard dry soil, and in such a manner as to throw off water. The edge should be level with the turf border. The paths on the lines from base to base—three feet in width—should be laid with hard soil, and also a circle around each base.

"On a line from the home to the second base and distant from the former 45 feet, is the pitcher's first point, the second point being six feet farther on the same line."

Then, having specified the cut and the outline of the grass and the length and breadth of the ball park, Chadwick enunciated the rules of the game in loving and microscopic detail. To wit:

"The ball must weigh not less than 5 nor more than $5\frac{1}{4}$ ounces avoirdupois. It must measure not less than 9 nor more than $9\frac{1}{4}$ inches in circumference. It must be composed of woolen yarn and shall not contain more than one ounce of vulcanized rubber in mold form and shall be covered with leather and furnished by the secretary of the league.

"When the ball becomes out of shape, or cut or ripped so as to expose the yarn, or in any way so injured as to be unfit for fair use, a new ball shall be called for by the umpire at the end of an even inning, at the request of either captain."

No mention of the pitcher calling for a new ball because he didn't like the feel of the old one. Or, of the umpire tossing out the ball because it hit the ground while the pitcher was warming up. In the primeval days, if the yarn was exposed, throw it out—at the end of an even inning.

For the *pièce de résistance*, and covering all eventualities, Chadwick conjured the worst possible scenario and decided: "Should the ball be lost during a game, the umpire shall, at the expiration of 5 minutes, call for a new ball."

The Nestor of base-ball

Henry Chadwick, who came to America from England in 1837, became the foremost baseball historian and "father" of the game. "Should the ball be lost during a game," he wrote in 1877, "the umpire shall, at the expiration of 5 minutes, call for a new ball."

CHAPTER 3

"Baseball," Henry Chadwick observed in 1877, "dates its origin from the old English game of rounders, to which, however, it now bears as much resemblance as chess to draughts or 'chequers.' In this country, the early history of the game shows it to have been little else than a schoolboy pastime. In 1845 it began to occupy a more important position in the record of American field-sports, and about that time it became a regular club game, the Knickerbocker Club of New York being regarded as the Nestor of base-ball."

The Knickerbocker Club of New York may have been the Nestor of base-ball, and Alexander Joy Cartwright may have been the spirit behind Nestor. But other clubs in other cities in other years left imprints on what Chadwick now was calling "the national game of base-ball." It earned that title without much quibbling because no other professional team sport was played in America at the time, and no other team sport of any kind was played so simply and probably so inexpensively. All it needed was a field, a ball, a bat and a bunch of boys.

The "traditional" American sport was horse racing, but that remained more of a class sport than a mass sport. The first Kentucky Derby was run in 1875 in Louisville, the year before Hulbert raided the National Association to ruin, and the first Derby crowd in history was estimated at about 10,000. But thoroughbred racing was part of a way of life, mainly a pastoral life, an aristocratic and a privileged life.

Football appeared as a college sport in 1869, but went through turbulent times and was even prohibited at times. In 1873, some Cornell students got into an exchange of letters with some Michigan students, and a football match was arranged on a neutral site: Cleveland, with 30 players permitted on each squad. But President White of Cornell vetoed the project, saying: "I will not permit 30 men to travel 400 miles merely to agitate a bag of wind." And, even as late as 1905, Theodore Roosevelt denounced the savagery of football from the White House, prompting a sweeping overhaul of the rules that banned massed formations and allowed the forward pass.

Basketball did not make the scene until 1891, and ice hockey came by way of Canada, where the McGill University club was organized in 1880. But it was not until 1917 that the National Hockey League was formed in Montreal and it was not until 1924 that the Boston Bruins joined the league as its first team from the United States.

So, there was little doubt that baseball grew as *the* team sport, and it grew at a time when the railroad was growing as the chief link between East and West. In fact, "town ball" may have been the ultimate expression of baseball's appeal to the whole town: Everybody got into the game. Chadwick even credited the Olympic Club of Philadelphia with being "its principal exemplar" around the year 1840.

"At a later time, too," he related, "a phase of base-ball was popular in the Eastern states under the name of the 'New England Game,' a title given it in contradistinction to the New York game of the period; the former being played with a small, light ball, which was thrown overhand to the bat, while in the latter a large elastic ball was used with long heavy bats, the ball being pitched to the bat.

"Base-ball as now played, however, can only date its rise from the establishment of the National Association of Base-ball Players, organized in 1857, from which time only has it been played under a specially authorized code of rules."

In the earliest days, when the Knickerbocker Club was gathering on Madison Square in the afternoon, you threw the ball at a player to get him out. But people running to first base were getting winged so frequently, and so painfully, that the rule was changed: The ball now was thrown to the base.

"The first printed code of rules," Chadwick noted, "contained but 14 sections, and under it the pitcher could deliver the ball as wildly as he chose, and the batsman could strike at it at his option, thus making the game tediously dull and uninteresting, when the contesting nines were rivals or pretty evenly matched.

"The changes in the rules introduced, even at the first convention of the fraternity in 1857, were such as to materially improve the game; but these revised rules were nothing in comparison with the complete code of laws by which base-ball is now governed, and which now characterizes it.

"Up to the year 1860, base-ball—as played under the National Association rules—was chiefly confined to New York and its vicinity, though a few clubs existed in other states. But in 1860 the then brilliant career of the Excelsior club of Brooklyn created quite a furor, and the tour of this club through New York state, and afterward to Philadelphia and Baltimore, led to a wide extension of the popularity of base-ball; and a year or two later the same club established the 'New York Game'—as it was then called—in Boston, and it gradually superseded the 'New England Game,' which is now almost unknown."

The New York Game had its greatest showcase, as might be expected, in New Jersey: at the Elysian Fields in Hoboken, where the Knickerbockers had made history back in 1846 in the first ball game on record. Now, a decade or so later, the Knickerbockers were joined by other clubs in the area, and the first series of games aimed at a championship of any sort took place in 1857, then again in 1858, and again in '59. The Knickerbocker, Eagle, Gotham and Empire Clubs were the best by far, at least until the Atlantic Club of Brooklyn began to win regularly. And, after that, the Atlantic Club ruled the roost until dethroned by the Excelsior Club, which Henry

Chadwick portrayed in this elegant way:

"In the season of 1860, the Excelsior Club of Brooklyn, ranking second to none at the time in social standing, then occupied the highest position in the country as the leading exemplars of the beauties of the game; and, by the way, this club did more to establish base-ball on a permanent and reputable footing than had before been attempted by any other club; other noteworthy organizations, such as the Knickerbocker Club of New York, for instance, having been more limited in their sphere of operations."

But the "memorable season" of 1860, as Chadwick rated it, was the prelude to the storm: "The great rebellion of 1861, of course, materially interfered with the progress of base-ball; indeed, in effect, it put it back several years; and it was not until 1864 that the game began to recover its lost ground."

If so, baseball on all counts was more fortunate than the rest of the country, which did not recover its lost ground for many years after the Great Rebellion. But the Civil War, while it fragmented the organized sport of baseball for a while, added more to the game than it subtracted. For the first time in many lives, young men left the towns and the family farms and "joined up." They traveled from one region of the land to another, and they traveled with their customs and manners and even their games. The Excelsiors may have carried the sport of baseball from Brooklyn to Upstate New York, but the armies carried it from the North to the South and to the West, and the game was played in Union army camps and in Confederate prisoner-of-war camps. And President Lincoln, one summer afternoon in 1862, even wrenched himself away from his agonizing chores and took his son Tad to a baseball game.

After the war, the sporting life returned to the social clubs, and baseball revived with a rush as people craved and pursued some leisure-time pleasures after four years of bitterness and booty. The Resolutes of Brooklyn began playing ball even before the fighting ended, and the Rockingham nine of Portsmouth, N.H., took the field in 1865 as soon as the fighting ended.

The Mutuals of New York were formed in '64, reached a peak after the war and played from 1869 to 1871 under a celebrated president who was far along the path to fame and fortune in other pursuits: Boss Tweed.

The Forest City nine of Rockford, Ill., arrived in 1867 and became known as "the Champions of the Northwest." They did have a glittering cast led by the teen-age pitcher Albert G. Spalding, Ross Barnes, Bob Addy and Fred Cone, who all played on the great Boston Red Stockings in the next decade.

The dominant club in the decade of the 1860s, the Atlantic Base Ball Club of Brooklyn, won five championships between 1864 and 1870, losing only to the Unions of Morrisania in '67 and the Cincinnati Red Stockings in 1869. And upstate in New York, out where farmland stretched to the horizon, the Niagaras of Buffalo made their debut in '67, and three years later the Haymakers of Troy were in action, playing against visiting teams like the Athletics at places like the Bull's Head Tavern field in nearby Bates-town.

To the west, the Independents of Mansfield, O., were in action in '69. And so was the Antioch College team, which even scheduled the Cincinnati Reds in a fine display of bravery mixed with undergraduate innocence.

Still, these were mostly social clubs and amateur athletes, and the distinction was not drawn until the National Association convention of 1868: There would now be amateur teams and there would be professional teams. But even this distinction was late.

"Up to 1868," Chadwick reported, "the laws of the National Association prohibited the employment of any paid player in a club nine; but so strong had the rivalry become between leading amateur clubs of the principal cities where the game was then in full operation, that the practice of compensating players had worked its way to an extent which entirely nullified the law."

In other words, rivalries between cities had become so fierce that the contending clubs began to recruit and pay players, rules or no rules. But now, in 1868, with the country healing its wounds and lifting its spirits, the true professional came out of hiding, accepted the public anointing and created an industry.

And one team of professionals, the Cincinnati Red Stockings, promptly took the opportunity, dramatized it and achieved the fullest measure of success in the very next season, the rousing summer of '69.

It was rousing because the city of Cincinnati was determined to have a rousing summer to erase a bad memory: Two years earlier, the Washington Nationals baseball team went barnstorming across the Midwest, 2,400 miles in three weeks, and took no prisoners. So now, rising above the debris of local humiliation, Cincinnati plotted its redemption.

The chief instrument of that redemption was a jeweler and cricket player named Harry Wright. He was born in England in 1835, came to America with his family and joined the Knickerbockers as an outfielder in 1858. He was, in the custom of the time, an amateur. But he also was, in the custom of the time, an operator. In 1863, he staged a "benefit" game at 25 cents a head, and came away with $29.65, and a desire for more.

Two years later, as the war was ending, Wright accepted a job as cricket instructor at the Union Cricket Club in Cincinnati for $1,200 a year. And, one year later, in July of 1866, he trotted out the old enterprise and organized the Cincinnati Red Stockings, an amateur club of local athletes. He was named the captain, and the stage was set.

It was set for the revival of 1869, when Wright was called upon to create an all-star team and redeem the honor of Cincinnati. He was enlisted for the job at $1,200 for a dual role as the center fielder and manager, although some accounts suggested that he actually got closer to $2,000.

The only man on the team from Cincinnati was the first baseman, Charlie Gould. The others were imported, for a price. Harry Wright's first choice was his brother George, who arrived from New York and signed as the shortstop for $1,400. Asa Brainard, the pitcher, came for $1,100. Fred Waterman, the third baseman, got $1,000. Gould at first base, Charles Sweasy at second base, Douglas Allison at catcher and Andrew Leonard and Calvin McVey in the outfield, all were enlisted at $800 apiece. The substitute, Richard Hurley, signed for $600.

They were the first acknowledged "pros," and they made the most of it. They traveled 11,000 miles, they won 57 straight games, they even were accorded a private interview with President Ulysses S. Grant. They were undefeated and unbridled, and they bowled their way across the country drumming up business with their own theme song, composed by one of the players:

> We are a band of baseball players
>> From Cincinnati city.
> We come to toss the ball around
>> And sing to you our ditty.
> And if you listen to the song
>> We are about to sing,
> We'll tell you all about baseball
>> And make the Welkin ring.
> The ladies want to know
>> Who are those gallant men in
> Stockings red, they'd like to know.

At the close of their summer of barnstorming, they were famous. But not rich: After salaries and expenses, the club showed a net profit of $1.39. Still, Aaron Chapman announced that he would rather be president of the Cincinnati Red Stockings, which he was, than President of the United States, which he was not. And Henry Chadwick saluted the team's success in an account titled "The Inauguration of Professionalism," depicting them as the "first regular professional club" and reporting their success in these words:

"The Cincinnati Red Stockings took their place upon the field, and during the campaign of that year they encountered every strong club in the country from Maine to California, and they met with such remarkable success as to make their career in that year noteworthy in the history of the game."

The streak reached 92 the following season before reality returned to the Red Stockings. It was on June 14, 1870, and they went 11 innings on the Capitoline Grounds in Brooklyn before the streak died. Tied 5-5 after nine innings, the Red Stockings scored two runs in the first half of the 11th, but the Atlantics came back with three runs in the home half and, by the score of 8-7, the Red Stockings no longer were undefeated.

The streak was gone, and so was the glamour, but not the high salaries and travel expenses. And, as a result of those conflicting currents, the Red Stockings disbanded a year later and took their place on the shelf of the history and legend of the sport they had helped to dramatize. They were resurrected, however, as charter members of the National League in 1876. Harry Wright was named the first secretary of the league. And Henry Chadwick even titled him "the father of professional baseball."

The runaway success of the Red Stockings also created a boom in baseball. The Red Stockings were acknowledged and unrelenting professionals, and they were celebrities, no longer slyly and privately on the payroll. And they were soon being followed and imitated by so many other clubs and "nines" around the country that the next step was inescapable: Ten clubs met in Collier's Cafe on March 17, 1871, and formed the first league of strictly professional teams. It was called the National Association of Professional Base Ball Players, which took it into a new dimension beyond the National Association of Base-ball Players in 1857, back in the days when only amateurs need apply.

The National Association may have been the first professional baseball league, but it stopped short of becoming the first major league for a number of reasons. It was loosely knit, for openers. It tended to attract drinkers and gamblers, and ultimately bribers. And it was so heavily dominated by one team, the Boston Red Stockings, that the public soon lost interest.

It was ironic that the stars of the cast were the Wright brothers, Harry and George, who took the path from England to New York to Cincinnati, where they put life and muscle into the Red Stockings of 1869, and on to Boston, where they put life and muscle into the Red Stockings there in the 1870s. It took them one season in Boston to get the knack, but once they did, they didn't lose it. For the four years after that, Boston was the master of the National Association and the Wrights were the masters of great teams that outdistanced and finally outlived the National Association.

Harry Wright, the manager, was a gentleman who did not berate his players or argue with umpires. He opposed Sunday baseball on religious grounds. He was enterprising almost beyond belief, representing at various times a turnstile company and a manufacturer of baseballs and obtaining the patent on the score card used at all home games in Boston.

He was 12 years older than his brother George, who was a year or so older than brother Sam, and all three eventually played in the big leagues. Harry was the organizing genius; George was the exceptional athlete. George was born at 110th Street and Third Avenue in New York in 1847, and lived until 1937, which was Joe DiMaggio's second season with the New York Yankees.

Their father was a professional cricket player in Sheffield, England, who came to the United States in 1836. He also played professional cricket with the St. George Cricket Club of Hoboken, which must have been a hotbed of all games played with stick and ball. All three of his sons played cricket, too, but made their names when they went more deeply into baseball.

When he was only 17 years old, George was playing for the Gothams of New York, using Cartwright's rules. A year later, he played for the Philadelphia Olympics. Then back to the Gothams the year after that and, since they had only nine or 10 men on the roster, George played every position on the field. But he was best at shortstop, and that's where he played his most memorable games.

In 1866, he switched again, this time to the Morrisania Union of the Bronx. Then, a year later, he made the big switch to the Washington Nationals, who listed him as a "government clerk" to preserve the fiction that this was a team of amateurs.

They even listed an address for him: 238 Pennsylvania Ave., which happened to be a public park. Even if the park had been his true address, he wouldn't have spent much time in it that year. That was the summer when the Nationals barreled across the country, knocking off the local teams, including the one in Cincinnati that was soon to conscript both Harry and George Wright to help the city atone.

The next year, 1868, George returned to New York and the Morrisania team, and became known as the best player in the East. The irrepressible Henry Chadwick named him to the first "all-star team" that year. Then, it was off to Cincinnati at Harry's urging, and the Cincinnati Red Stockings took shape.

After the Cincinnati club folded, the Wrights moved on to Boston in 1871 and launched the Red Stockings there, Harry as manager, George as shortstop. The team ran third that season, but won the pennant the next four years and, in 1875, finished with the unarguable record of 71 and 8.

By then, George Wright was a player of titanic achievement. Standing only 5-foot-9½ and weighing 150 pounds, he had a bushy mustache and a dashing image—and he could play. He was credited with having invented the trap-fly play, trapping a pop fly on the first bounce in order to lull the other team's baserunners into a double play. Years later, the trick was nullified when the infield-fly rule was adopted: With runners on first and second base (or first, second and third) and fewer than two out, any pop fly to the infield is declared by the umpire to be an automatic "out," no ruse allowed.

George also was credited with being the first shortstop to cover second base when the second baseman was off the bag.

He could hit, too. True, he was swinging against underhand pitching with no curveballs. But he still posted extraordinary numbers during his five years in the National Association—.409, .336, .378, .345 and finally .337—before moving on to Boston's National League team with brother Harry.

Some of Harry's enterprise rubbed off on George in 1872, their second year in Boston, when he and Harry Ditson opened the Wright & Ditson Sporting Goods store, the largest in New England. They sold cigars and baseballs, later sold tennis and golf equipment and became so successful that they eventually were bought out by Albert Spalding, whom they joined in 1876 as founding members of the National League.

Spalding by then was William Hulbert's chief prize on the Chicago White Stockings, the team that swept to the National League's first pennant. Boston was an also-ran, but George Wright had the distinction of appearing as the first batter in the history of the "big" league. Leading off the Boston batting order made out by his brother, the manager, George grounded out to shortstop in Philadelphia on April 22, 1876.

The Red Stockings finished only fourth in the National League's inaugural season, 15 games behind Al Spalding and "Cap" Anson, the newly installed captain of the White Stockings. But they won the league's second pennant, and the third, and now the Wright boys had played and managed for six championship teams in seven years in two leagues. And they weren't done yet. The following year, 1879, George jumped from Boston to the Providence Grays as shortstop and manager, and beat out Harry's Red Stockings for the pennant by six games.

George wasn't done yet, either. Later, he played in the first golf match held in New England and, in 1884, bought the Boston franchise in the Union Association, one of several leagues that tried with mixed success in the 1880s to muscle in on the National League. The Union Association lasted only one season, but George Wright found it wasn't a total loss: He had persuaded the new league to use only Wright & Ditson baseballs as long as it was in business.

But the Union Association was the least of the challenges that besieged the National League during a decade of almost nonstop confusion. Baseball as a business was having growing pains, and part of the reason was that the National League had a fairly austere outlook: still no Sunday baseball permitted, no beer allowed in the grandstand, no ticket-scalping countenanced. For all three reasons, dissent was sure to set in, and it did after just six years.

The first challenge came in the form of a rival league, the American Association, which attacked the National League owners as fat cats who thrived on exorbitant ticket prices (50 cents) and saddled the public with restraints. The Nationals replied by attacking a "beer and whiskey" organization that included teams in Baltimore and Louisville that were owned by breweries and distilleries. Not only that, but the new league's St. Louis club was owned by a prosperous saloon keeper, Chris Von der Ahe. And the American Association was waging economic war by charging only 25 cents for a ball game.

The feuding began in 1882 and it was inflamed at the close of the season when the Chicago club of the National League challenged the Cincinnati club, the best in the American Association, to play a "world series." The Association had forbidden its teams to compete against the "rowdy" National League, but the Red Stockings ignored the injunction and knocked off the White Stockings, 4-0, causing dancing in the streets of Cincinnati and consternation in the older league.

Chicago regained its poise the next day, though, and scored a 2-0 victory. But that was as far as the match went. The president of the Association, H.D. Denny McKnight, threatened to expel the Cincinnati players if they continued. So, the first "world series" ended in a 1-1 tie.

Feelings ran high between the leagues because the rivalry was accompanied by a lot of name-calling and finger-pointing. Three years earlier, the National League had settled on a 50-cent admission to assure itself a somewhat solid financial base. The single-admission policy came under immediate fire, notably in Syracuse, N.Y., where it was charged that the policy would "throw the entire assemblage into promiscuous relations with drunken rowdies, unwashed loafers and arrant blacklegs."

Then the National League's Cincinnati club, playing in a city with 27 breweries and distilleries, insisted on playing Sunday ball and selling beer in the ball park. The league replied by affirming its policy and voting specifically to forbid Sunday ball and the sale of liquor on the grounds. Cincinnati did the only sensible thing under such non-negotiable conflicts: It dropped out of the National League after the '80 season and, two years later, surfaced in the American Association.

The Reds left the National League with some parting shots, particularly at Worcester, Mass., one of the louder voices raised against beer on Sunday. One Cincinnati newspaper, joining the fight with flags and phrases flying, wrote:

"Puritanical Worcester is not liberal Cincinnati by a jugful. What is sauce for Worcester is wind for the Queen City; beer and Sunday amusements have become a popular necessity in Cincinnati."

The Reds returned to the National League fold in 1890. But, by then, several more battles had been fought for the soul and the business of baseball. They broke out, ironically, after the two rival leagues had reached a truce of sorts in 1882: There would be no more raiding of player contracts, with each club allowed to exert firm control over its players.

This was even stricter than the "reserve clause" policy adopted three years earlier, which established the idea that players' contracts were *reserved* to their teams. And, for the players now, the truce between the leagues suggested a truce at their expense. They took the first step toward common action in 1885 when they organized the Brotherhood of Professional Ball Players. It was a kind of union that tried to reverse the economic strictures that the club owners in both leagues were invoking, now that they had reached their truce and agreed to stop raiding each other's talent. And the strictures came wrapped in dollar signs: Salaries were limited, fines

The Cincinnati Red Stockings of 1882 won the championship of the American Association and played a two-game "world series" against the Chicago White Stockings of the rival and "rowdy" National League.

were imposed and, most important of all, the "reserve clause" bound the players to their teams for life.

So, sensing that it was making only small progress, the Brotherhood took another step in 1890, and that one was a giant stride: It formed the Players League, and promptly challenged the two other major leagues. It was a mutiny, all right, and it survived only one season. But the Players League actually outdrew its rivals, 980,887 customers to 813,678 for the National League and about 500,000 for the American Association.

More than that, it stayed long enough to weaken the American Association to the point of collapse, which it did after the 1891 season. And, three-quarters of a century before professional athletes in almost every major sport formed labor unions that revolutionized the business, it cast a long shadow down the corridors of baseball history.

The main idea 4

The Baltimore Orioles revolutionized the game in the 1890s with their dashing style and all-out offense. Two of the team's rockets were John McGraw (front row, left) and Willie Keeler (front row, right).

CHAPTER 4

In late 1891, just 16 years after William Ambrose Hulbert had organized it, the National League finally stood alone. The pretenders were gone—the National Association, the Union Association, the American Association, the Players League. At least, it stood alone for 10 years until the American League arrived and won equal rank. But, for most of the decade of the Nineties, there was one—one *big* league.

For that matter, it was bigger than ever. After the Players League folded in 1890, and the American Association a year later, the National League swept up four teams from the Association and opened the season of 1892 with one dozen clubs. It now stretched from Boston to St. Louis, with two teams in New York and one in Washington, and it was passing milestones with almost every performance.

Some of the milestones may have been small, some were absolutely strange and some preceded the formation of the National League, but they all supplied footnotes to the development of the sport and its impact on the public:

The first score card printed for a ball game, as far as anyone could tell, appeared on October 11, 1866, in Brooklyn and it had the ringing title: "The Great Game for the Championship of the United States." That may or may not have been true, but 30,000 people turned out to watch the Athletic and Atlantic clubs play their game at 15th and Columbia Avenue. The Athletics won, 18-9.

The first switch-hitter reportedly was Bob Ferguson, an infielder with the Atlantics.

The first curveball supposedly was thrown by Candy Cummings, who pitched for New York, Baltimore, Philadelphia and Hartford in the National Association from 1872 through 1875, and for Hartford and Cincinnati in the first two seasons of the National League in '76 and '77. At least, he is generally credited with having developed the curveball, although it was delivered underhand in those days and was not really the first breaking ball on record.

The first one—at least, the first one confirmed by Henry Chadwick when he was writing for the Brooklyn Eagle and growing into the historian of the game—was thrown or demonstrated on August 16, 1870. And this is how Chadwick reported this footnote:

"Yesterday, at the Capitoline Grounds, a large crowd assembled and cheered lustily as a youth from New Haven, Connecticut, Fred Goldsmith, demonstrated to the satisfaction of all that a baseball could be so manipulated and controlled by throwing it from one given point to another, as to make a pronounced arc in space."

To clinch his point, Goldsmith drove a pair of 8-foot poles into the ground—one halfway from the pitcher's mound to home plate, the other just to the right of the plate. Six times, he pitched a ball outside the first pole, and bent it around toward the second one, "and that which up to this point seemed an optical illusion and against all rules of physics was now an established fact."

In 1878, turnstiles were introduced, although three years later only 12 persons went through them to see Chicago play Troy in a driving rain on the last day of the season.

In 1881, the pitcher's mound was moved back from 45 feet to 50 feet from the plate.

In 1882, umpires were told to stop soliciting the views of players and spectators, and to make up their own minds. Also in 1882, Will White of the Cincinnati Reds, the champions of the American Association, became the first player known to wear eyeglasses.

In 1884, pitchers were allowed to throw overhand. That didn't seem to bother Ned Williamson, the shortstop for the Chicago White Stockings, who hit a record number of 27 home runs. One of Williamson's teammates was a reserve outfielder from Iowa who hit four home runs and later followed another calling with far more resounding success: Billy Sunday, the evangelist.

In 1888, DeWolfe Hopper recited "Casey at the Bat" for the first time on the stage. And, in another performance that spread the game before the public, Albert Spalding took two teams on a tour of Hawaii, Australia, Ceylon, Egypt, Italy, France, England and Ireland.

In 1889, bad news for the pitchers. Nine years earlier, they were allowed to throw eight balls off the plate before being charged with a walk on the ninth. Now, four wide ones and the batter strolled.

In 1893, the pitching distance was moved back one more time, for the last time, and it was fixed at 60½ feet from home plate. And, in a footnote to that footnote, the precise distance was set by accident. It was supposed to be 60' 0" and no more. But a surveyor with weak eyes misread the blueprint, took it to specify 60 feet, 6 inches and that was that.

The first professional league didn't appear until the National Association took the field in 1871 but, a decade or so later, teams and leagues were proliferating from one end of the country to the other. Or, at least, east of the frontier.

In 1884, for example, there was the National League at the tip of the pyramid with its eight teams. Then, the American Association with 13. The Northwestern League had 12, a bit off the mainline: Evansville, Saginaw, Peoria, Grand Rapids, Terre Haute, Milwaukee, Minneapolis, Muskegon, Stillwater, St. Paul, Fort Wayne and Quincy.

In the East, seven clubs in the American Alliance in New York, New Jersey and Pennsylvania formed a league called the Inter-State Association and played ball in Brooklyn, Harrisburg, Reading, Trenton, Washington, Camden and Pottsville (where the team was endowed with the local treasure as the Pottsville Anthracite).

The Western League was organized that year, and "after a spirited debate, it was resolved to take in cities as far north as Dubuque and south to Sedalia, Mo., with clubs in Dubuque, Clinton, Ottumwa and Keokuk in Iowa; in Rock Island, Peoria, Springfield and Quincy in Illinois; in Kansas City, Sedalia, St. Joseph and Chillicothe in Missouri, and in Atchison in Kansas— all represented by delegate or letter."

Nine of the cities were elected to franchises in the league, annual dues were placed at $40, the visiting team was allocated 40 percent of the gate receipts (or a guarantee of $60) and Spalding's Official League Ball was adopted as the official ball, just as its name stipulated.

The Iron and Oil Association made the scene, too, making no secret of the sources of its local wealth. At its organizational meeting in the St. Charles Hotel in Pittsburgh, it first voted to call itself the Ohio Valley Base Ball Association. But, reminded that there was already an Ohio League in business, the new league changed and dramatically improved its name, and established clubs in Oil City, Franklin, East Liberty, New Brighton and New Castle in Pennsylvania, and Youngstown in Ohio.

In a sense, baseball was still "town ball," with the local pride and sometimes prosperity riding with the fortunes of the town's team. And one of the towns where it was flourishing most was St. Louis, which had two teams with wide-ranging fortunes. In 1885, the National League team in St. Louis finished eighth and last; the American Association team, the Browns, won the pennant.

Baseball was booming on the banks of the Mississippi, and one of the reasons it was booming was Alfred Henry Spink, one of the eight children of William Spink, once a member of the Canadian Legislative Assembly. The family migrated from Quebec to Chicago after the Civil War, and the four Spink sons were thrust into an atmosphere charged with the baseball feats of Cap Anson and Al Spalding.

When they grew up, the boys began to move south again. Billy, an expert telegrapher, became sports editor of the St. Louis Globe-Democrat. At his prodding, his brother Al joined him in St. Louis and became a sportswriter for the Post-Dispatch. He also orchestrated the efforts by local sportsmen to form a professional team, which became the St. Louis Browns, and to enlarge and renovate the team's ball field, which became Sportsman's Park.

But Alfred Spink made one more move that put him in the mainstream of baseball and that helped put baseball in the mainstream of American life. He started a weekly newspaper, The Sporting News, sold it at newsstands in the United States and Canada, and began to cover sports with a tight focus as part of the national scene.

The first issue was printed on March 17, 1886, and was sold for 5 cents for the single copy or $2.50 for the yearly subscription. Its stories were filed as though they were letters: "Chicago, March 11—Editor, Sporting News." Its front page that day had three stories at the top, two of them on baseball. On the left, the headline read: "The Game in Gotham. The Coming Base Ball Season to be the Liveliest the Metropolis Has Ever Known." In the center: "The White Stockings—Chicago's Great Team Getting Ready for the Trip to Hot Springs." And, on the right side of the page: "Ready for the Road. The Gentlemen's Driving Club Waiting for the Word."

The road riders did their riding with trotters, just as later generations did their road riding in sports cars, and the lead of the story reflected the local fervor: "The Gentlemen's Driving Club of St. Louis is now entering upon the fifth year of its existence with brilliant prospects of having a most successful season." The report also noted that the club has "the most prominent road riders of the city," and did not restrain its enthusiasm when it added that the sport "has become one of the most popular institutions of its kind in the West."

The tone was eager and exuberant, and it was sounded in the lead editorial, which reported greetings from writers and ball players, and then said: "And now, in view of all these kind wishes, how could we in return promise anything but to publish a paper saying good things of all men and ill of none?"

Other columns and roundups were devoted to The Turf, with a report from Memphis; to The Ring, witth a cut of Ed Kelly, the middleweight champion of Missouri, and to The Stage, with nearby two-inch ads for Fanny Davenport in "Fedora" at the Olympic Theater in New York, and for Kersand's Minstrels and Koerner's Oyster House Restaurant and Saloon in St. Louis.

But the main event was baseball, and Spink's weekly began to cover it in loving and even extravagant detail just as the sport began to boom.

Five years later, the feuds and wars of the 1880s ended with the collapse of the Players League and then the American Association, and by 1891 the stage was set for new stars to lead the performance into the next century. And, in August of that year, the brightest and longest-lasting star of the time was delivered onto the stage when a train pulled into Baltimore carrying an 18-year-old country boy named John Joseph McGraw of Truxton, N.Y.

He was a graduate of the Iron and Oil Association, he already had played for meal money in Upstate New York, for $60 a month on an exhibition tour of Florida and Cuba and for $125 a month in Cedar Rapids, Ia., in the Illinois and Iowa League. The towns were Joliet, Quincy, Ottawa, Aurora, Rockford, Davenport and Ottumwa, they ranged from 5,000 persons to about 20,000, and they seemed to live for the summertime thrill of seeing a famous baseball team on tour, like Cap Anson's Chicago White Stockings.

Meanwhile, in Kansas City, a child named Casey Stengel was one year old. In the East, the great P.T. Barnum left a world that he had helped to enliven with folk heroes like General Tom Thumb and Jenny Lind, phenomenal imports like Jumbo the elephant and the great traveling circus. And at the corner of 57th Street and Seventh Avenue in Manhattan, the new Music Hall, later renowned as Carnegie Hall, opened its doors on May 5, 1891, with an all-star gala of its own that featured the Symphony Society Orchestra, the Oratorio Society Chorus, the Boys' Choir of 100, Walter Damrosch conducting it all and "P. Tschaikowsky, the eminent Russian composer, who will conduct several of his own works."

It was three months later in that summer when John McGraw bounced down from the day coach and reported to Billy Barnie, the veteran manager of the Baltimore Orioles, who stared at the short, slender teen-ager who weighed exactly 121 pounds, and said: "Why, you're just a kid. Can you play ball?"

McGraw could, although he was a boy among men as he made his debut on the scene. The Boston Nationals had just taken a "census" of their players and learned that the youngest was 22 and the average was 28. But here was McGraw, ready to make it in the majors at 18. In his first time at bat, he struck out with the bases loaded.

But for the next 11 years, Baltimore was home for John McGraw, as he led the Orioles into a revival that became a renaissance and that endowed baseball with some of its most talented and storied characters.

The Orioles were playing in the American Association when he arrived that August, but they were gathered into the National League when the American Association folded at the end of the season. After a so-so 1892 season, McGraw played in 127 games in 1893, went to bat 475 times, made 156 hits, scored 123 runs, hit .328 and stole 40 bases. The kid who had appalled Bill Barnie had grown into a young professional, and the Baltimore Sun put it this way:

"McGraw is one of the youngest and most promising youngsters in the business, and undoubtedly has a brilliant baseball future. He is as lively as a cricket."

This cricket wasn't just lively; he was hellbent. And "Oriole baseball," as it became known, began to flourish in 1894 as a mixture of imagination, speed and piracy. It was practiced by one of the great roistering gangs of men, too, and they frequently started "practicing" at 8 o'clock in the morning for games that didn't begin until late in the afternoon—not until 4:30 in Washington, for example, in order to "get the crowd" from the federal departments as they left work. But the Orioles spent the long pregame hours perfecting their skills, strategies and tricks.

The team had finished in 12th and last place in 1892 and eighth in 1893 in the 12-team alignment, but now was about to begin a spectacular rise to the top. The Orioles were driven by a new manager, Ned Hanlon, and they were goaded by McGraw and his close friend, Hughey Jennings. And when William Henry (Wee Willie) Keeler joined the club from Brooklyn during spring training in Macon in March of '94, they were now reinforced by one of the best, beady-eyed, lefthanded hitters in the business, a man who would achieve a .345 lifetime batting average.

Dan Brouthers, also obtained from Brooklyn in the Keeler deal, was Baltimore's first baseman. Heinie Reitz was the second baseman, McGraw played third, Jennings was at shortstop. Steve Brodie and Joe Kelley played the outfield along with Wee Willie, and Wilbert Robinson was the catcher. After Brouthers moved on, "Dirty Jack" Doyle took over first base. And Joe Corbett, who joined the team in 1896, pitched 24 victories a year later as a full-fledged member of the Lavender Hill Mob of Mob Town.

They were as physical as a college football team. McGraw remembered going 10 weeks without a rubdown, mostly because trainers pampered no one in those days. Keeler once saved a game in Washington by chasing a long drive to the outfield fence, plunging his hand through the barbed wire on top and making the catch—although his arm was ripped to the elbow.

Corbett once missed spring training because he had a prior commitment: He served as a sparring partner for his big brother, Gentleman Jim Corbett, the heavyweight champion. And Jim even suggested that Joe give up baseball because it was growing too rough.

It was rough, all right. McGraw always stood on the inside corner of third base as a runner approached, forcing him to swing wide around McGraw rather than pivot on the bag itself. Sometimes, when a runner tagged up at third so that he could score after a fly ball, McGraw would hook him by the belt and hold on. The Orioles perfected the bunt, the running game, the Baltimore chop, the cutoff throw from the outfield. They called it "inside baseball," and they even included the groundskeeper, Tom Murphy, whose role in "inside baseball" was cast by McGraw himself. Build up the third-base foul line, Murphy was told, so that bunts would roll down-slope and curl fair.

During one stretch, they reportedly worked the hit-and-run play successfully 13 straight times and John Montgomery Ward, the manager of the New York Giants, said: "That isn't baseball the Orioles are playing. It's an entirely new game."

"Jennings, Kelley, Keeler, Wilbert Robinson and myself organized ourselves into a sort of committee," McGraw remembered. "We were scheming all the time for a new stunt to pull. We talked, lived and dreamed baseball. We met every night and talked over our successes and failures. If it was a trip to the theater, all of us went and sat together. Every year later on, we had a reunion. The players even looked after each other for years afterward. It was like an old college football team."

Whatever it was, it paid off. In 1894, the Orioles soared into first place with this remarkable lineup:

	Position	Age	Average
John McGraw	3b	21	.340
Willie Keeler	rf	22	.368
Joe Kelley	lf	22	.391
Dan Brouthers	1b	36	.345
Hughey Jennings	ss	25	.332
Steve Brodie	cf	26	.369
Heinie Reitz	2b	26	.306
Wilbert Robinson	c	30	.348

Jennings stole 36 bases, McGraw 77, Kelley 45 and Brodie 50. The Orioles won 18 straight late that season, lost one, then won six more games in a row—giving them 24 out of 25 and the National League pennant.

"We would have won all 25," McGraw murmured, not fully satisfied, "if Robbie hadn't slipped in the mud chasing a foul fly. The big lummox."

When the Orioles returned home from the West with the pennant, they were greeted at the Camden Street Station by a roaring celebration. A dozen carriages rolled up to the platform to carry the team through the streets in a town that had already gone wild. National Guardsmen, armed with bayonets, were called along with the entire police force to restrain the crowds surging along the 10-mile parade route, with 200 floats and two hours of winding through the streets of downtown Baltimore. And finally, in full evening dress that night, the Orioles were lionized at a civic banquet.

McGraw, though, felt that the season was just beginning, since the two top teams in the league were scheduled to meet in a postseason series for the Temple Cup, which had just been donated by William C. Temple, the president of the Pittsburgh club. Besides, the No. 2 club was the New York Giants.

"It is a disgrace to baseball," the 21-year-old "Little Napoleon" said. "I have kept myself in trim for these games, notwithstanding the temptations that have beset me every hour since out return to Baltimore. The team is not in fit condition to play, and we should forfeit the Temple Cup."

They didn't have to: The Giants, behind the relentless pitching of Amos Rusie and Jouett Meekin, swept four games and the cup. They won, 4-1 and 9-6 in Baltimore, and then 4-1 and 16-3 in the Polo Grounds in New York.

The townspeople of Baltimore, though, were forgiving in their disappointment. They realized that baseball contracts ran from April 1 to September 30, and that the players had been paid poorly for the Temple Cup series. So, they staged benefits at Ford's Opera House and the Music Hall to raise the postseason ante and reward the practitioners of "Oriole baseball."

One of the remarkable things about the Orioles was that they had only one really senior player, Dan Brouthers, and he played only that one full season for them. The following May, he was sold to Louisville for $700. But

Brouthers cut a heroic figure as *the* power hitter of his time—he was the "Babe Ruth" of the 1880s—and he was still fearsome at the age of 36.

Brouthers also looked the part: He stood 6-foot-2 and weighed 200 pounds, he had a bushy mustache and he had the dramatic full-form look of that era's man of distinction. He also won four major league batting titles outright and shared another during a career that began in 1876 when he played semipro ball for the Wappingers Falls Actives up the Hudson River in New York state, not far from where he was born in 1858.

He was a lefthanded pitcher with a curveball—which was rare enough then. But he also could hit with power, which was even rarer. So, he was converted into a first baseman and established as a cleanup hitter, and he stuck to those roles for most of the next quarter of a century.

Brouthers played in the Hudson Valley for three years before signing with the Troy Haymakers of the National League in 1879. Troy finished last in the league, but not because of Dan Brouthers. He pitched three games before going back to first base full-time. But the Haymakers were mis-named: They hit only four home runs all season—all by Dan Brouthers.

In the custom of the day, Brouthers skipped around a great deal, play-ing with independent teams in Baltimore and Rochester for most of one season before getting back into the National League with Buffalo in 1881. He hit a league-leading eight home runs in '81 and anchored the "Big Four" of the league: Hardie Richardson in center field, Deacon White at third base, Jack Rowe the catcher-shortstop and Brouthers at first base, all big hitters. And, one year later, he hit .368 and won his first batting title.

One year after that, he hit .371 with 156 hits (17 triples) in 97 games, and repeated as the batting champion. And the year after that, in 1884, he averaged .325.

Then, in 1885, Brouthers played a lead role in a strange scenario that embroiled the entire league. The Buffalo club was in financial straits, so it sold Brouthers, Richardson, Rowe and White—yes, the "Big Four"—to De-troit for the sensational sum of $7,500. The only thing wrong with that was the timing: It was the middle of September; that is to say, the heat of the pennant race. The president of the league, Nicholas Young, tried to cancel the deal because it obviously would have a tremendous impact on the pen-nant race. But the "Big Four" refused to return to Buffalo.

So, Young made a remarkable decision in a remarkable situation: He let them remain property of the Detroit club, which finished sixth, anyway. But he ordered them not to play in any games against contending teams. In the confusion, the four big hitters missed all the games for the final three weeks of the season. And, with the $7,500 in the till, but with the "Big Four" gone from the scene, the Buffalo club collapsed when the season closed.

It didn't take long for Detroit to reap its rewards, though. In 1887, the team won the pennant while Brouthers bloomed as a power hitter in an era of the dead ball. He hit one momentous home run in Washington that for years was invoked as the standard of distance. In Boston, he hit one that bounced off a wooden structure beyond the fence known as the "Sullivan Tower," and a number of fans tumbled off the tower when the missile struck. He also batted .419 with 239 hits (in a season in which bases on balls were counted as hits), but somehow lost the title to Cap Anson by two points.

He was one of the first lefthanded hitters, he was the first hitter from either side of the plate to win the batting title in consecutive years and he was one of the earliest and most romantic power hitters—a kind of Casey at the Bat. He even became active in labor matters, speaking for the players in 1889 when they announced the formation of the Players League. And he put his money where his mouth was in 1890, hitting .345 in the league's only year of existence and helping the rebel Boston team to the pennant.

He was so good that he bounced back without missing a beat when the Players League quit. He signed with Boston of the American Association the following year, and won the hitting title in that league, too. And, since he had played for Boston in the National League in 1889, he now had the distinction of having played for three different Boston teams in three leagues in three years—and of hitting .373, followed by .345, followed by .349.

Brouthers got back into the National League in 1892 with Brooklyn, and tied for the batting title with a .335 average. Then, in January of '94, he and Willie Keeler were traded to the Baltimore Orioles.

Brouthers was everything that the ultimate hero might properly be in baseball. He played on nine teams in the National League alone, and that stands as a record. He hit .415 at the age of 39 in the Eastern League, and won the batting title. He hit .373 at the age of 46 for Poughkeepsie in the Hudson River League, and won the batting title there, too.

That was in 1904, and he even appeared in two games for the Giants as a favor to McGraw, who was the manager of the Giants then and who figured the return of the old National League hero would be a gate attraction. And for 20 years until his death in 1932, Brouthers worked as a night watchman and press-box attendant in the Polo Grounds, a .349 lifetime major league hitter, a man with 2,349 hits in 1,658 games and 103 home runs, and the most accomplished player of his time.

But, having helped McGraw launch "Oriole baseball," Dan Brouthers was gone when the Orioles consolidated their success of 1894 by winning the pennant again in 1895. They once more were foiled in the Temple Cup series, this time by Cleveland and Denton True (Cy) Young.

But, in 1896, the Orioles won the pennant for the third straight year, and this time satisfied even McGraw by overpowering Cleveland for the Temple Cup. And, the year after that, they not only survived a rock-throwing, punch-throwing summer but also won the cup again, this time from the Boston club, which had beaten them out for the pennant. The Orioles, given their shot after running a tight second in '97, made the most of it.

"The main idea," John McGraw said, "is to win."

Julius Caesar's league

John McGraw went from Baltimore to New York where he fought Ban Johnson, the American League and everybody else and established the Giants as a stronghold in the National League.

CHAPTER 5

On February 15, 1898, the day the battleship Maine exploded in Havana harbor, John McGraw and Wilbert Robinson were teaching "Oriole baseball" in the gymnasium at Johns Hopkins University. They were not alone: Other members of the Baltimore Orioles, the demons of professional baseball, were busy in similarly peaceful pursuits in the days before spring training began. Hughey Jennings was tutoring at the University of Georgia, Joe Kelley at Georgetown and Bill Clarke at Princeton.

They were a remarkably close and partisan bunch. One afternoon in Boston late in the previous season, they had to fight their way back to the team's hotel against snipers who pelted their horse-drawn carriages with rocks from the sidewalks and houses. It was a pitched battle that had escalated in this sequence: Jack Doyle, the first baseman, jockeyed umpire Tom Lynch so long and so vigorously that Lynch threw him out of the game. Doyle left by firing an insult, whereupon the umpire responded by firing a right to the head, and they then were joined by Kelley and Joe Corbett and waves of Boston fans.

Now, it was another year and another season, and the Orioles and their chief antagonists were girding for another bare-knuckles campaign in the National League. But, on April 24, about a week after the season opened, war was declared by the United States.

Then the ball-park crowds disappeared, and a runaway race by Boston and Baltimore did nothing to bring them back. The Orioles one afternoon in Cleveland played before 75 cash customers. Clearly, some franchises were in disarray.

The Louisville club was the first to change hands, being taken over by Barney Dreyfuss, later the owner and impresario at Pittsburgh. Next: Chris Von der Ahe, who from his saloon days had built the St. Louis club (an American Association team until its absorption into the N.L. in 1892), was pursued and jailed by his creditors and his ball park was sold from the courthouse steps. In Brooklyn, the executive reins were passed when Charles H. Byrne died and was succeeded as president of the club by Charles Ebbets, a onetime office boy, ticket-taker and schedule-maker.

In New York, the Giants, still headed by their original owner, John B. Day, also had been sinking into money problems, not the least of which was the fact that a professional team was playing its games on Manhattan Field, next door to the Polo Grounds. Thrashing around for help, Day exchanged stock with Albert Spalding of the Chicago club and also with John T. Brush of the Cincinnati club, which in turn "sold" him the Indianapolis club. Even Arthur H. Soden of the Boston team held shares in the Giants, whose stock was now scattered all over the map. They were, in effect, a National League co-op.

This was "syndicate baseball," and it soon became the great issue of the day in professional sports because it scrambled the lines of ownership and of loyalty. And, before it was settled, the pattern of professional baseball was revolutionized.

The trigger was pulled by Harry Von der Horst, the owner of the Orioles. He was a beer wholesaler who organized the club 16 years earlier with the absolutely sound idea that he might now sell more beer through his own team. He leased a lot, built Union Park, installed 6,000 seats and a beer garden, charged 5 cents a head and in his second year of operation made $30,000 from the crowds that swarmed from the horsecars into his stadium.

. But now, in the winter of 1898-99, as the Spanish-American War strained the economy of sports along with the economy in general, Von der Horst bought an interest in the Brooklyn club. His goal this time was also absolutely sound: to switch his best players there, to reap the benefit of Brooklyn's booming population and to run the Orioles as a kind of super farm team.

The Baltimore manager, Ned Hanlon, executed his part of the plan by switching to Brooklyn and taking with him the heart of the great Oriole teams—Keeler, Kelley and then Jennings, and three pitchers who had been 20-game winners. They set up shop in Brooklyn's Washington Park, and now they had everything—except McGraw and Robinson.

They simply refused to switch. They were the Orioles. Besides, they owned the Diamond Cafe and were in no position to move. They resisted so furiously that Von der Horst let them stay, with McGraw now the manager of the Orioles and Robinson as his deputy.

This was "syndicate baseball" at its worst, and Von der Horst waged it so outrageously that he even sent four mediocre hitters to McGraw from Brooklyn, along with three pitchers who had won only a handful of games the season before. "The main reason for the deal," McGraw reflected, "was to make Brooklyn the dominating power in New York baseball, and we sure did."

Before the next season was over, the National League was feeling the effects of the deteriorating economy and the confusing baseball situation. The Louisville park burned in that summer of 1899. Brooklyn was struggling to get the upper hand promised by the syndicators. And the Cleveland club's owners bought the troubled St. Louis franchise and transferred their best players there (while maintaining control of the Cleveland entry), and Cleveland won only 20 of 154 games.

As if all that weren't enough grief, a new threat was gathering outside: The Western League, the best and most prosperous minor league, was starting to crowd the National League when it could least stand the pressure. As a result, the National League decided to pull in its horns to minimize its vulnerability and to drop four of its 12 clubs, and one of them was Baltimore.

The Western League may have been a minor league, but it had a major league mind behind it: Byron Bancroft Johnson. He got into the league in 1894 when he was only 30 years old and sports editor of the Cincinnati Commerical Gazette. He also was a longtime critic of John T. Brush, owner of the Cincinnati team, who once suggested sarcastically that Johnson take over the Western League and try straightening it out himself. And, urged on by Charles A. Comiskey, the manager of the Reds, that's exactly what Johnson did.

Johnson was tough, vain, heavy-handed and successful. He picked up the pieces of several National League fiascos, annexed the Cleveland territory to his league, moved his St. Paul club to Chicago with Comiskey in control, got Connie Mack to run the Milwaukee club and tried to persuade John McGraw to direct the Baltimore team as a new entry in a new league that Johnson was visualizing: the American League.

McGraw happened to be available because the National League had just pulled the rug out from under him again. At the close of the 1899 season, it dropped the Baltimore franchise (as well as Louisville, Washington and Cleveland), and McGraw and Robinson once more received marching orders: sold to St. Louis. But, once more, they refused to go, just as they had refused to go to Brooklyn a year earlier. Even when McGraw was offered the manager's job in St. Louis, he refused to go. In fact, he even stayed home when the clubs went south for spring training in 1900, a new century opening, an old league stumbling, a new rival growing.

One month into the season, St. Louis tried again, and this time McGraw recited terms: $100 a game and *no* reserve clause—that is, his services were not to be reserved to St. Louis at the end of the season. He wanted to be a free agent, and he was exactly 75 years ahead of his time.

So, he and Robinson packed their gear in their adjoining houses on St. Paul Street, and headed through baseball's no man's land for St. Louis. They spent a lot of time at the racetrack across the street from the ball park that summer, and they made sure that they did by getting themselves thrown out of ball games fairly often and then simply hiking across the street.

When the season ended, with the St. Louis club tied for fifth place, McGraw had a batting average of .337 with 28 stolen bases. But he and Robinson promptly took a longer hike, all the way back to Baltimore, where they had front-row seats at the gathering war between the National League and Ban Johnson's Western League, which had been anointed as the "American League." And both leagues were making strenuous efforts to land McGraw, who was already a towering figure at age 27 as the star player and chief evangelist of "Oriole baseball."

McGraw attended an American League meeting in Chicago, and was impressed by Johnson's somewhat self-serving analysis of the situation: "The National League is being administered to death. The American League is the only thing that can keep baseball alive."

Then, keeping his options open, he attended National League meetings in New York and Philadelphia. The club owners chided him for having left St. Louis, and assured him that he had a bright future in the National League—even though Baltimore no longer had a club.

At least, it had none in the National League. In 1901, Ban Johnson made it official: He was now in business as a "major" league. Chicago, Milwaukee, Detroit and Cleveland would remain in Johnson's league, with Baltimore, Washington, Philadelphia and Boston replacing Indianapolis, Kansas City, Buffalo and Minneapolis.

Baltimore's chief stockholder and manager? The old Oriole, John Joseph McGraw.

"A real baseball war was on," McGraw remembered. "We immediately started a raid on the National League, and I managed to get most of the players that I had wanted off my former Baltimore club."

One of the players he retrieved was Joseph Jerome McGinnity, a blond giant from the Indian Territory who was later known as "Iron Joe" for good reason. He won 57 games in two seasons while pitching for Baltimore and Brooklyn before McGraw got him back, and he wound up winning 247 games during 10 years in the big leagues. Five times, he pitched both ends of doubleheaders. Three times in one month in 1903, he won doubleheaders. He won 31 games for McGraw one year and, more astonishing than that, he did it while pitching 434 innings. If that performance hurt his arm, it wasn't immediately apparent: The next year, he came back and won 35 games. And he was still pitching in the minor leagues at the age of 54.

McGinnity also was one of the first players to cross from the National League to the American. Johnson opened the doors for a large switch-over by waiving the $2,400 salary limit that prevailed in the National League. He had eight strong franchises and an exceptional lineup of managers that included Clark Griffith, Jimmy Collins, Connie Mack, George Stallings, Hugh Duffy and McGraw.

He also had a 10-year term as president of the new league, a term that was extended in 1911 to 20 more years. He established his headquarters in the Fisher Building in Chicago, where nobody doubted that this was a "major league" office with a major league boss who had become well known for his strict rules—no liquor in the ball parks, no profanity in the ball parks, lots of paint and brightness in the ball parks, full authority for the umpires and maximum encouragement to the women to attend games.

The National League resisted Johnson and denied that he was running a "major" league. But 60 percent of the players in the new league in 1901 were former National Leaguers, including Cy Young, Napoleon Lajoie and Wilbert Robinson, and the American League eventually collared Ed Delahanty and Willie Keeler, among others.

The new league opened for business on April 24, with ceremonies in Chicago but with rain in Baltimore. In fact, it rained for two days in Baltimore before McGraw got his season rolling with Ban Johnson throwing out the first ball before 10,371 fans.

The Orioles beat the Red Sox that day, 10-6, and the war was on.

But so was the war between McGraw and Johnson, which started as a clash of personalities between two relentless personalities. It may even have started with Johnson's first memorandum: "Clean ball is my main plank. I will suspend any manager or player who uses profane language to an umpire." To a man of McGraw's violent style on the ball field, that was a challenge by any definition.

But economics soon joined politics and personalities as sources of conflict. The American League still needed a team in New York, and the expectation was that it would quickly establish one, with McGraw in command. But, as the league's first summer passed, the gulf between him and Johnson widened—and then he began to hear new overtures from his old home, the National League.

As early as June, McGraw had been sounded out about his possible return "under ideal conditions," and he even had been sounded out by the owners of the New York Giants. By August, though, he was still playing third base for the Orioles and hitting .352, with the Orioles running third behind Chicago and Boston. Then he pulled tendons in his right knee, and returned from a Western trip with his leg in a cast and the Orioles in fifth place.

Both leagues were now cutting each other's financial throats, and Ban Johnson was growing increasingly peevish about McGraw and his official flirtations. He issued a statement accusing McGraw of "crimes" like dickering with his enemies, and added in ringing tones: "We want no Benedict Arnold in our midst." And McGraw, also reaching into history for venom, replied: "So the Julius Caesar of the league calls me a Benedict Arnold, does he?"

The sniping continued into the following season, and reached a peak in July. By then, Ban Johnson was pushing his plan to install a team in New York to invade the territory of the Giants. And, by then, McGraw was getting the old feeling that he would be left holding the bag again in Baltimore. So, he executed a stunning coup: He beat Johnson to the punch, and jumped to New York himself as playing manager of the Giants.

The coup was actually executed by an ally of Andrew Freedman, chief owner of the Giants, a terrible-tempered real-estate lawyer with Tammany Hall connections but little redeeming personality. The ally was John T. Brush, the owner of the Cincinnati club, who had held stock in the Giants since the middle of the 1890s when "syndicate baseball" resulted in interlocking control of teams by other teams.

Brush called McGraw to Indianapolis, where he lived in a large house on eight acres of forest. It had been named Lombardy by James Whitcomb Riley, "the Hoosier poet," in a toast to Brush's wife, the former Elsie Lombard. The setting was pastoral and secretive. McGraw was instructed to reach Indianapolis by a train that would arrive before dawn, then to walk quickly from the depot to a street corner a couple of blocks away. There, *Mrs.* Brush would pick him up in a carriage and whisk him off to Lombardy.

"All this," recalled John B. Hempstead, the son of Brush's son-in-law, "so that neither the press nor the baseball world would discover the pending deal between them."

The pending deal was settled in the dining room, and the contract was signed on the dinning-room table. Brush's daughter Natalie, who was a child then, remembered years later that the scene was turn-of-the-century classical: The long driveway edged with a double row of iris, the walls covered with tapestry, the draperies of heavily brocaded rose satin and velvet, the inlaid mahogany of the Adam period, the conservatory beyond the door past the dinning-room table where a bit of baseball history was being made.

So, on July 16, 1902, the deed was done. McGraw jumped from Baltimore, switched leagues and took over "absolute control" of the New York Giants. And, as he said farewell to Byron Bancroft Johnson and his league, Benedict Arnold fired a parting shot at Julius Caesar, saying: "He picked on me—and I couldn't stand his umpires."

★　　　★　　　★

In New York, the headlines read: "Latest Baseball Deal. Freedman Practically Buys Baltimore American League Team. Players To Join New York."

Half a dozen players, in fact, led by the strutting little boss himself. And Ban Johnson hustled down to Baltimore, announcing that he had been expecting "this emergency" and was "fully able to meet it."

But he was whistling Dixie, so to speak. The next day, the Orioles didn't have enough players for their game against St. Louis. So, the visiting players "took their positions on the diamond and went through the formality of playing the game while none of the Baltimore players appeared in uniform on the grounds, forfeiting the game." The headline there said: "No Baseball In Baltimore."

Back in New York, though, the Giants were on the road but the invasion was in full swing. On the morning of July 17, McGraw made his first appearance to headlines that said: "McGraw At Polo Grounds. Andrew Freedman Gives The New Manager Power To Strengthen The Local Team."

The local team certainly needed strengthening: The Pittsburgh Pirates were in first place in the National League that day with a spectacular record of 54 victories, 15 losses and a 16½-game lead. At the bottom of the league, the Giants reposed with a record of 22 and 50, and they were 33½ games behind and incontestably last, and this was only the middle of July.

"Of course," McGraw said, disassociating himself from this disaster, "the pennant is out of our reach as far as this year's playing season goes.

But look out for us next year."

Then he turned to Freedman, the man who had just hired him and endowed him with the cudgels of office, and produced the list of 23 players on the New York roster. He crossed nine names off the list, and said: "You can begin by releasing these." Freedman replied that they had cost him a total of $14,000. But McGraw, wasting neither time nor tone in his first day on the job, said: "If you keep them, they'll cost you more. I've brought real ball players with me, and I'll get some more."

Two days later, the Giants were home from Cincinnati and they took the field on July 19 for the first time with McGraw and his migrated professionals in uniform. "According to officials," reported The Times, "16,000 persons passed through the turnstiles" that Saturday afternoon.

In the New York Evening World, the great day was reported in these words: "John McGraw and his Baltimore recruits made their local debut before nearly 10,000 people." That was a pretty hefty range of figures on the crowd, but nobody could dispute the mood: Revival was in the air. And, even though the Giants lost the game to Philadelphia, 4-3, curiosity and anticipation ruled along with a kind of patriotism, and The Times said:

"New York's baseball team played its first game at the Polo Grounds yesterday under the new management of John McGraw. The Philadelphia nine were the opposing players. With the new management and the infusion of new blood, the New Yorks played much better ball than they had been doing. They did not win, but the home players lost the game by only one run and *put up a good article of the game.*"

McGraw's first lineup in New York had McGraw playing shortstop and batting second, Dan McGann at first base batting third, Roger Bresnahan catching and batting eighth and Iron Joe McGinnity pitching and batting ninth. They were the newly recruited old Orioles, and they gave the crowd something to take home: hope. Also in the lineup, and batting fourth, was the center fielder Steve Brodie, an Oriole star of the past who had been with the Giants since the beginning of the season.

"That the people of New York want to see good baseball," The Times concluded, "and will liberally patronize the same was proved by the crowds that went to the Polo Grounds to see what their new team would do under the new regime. And they had nothing but encouragement for the home players. Although beaten, the crowd applauded the home team as it left the ground."

The game was not only the first for McGraw in New York as the Giants' playing manager, but the first for him anywhere in three weeks after a series of typically violent skirmishes that spiced his departure from Baltimore and his arrival in Manhattan.

Nearly two months earlier, he was spiked at third base by an outfielder for Detroit named Dick Harley. His orange-and-black stocking was soaked with blood, but McGraw still leaped at Harley's throat while a Saturday crowd of 4,000 went wild.

The spike wound kept him on the sidelines for five weeks. Then, in his first game back, he plunged into an argument with the umpire over a tag that he either made or did not make during a rundown. He was thrown out of the game, refused to leave, was thrown out again, then was told the game was being forfeited. Ban Johnson thereupon suspended him indefinitely, but McGraw kept the argument going in the newspapers for two weeks and then played his ace: Off to New York with half the Orioles' stars.

Johnson, who also did not mince words, fired a few parting shots himself as McGraw departed: "The McGraw-Baltimore incident is closed. It took a long time for the patrons of baseball in Baltimore to learn McGraw's peculiar curves and angles, but they learned fast. The National League sent a good, kind angel in the form of Freedman's certified checks and the angels had wings enough to carry McGraw away. So, Baltimore and the American League rejoice."

So, McGraw caused rejoicing in two cities at the same time. But his first mission was to resurrect the Giants in the biggest market in the country, and he did. One thing he did was to express outrage when he found Christy Mathewson alternating at first base or the outfield on days when he was not pitching, and he put a stop to that on the spot.

Mathewson was 22 at the time, the oldest of five children of a gentleman farmer in Factoryville, Pa., and a really big man on campus at Bucknell University: star in baseball, football and basketball; president of his class; a member of two literary societies and the glee club, and a semipro pitcher in the summertime. He left Bucknell in 1899 and signed his first professional contract for $90 a month to pitch for Taunton, Mass., in the New England League. While he was there, a teammate showed him how to throw the "reverse curve," or "fadeaway," as it became known, really a screwball that broke in to a righthanded batter.

"All batters who are good waiters, and will not hit at bad balls," he wrote in his memoirs, "are hard to deceive, because it means a twirler has to lay the ball over, and then the hitter always has the better chance. A pitcher will try to get a man to hit at a bad ball before he will put it near the plate.

"Many persons have asked me why I do not use my 'fadeaway' oftener when it is so effective, and the only answer is that every time I throw the 'fadeaway' it takes so much out of my arm. It is a very hard ball to deliver. Pitching it 10 or 12 times in a game kills my arm, so I save it for the pinches."

He saved it for the pinches often enough and successfully enough so that the offers came in from both the Phillies and Giants one year later, in 1900. He figured that he would do more pitching in New York, signed for $2,000 and pitched for a last-place team. He didn't pitch much, or well: six times, no victories, three defeats, and he walked 20 batters in 34 innings.

The Giants, not too thrilled, sent him back to Norfolk in the Virginia League, where he had opened the season and where he had won 20 of 22 decisions. This time, he didn't stay long enough to stun people. Cincinnati drafted him for $100, then sent him back to the Giants in a trade for Amos Rusie, who had won 241 games in nine seasons but who now was fairly crippled by a chronically sore arm. And this time, Mathewson thrived. In 1901, he won 20 games for a seventh-place team, including a no-hitter a month short of his 21st birthday. And he was pitching and filling in occasionally elsewhere when McGraw arrived in the summer of 1902 and formed an alliance that lasted for the rest of their lives.

But McGraw made his first imprint on New York baseball when he first took the Giants to Brooklyn for two games against the Trolley Dodgers, a team stocked with players from his prime days in Baltimore. A great rivalry was born, and a good crowd of 7,000 showed up on a Wednesday afternoon to watch the Giants beat the Dodgers, 4-1. It was their first victory as McGraw's men, and they followed it the next day by winning, 2-0, with Mathewson pitching a five-hitter and striking out 11 batters.

For the rest of the season, the Giants were the best last-place team in the business. They won 25 games and lost 38 after McGraw took charge, and the box office began to pick up, too. McGraw, meanwhile, moved into the Victoria Hotel at Broadway and 27th Street, two blocks from the Giants' office in the St. James Building, in the neighborhood where most of the theaters were clustered. He became a familiar and frequently bare-fisted figure in the night life of the city. But, by day, he was a fanatic for the business at hand. He would drop into the office early each morning, then would head directly for the Polo Grounds, where he would arrive at 10 o'clock for a game that did not begin until 4 in the afternoon.

Two things happened that winter to further shape the pattern of New York baseball. Andrew Freedman sold the Giants for $200,000 to John T. Brush, the clothing man who had bought the Indianapolis team in 1888 and the Cincinnati team after the 1890 season. Brush didn't have the money for the Giants, but he knew where to get it—from the other National League owners, who were not too regretful to see Freedman go, and the Fleischmann brothers, Julius and Max, the yeast kings, who took the bankrupt Cincinnati Reds off Brush's hands.

The second development that winter involved McGraw's old antagonist, Ban Johnson, who finally landed an American League team in New York. They were the Highlanders, so-called because their first president was Joseph Gordon, and the Gordon Highlanders were then the best-known regiment in the British Army. They also played their games at Broadway and 165th Street, one of the highest points of land in Manhattan.

The Highlanders actually came from humble stock, despite the implications of their nickname. They were financed by seven Democratic politicians led by Captain Bill Devery of the New York police and Frank Farrell,

The tough, vain and heavy-handed Ban Johnson met the challenge of competing against the National League, but battling with John McGraw was another matter.

the pool-room king of Manhattan, who was basically a bookmaker with Tammany connections.

The Highlanders went to work under a celebrated manager, Clark Griffith, "the Old Fox," who had been born in 1869 in a log cabin in Missouri after his parents had traveled there by covered wagon. He worked his way up the scale of success as a pitcher, earning $10 from his local team in Illinois after his family moved there, then $50 a month in the low minors, then $225 a month in the high minors in 1888.

During the 1890s, he pitched in the National League as a star with the Chicago club, which was run for most of that period by Cap Anson, and he developed a bristling rivalry with McGraw. Now, Griffith was being installed as manager of the new team in town—McGraw's town. And within a couple of years, Griffith's Highlanders began to be called the Yankees.

The World Series

The uniform was black but the mood was upbeat when Giants Manager John McGraw (left) greeted Philadelphia A's Manager Connie Mack before the 1911 World Series in a replay of the first Series meeting (1905) between the two teams.

CHAPTER 6

Maybe it was the temper of the times that set the tone for the new century. Maybe it was the number itself that romanticized the tone: the 20th Century. Maybe it was the obvious fact that the decade of the 1890s needed something special for an encore, and this was it. Or maybe it was the turn of the national mood at the turn of the century, the mood surging with Theodore Roosevelt as he went surging up San Juan Hill with his volunteer cavalry regiment, and even the name symbolized the mood: Rough Riders.

Now, as the new century opened, Roosevelt was back behind the desk as governor of New York, soon to become vice president of the United States and, before September was gone in 1901, advancing to President on the assassination of William McKinley in a kind of one man's manifest destiny.

It may have been a new century, with new heroes and new villains, but it looked back and cherished the old spirit—the spirit of the frontier. It was as though the frontier style of life had spilled into the 20th Century and its cities. Street gangs in Manhattan sometimes mobilized as many as 1,500 bare-fisted brawlers for main events. Bat Masterson, no longer the law of Dodge City, as he had been a generation before, no longer the Indian fighter and scout of life on the trail, now worked as a 50-year-old sportswriter on the New York Morning Telegraph, still a formidable figure in a black derby as he made the rounds of the West Side saloons.

Out where the frontier was still a fact of life, and not just a figment of memory, the Fourth of July show at Sheridan, Wyo., in 1902 featured a "lifelike reproduction of the slaughter of General Custer and his men," a replay from 26 years before, but a replay that did not cut corners: The "heroic Seventh Cavalry" was surrounded by 1,500 Crow and Cheyenne Indians in "hideous warpaint who swooped down upon the 200 men from Fort McKenzie and cut down and annihilated them in the presence of thousands of spectators."

The New York Times reported "an increase of hostility" toward a newer enemy: the automobile. One farmer shot at a passing motorcar because it was frightening his horses. In Manhattan, "automobilists" were lobbying for an increase in the speed limit, from eight miles an hour, as currently enforced, all the way to 12 or even 15. But, in the best frontier spirit, citizens were forming vigilante committees to fight the threat of reckless speed. And outside Chicago, in the suburb of Winnetka, the mayor stretched a rope across the street and began timing cars with a stopwatch.

John Nance Garner, a young country judge from Texas, was elected to the House of Representatives in 1902, and later remembered that "the autocratic leaders of the Democratic Party thought I was just another cow thief from Texas." He wasn't, although he did spend a great deal of his time fighting the railroads in Texas on behalf of his constituents, most of whom were farmers. And, when he wasn't doing that, he was chiefly interested in baseball, growing pecans and playing poker, a game at which he became so skilled that his winnings in some sessions of Congress reportedly exceeded his pay of $10,000 a year.

It may not have been the frontier spirit, but one of the highest prices on the New York Stock Exchange was commanded by American Snuff at $123 a share. And it may not have been the frontier spirit, but something very much like it energized the throngs of gamblers who flocked to places like Richard Canfield's casino on 44th Street off Fifth Avenue in New York, and the same surge of civic energy filled Delmonico's restaurant two doors away, as well as Rector's and the roof garden of Stanford White's Moorish castle and tower that had become the second Madison Square Garden.

It was a time when nicknames captured the man, and sometimes the woman. Bet-a-Million Gates was there, more formally known as John W. Gates, which in a way was too bad. Gentleman Jim Corbett was there, one decade after he had won the heavyweight title by knocking out the legendary John L. Sullivan in 21 rounds in New Orleans. Outweighed 212 pounds to 187 by Sullivan but a fetching figure of a man, tall and slender and handsome, Corbett was a bit of a dandy, but nonetheless the Gentleman Jim who had rescued prize fighting from the riffraff of sports. Well, he rescued it *temporarily* from the riffraff of sports. And the timekeeper at ringside on the day Corbett destroyed the legend of the Boston Strong Boy? Bat Masterson, of course.

Diamond Jim Brady was there, too. James Buchanan Brady, who went a long way for a railroad-equipment salesman and who spent many of his evenings presiding over feasts at Rector's, frequently accompanied by Miss Nellie Leonard of Clinton, Ia., who was immensely better known as Lillian Russell, the "Belle of Broadway." Or, to Diamond Jim and her four husbands: Nell.

Diamond Jim and the Belle of Broadway were a weighty pair who set the tone, the pace and probably the record for night life in *la belle époque*, particularly for that phase of night life that could be pursued at the dinner table. They would descend on Rector's before heading for the theater, and would pitch into a feast that might open with several dozen oysters, half a dozen boiled crabs and a few ducks. Then they would get down to the serious eating. And they would return for supper after the theater, and resume the marathon.

When a little more action was needed to spice the menu, Diamond Jim would join the elegant stampede to the lavish, million-dollar casino built by Richard Canfield and endowed with one of the best art collections anywhere in the land. Canfield sort of set the tone here, the way Brady did at Rector's groaning board: He was tall and imposing, a self-made achiever with a grammar-school education and a prison record, a wide knowledge of art and literature, and close relationships with J.P. Morgan, James McNeill Whistler, Diamond Jim Brady and Stanford White.

They shared an interest in acquiring things of value, and they even shared stock-market tips at the gaming table. They also shared the respectability that is frequently bred by celebrity. Whistler, in fact, once painted Canfield's portrait, which later was purchased by the Cincinnati Museum. And Canfield probably expressed the prevalent attitude when he observed: "I do not know that I have any code of ethics. As morals are considered by most people, I have no more than a cat."

The seats of power were often those at the Casino Theater, where the city's men of means would gather in the evening to share an appreciation of beauty on stage. And there was no more beauty on any stage than there was at the Casino when the Floradora Sextette appeared in pink walking costumes, huge black picture hats, long black gloves and smiles, strolling onto the scene carrying parasols, and doing it all so fetchingly that the group filled the theater for 500 nights. All six of the original Floradora girls married millionaires: One became the spouse of a silk manufacturer, another married a financier, another a diamond miner, another a Wall Street broker, one even took the vows with the nephew of Andrew Carnegie. The sixth, Marie Wilson, married Freddie Gebhard, formerly the suitor of Lillie Langtry, and a society horseman whose jumper set an indoor record at the National Horse Show in Madison Square Garden.

It was in the Garden, in fact, that the surging life of the new century surged to a peak of drama on the night of June 25, 1906. They were all gathered there in the roof theater of Stanford White's tower, one of the town's favorite meeting and eating places. It was not far from the luxury apartment that White had designed for himself when he drew the architectural plans for the Garden and its tower, where he had lived and loved since its formal opening in 1890. It was also the centerpiece of the landscape that he had created for New York, landmarks that included the Brooklyn and Metropolitan museums, the Pennsylvania Station and the Washington Arch, as well as the Moorish Castle on Madison Square.

It was there, in the spectacular tower adjoining the main arena, that he had wined and dined brigades of beauties, and most especially the 21-year-old Floradora and Gibson girl Evelyn Nesbit, the storied "girl on the red velvet swing," and later the wife of the unstable millionaire Harry K. Thaw. And Thaw brooded at length about what might have happened in the days when his bride had been one of the trophies won by Stanford White.

The final act was played on that June night in 1906. White was having dinner at one table with his 20-year-old son Lawrence and a group of friends. At another table, Thaw sat with his wife. On stage, half a dozen girls in pink tights were dancing around an immense bottle of champagne while a tenor sang "I Could Love A Thousand Girls," and that may have triggered

Harry Thaw's hair-trigger temperament.

Thaw rose from his table to leave, near the end of the second act, and Evelyn Nesbit dutifully rose and left with him. Then, Thaw turned and walked back inside, straight to the table where White was sitting. From beneath his black cloak, Harry Thaw drew a pistol, and he fired it three times at Stanford White's imposing red head.

At the trial, Evelyn was dressed demurely in a middy blouse and pleated skirt with a large bow at her throat. She testified that she had met White in 1901, when she was barely 16. She said that the architect had drugged and seduced her in an apartment over the F.A.O. Schwarz toy store on 24th Street. And, she went on, she later had described this ordeal to Harry Thaw just before their marriage.

Her testimony caused a rise of 100,000 copies a day in the combined circulaton of New York's newspapers. Her testimony also caused a deadlock on the jury. And, as a result of that, a second trial was called in 1908, and that time Harry Thaw was found not guilty by reason of insanity.

Irvin S. Cobb, who covered the trial for the World, wrote that Evelyn Nesbit was "the most exquisitely lovely human being I ever looked at." The jury apparently agreed.

★   ★   ★

By day, the action took place uptown and outdoors; in New York, chiefly at the Polo Grounds. By night, it switched downtown and indoors, chiefly to the casinos and cabarets, or to Stanford White's renowned "central palace of pleasure" on Madison Square. On balance, it was a perfect arrangement: The lions of Broadway's night life and the theater flocked to the ball park in the late afternoon, and John McGraw led the return parade back down Broadway in the evening.

But, for baseball to fulfill its role in the social and national cast, some order had to be imposed in a business that was wracked by bitterness and warring between the old National League and the new and thriving American League.

The warring carried back and forth across cities and states, and even embroiled the courts, sometimes in comic ways. The great Napoleon Lajoie jumped from the National League to the American League without leaving Philadelphia: He simply jumped from the Phillies to Connie Mack's Athletics. There was no great mystery to his switch: He was a .349 career hitter making $2,400 a year, the maximum salary allowed in the National League. So, Mr. Mack raised the ante to $6,000, and hired a star, who promptly justified the stakes by hitting .422 in the American League's inaugural season of 1901.

The Nationals, firing back with writs and *mandamus* clauses, hustled into court and demanded the return of their property. They based their action on the reserve clause, and they were upheld by the Pennsylvania

Supreme Court, which ordered Lajoie back to the National League club in Philadelphia in 1902. But that was no call to surrender, not for Ban Johnson. He realized that the court ruling had weight only in Pennsylvania, so he arranged with Connie Mack for Lajoie to be shifted to the Cleveland club in the American League. Whenever Cleveland played in Philadelphia, the team's star second baseman sat. But, every place else, the best hitter in baseball played—and he did so in the American League.

The war raged until early in 1903, when a sort of formal peace was imposed. It was built on economic self-interest up and down the line, and it was engineered with tradeoffs: The American League, for example, would be allowed to enter New York (over the violent dissent of John McGraw and the Giants), but it would pledge in return to stay out of Pittsburgh, where the Pirates had the best team in the National League.

Beyond that, the urgent issue of territorial claims and territorial integrity was settled by recognizing eight cities as stipulated American League territories and eight as National, even though five of the cities had teams in both leagues. This was the geography:

American League: Boston, New York, Philadelphia, Washington, Detroit, Cleveland, St. Louis and Chicago.

National League: Boston, New York, Brooklyn, Philadelphia, Pittsburgh, Cincinnati, St. Louis and Chicago.

Once the cities were recognized, the clubs had to decide on the players, especially the players who had jumped from one league to the other during the war. This was a tough one, and it was made even tougher when John T. Brush signed Ed Delahanty to a contract with the New York Giants almost on the eve of the peace conference between the leagues. It was provocative because Delahanty, one of five brothers who played in the big leagues, had just won the American League batting championship by hitting .376 for Washington. And Brush was warning everybody that Ed Delahanty would hit for the Giants in 1903 even if he had to break up the peace conference to do it.

When the owners and other delegates of the clubs met in the St. Nicholas Hotel in Cincinnati on January 9, 1903, they broke into some highly charged bickering and sniping over the issue of stealing players. Things grew so tumultuous that Garry Herrmann, the chief owner of the Cincinnati Reds, walked out of the meeting with a warning to the other owners to cut out the backbiting and get down to work. They did, the next morning, and Herrmann even led the way by relinquishing his claim to "Wahoo Sam" Crawford, a .333 hitter for Cincinnati in 1902 and a future Hall of Famer, who recently had skipped from the Reds to the Detroit Tigers.

With that sort of encouragement, the owners worked out a formula for settling all such cases of piracy: The year 1902 was established as the base year. All players who jumped to the new American League before that season were now confirmed with their clubs. Players who jumped after the start of the 1902 season were now ordered back to their original clubs, if the original contract claims were indisputable.

As it turned out, 16 contract claims were not indisputable, and they were settled this way: The American League was awarded Delahanty, Crawford, Lefty Davis, Kid Elberfeld, Willie Keeler, Wid Conroy, Bill Donovan, Dave Fultz and Napoleon Lajoie. The National League won the rights to Sam Mertes, Harry Smith, Vic Willis, Tommy Leach, Rudy Hulswitt, Frank Bowerman and the future ace of aces, Christy Mathewson. Final score: 9-7, American League.

The peace treaty was drafted in February 1903, and was put into words by Joe Flanner, the editor of The Sporting News, who also happened to have a law degree. Flanner translated the agreement into language that both sides could accept, and even set the National Agreement into type in the composing room of The Sporting News in St. Louis. Copies then were forwarded to Buffalo, N.Y., where representatives of the two leagues held a ratification meeting, and they adopted the agreement without changing a word.

They also entrusted the new *modus vivendi* to a three-man National Commission, a board composed of the presidents of the National and American Leagues, who happened then to be Harry C. Pulliam, formerly an official of the Pittsburgh Pirates, and the renowned revolutionary himself, Ban Johnson, plus a third member elected by the two presidents. They picked Garry Herrmann of Cincinnati, and even designated him as chairman of the commission. It remained the governing board of the big leagues until 1920, when Federal Judge Kenesaw Mountain Landis became the first commissioner of baseball. And, until Landis took charge, there was little doubt that the most influential and powerful member of the commission was not the chairman, but Ban Johnson, "the czar."

Johnson wasted no time anointing his American League as a fully certified major league, and he did it with a fine sense of drama by staging the home opener for the New York Highlanders with the kind of flair and pomp that would drive McGraw and his Giants a bit wild. The Highlanders spent the first week of the 1903 season on the road. But, when they made their debut in New York on April 30, they did it with gusto before a crowd of 16,000 fans. Johnson arranged for each fan to receive a small American flag as he went through the turnstile. The players lined up across the outfield at the stroke of 3 o'clock, and marched toward home plate while the Sixty-ninth Regiment band played the "Washington Post March." They halted in front of the grandstand, and stood at attention for "The Star-Spangled Banner." Act One, and not bad. Plus, New York won, 6-2.

The first teams to win championships under the new treaty were the Pittsburgh Pirates in the National League and the Boston club in the American. (Depending on the reportorial source, Boston was known as the Pilgrims, Puritans, Red Sox or, apparently most often, simply as the Boston

Americans.)

There was some irony in Pittsburgh's advancement to postseason play because the Pirates had won their third straight pennant that year despite the loss of two of their best pitchers, Jack Chesbro and Jesse Tannehill, who had defected to the American League. But they still had the dashing Fred Clarke in left field, Ginger Beaumont (the league batting champion in 1902) in center and the peerless Honus Wagner at shortstop.

The Pirates won the pennant by 6½ games over the Giants, who were making a powerful climb from last place to second place under McGraw, and after that straight into first place. And, in the American League, the Boston team won by 14½ games over Philadelphia, and did it mostly with players snatched from the National League.

Strangely enough, the treaty between the leagues did not include a series between the leagues. But, late in August, such a series struck Barney Dreyfuss of the Pirates as a smart idea. He surmised that the Pittsburgh and Boston clubs looked like winners, so he broached the idea of a postseason series to Henry J. Killilea, a lawyer from Milwaukee who owned the Boston team. Killilea went straight to Ban Johnson's office in Chicago and repeated what Dreyfuss had suggested, and Johnson got right to the heart of the matter by replying: "Do you think you can beat them?"

Killilea, who thought that he could, met with Dreyfuss early in September and struck the deal. They agreed to play until one team won five games, because Dreyfuss felt that the Temple Cup series had been too short at four-out-of-seven. They also agreed to split the gate, and to stipulate that neither side could use a player signed or otherwise engaged after September 1.

They also agreed that they would make their own arrangements with the players on each club, and that nearly sank the deal right there: The Pittsburgh contracts expired October 15, but the Boston contracts ended October 1, and the American Leaguers threatened to strike and skip the postseason series unless Killilea forked over the entire gate to the players. He won them over by awarding them two weeks of extra pay plus a share of his receipts.

This was, everybody agreed, the World Series. And the public responded with passion. They played the first game on October 1 in Boston, and a crowd of 16,242 jammed the grounds on Huntington Avenue, where ropes were strung across the outfield to restrain the overflow crowd. In the lobby of the Vendome Hotel before the game, bettors "with fistfuls of folding money" did business in the open while fans from the rival cities argued over the conflicting merits of Boston's Cy Young and Pittsburgh's Hans Wagner.

Young was 36 years old, but he was clearly the club pro: He won 28 games that season, pitching 34 complete games in 35 starts. But, in the first inning of the first World Series game, the Pirates, aided by Boston misplays, ripped into Young for four runs. Pittsburgh went on to win the inaugural game, 7-3, behind the six-hit pitching of their one healthy and accomplished pitcher: Deacon Phillippe, who pitched five complete games in the Series (which ran through October 13) and won three times.

But, the next afternoon, Boston rebounded and defeated the Pirates, 3-0, as Bill Dinneen pitched a three-hitter with 11 strikeouts. And the next day, still playing in Boston, the Pirates regained the Series lead when the gutsy Phillippe won again, this time outpitching Tom Hughes and Young, 4-2.

After three games in Boston, the teams boarded trains and switched the Series to Pittsburgh, where the American Leaguers were accompanied and fortified by the Royal Rooters, a clamorous organization of partisans who organized into a traveling and cheering section back in 1897 and who still beat the drums for Boston baseball. But, despite the tumult raised by 200 of the rooters, the strong-armed Deacon Phillippe pitched effectively once more for Pittsburgh, and prevailed once more for Pittsburgh. He outdueled Dinneen, 5-4, with the help of three hits by Wagner, who had won the National League batting title that season by hitting .355.

Now, Pittsburgh had a lead of three games to one, and hundreds of fans showed their appreciation by swarming onto the field and hoisting Phillippe onto their shoulders for a ceremonial trip around the ball park. After all, the Pirates had won three games, and he had pitched all three. And then, for an hour after, Phillippe was forced to sit around while his public lined up to shake hands with the hero of Pittsburgh baseball.

But neither fate nor the Boston bats treated Pittsburgh kindly after that. The Americans came back and overpowered the Pirates in the fifth game, 11-2. They did it mostly with the help of a six-run sixth inning and the pitching of old Cy Young, and they went on and won the next game, too, by a score of 6-3, and now the Series was tied.

Barney Dreyfuss then tried to hold back the tide by postponing the next game one day, invoking the privilege of the owner of the home team. He said it was too cold to play, but he was probably angling for an extra day of rest for Deacon Phillippe and for a Saturday crowd at Exposition Park. He got both, and Phillippe even got a diamond stickpin from his admirers in a ceremony at home plate before the game. But, with 17,038 customers watching in some dismay, the tiring Phillippe lost to the reviving Young, 7-3.

The clubs went back to Boston, waited through a rainy Monday, when Game 8 was scheduled to be played, and then the remarkable Phillippe pitched again on Tuesday with two days of rest. He was good, too, allowing eight hits and no walks. But Dinneen meanwhile was holding the Pirates to four hits and two walks, and Boston won the game, 3-0, and won the first World Series, five games to three.

Far into the night, the Boston faithful, especially the Royal Rooters, paraded around the ball park carrying their heroes on their shoulders. The Pirates slipped back to Pittsburgh, where Dreyfuss treated their wounds by tossing his entire share of the club's receipts into the players' pool. As a result, the Pirates collected $1,136 apiece for losing the World Series; the Boston players were paid $1,182 apiece for winning the World Series.

★   ★   ★

When the baseball season opened in April 1904, the "peace" between the two major leagues was about as fragile as John McGraw's temper. In five of the eight cities in each league, rival teams went head-to-head for the public's purse and passion, and this adversarial relationship was dramatized with the most passion perhaps in New York, where the National League had a blood rivalry of its own between the Giants in Manhattan and the Dodgers in Brooklyn. Then, whoever survived that encounter, if anyone did survive, the American League was waiting crosstown with its new and successful Highlanders.

Consequently, opening day in New York became an extravaganza of civic side-taking and ceremony. The Giants, opening the season in Brooklyn, made a spectacular entrance by parading down Fifth Avenue in two gasoline-driven cars rented for the occasion by Charles Ebbets, the owner of the Dodgers. The convoy moved across the Brooklyn Bridge to the ball park, where the crowd was already blasting at full pitch, and the ball players were immediately inundated by a wave of speeches, concerts and welcoming rallies. It was well after 4 o'clock when things quieted down, and then the Giants knocked off the Dodgers for the first of Christy Mathewson's 33 victories in 1904 and the first of the team's 106.

That was dramatic, too: The Giants had zoomed from last place in 1902 when McGraw arrived from Baltimore, on up to second place a year later and now they were taking the final stride to the top. McGraw himself played in only five games, but he was still the most visible and most audible of Giants as he took his stance in the coaching box and insulted his rivals, baited the umpires and primed the fans in a nonstop performance.

"Iron Man" McGinnity pitched 51 times, started 44 games, finished 38, won 35 and lost eight. And that was one year after he had won 31 games and lost 20, which may explain why he was called "Iron Man."

Then there was Mathewson, who started 46 games, finished 33, won 33 and lost 12. And that was one season after Mathewson had won 30 games and lost 13; and one season before he went 31-9. So, in three prime summers of pitching for the hellcat McGraw and his rousing team, Mathewson had a combined record of 99 and 34.

At the close of the season, the Giants had outdistanced second-place Chicago by 13 games. Cincinnati finished third, and Pittsburgh was fourth after three years of dominating the league. And, by then, sportswriters were speculating with some fervency about the likelihood of a "Nickel Series" between two hometown clubs linked by one 5-cent subway fare.

But the speculation did not exactly titillate Brush and McGraw, who clung to the position that the Highlanders were upstarts playing in a "minor league." To their consternation, though, the Highlanders clung to their position, too—and that was first place in the American League. In fact, they had a lead of half a game with only three days to play, and they also had Jack Chesbro, the spitball pitcher, who won 41 games that season. But the Giants were spared the ultimate agony when the Highlanders lost a critical game against the defending champion Boston club, and they lost it because Chesbro threw a wild pitch.

Chesbro's wife conducted a campaign years later, years after his death, to have the record of that pitch reversed: Not a wild pitch, but a passed ball charged to the catcher. It was a forlorn attempt at rewriting history, since everybody agreed that the ball had sailed far over the catcher's head. But, whatever it was, it cost the Highlanders the pennant and made Boston the American League champion once more.

John I. Taylor, the president of the Boston club, promptly fired off a telegram to John Brush, challenging the Giants to "a Series for the baseball championship of the world." Brush, goaded all the way by McGraw, sent back a reply that said: "Regret, we cannot meet you in any such series."

Brush actually was still peeved because Ban Johnson had installed the Highlanders in New York, and he had gone to some legal lengths in 1903 to try to prod the New York courts into issuing an injunction against the baseball "peace" treaty. McGraw still remembered his earlier battles with Ban Johnson, suspensions and insults and "Benedict Arnold" gibes and all. So, he had absolutely no emotional problems about the issue, which he stated succinctly in the closing days of the season:

"Why should we play this upstart club, or any other American League team, for any postseason championship? When we clinch the National League pennant, we'll be champions of the only real major league."

By now, the Giants had defied public pressure, insulted the rival league, violated the peace treaty and otherwise obstructed the hard-won progress between the two big leagues. That was their tantrum, and it worked. It also made them marked men, although that was a distinction they had held ever since McGraw strutted onto the scene and took charge of the team. But now, they were more like public enemies in the cities they visited, and McGraw enjoyed every minute of it.

"In those days," he recalled later, "it was not unusual for the papers to announce that 'the rowdy Giants, accompanied by representatives of the yellow press, got in town this morning.' We used to stay in the old Monongahela Hotel in Pittsburgh and from there drove in open carriages to the ball park, which was in Allegheny City across the river.

"To reach the bridge, we had to pass by the public market place. If we escaped a shower of small stones and trash outside the park, we were sure to get it as we passed the market. Understand, we dressed at the hotel then, not the ball park. If the fans started razzing, we would razz right back.

"One day we were greeted with a shower of old vegetables—potatoes, onions, tomatoes, even cantaloupes. That whole club had the skylarking spirit of college boys, and I was just as bad as any of them. On the field, though, they thought like men of affairs. Always they were on a hair edge, ready to get into a row if anybody pulled the trigger."

McGraw once offered to fight everybody in the Cincinnati ball park. Another time, he threw a ball at an umpire in Pittsburgh. And during the Pirates' first series at the Polo Grounds in 1905, he touched off a fight against his best rivals and worst enemies. He did that by sniping at the Pirates' pitcher, Mike Lynch, as Lynch passed him in the third-base coaching box. Fred Clarke, the manager of the Pirates, then threatened to fight McGraw, who was thrown out of the game by the umpire. Then, in the next inning, Christy Mathewson ran onto the field with fists cocked, and he was thrown out, too.

It didn't take long for Barney Dreyfuss, the owner of the Pirates, to send a petition to Harry Pulliam, the president of the league, saying: "Steps should be taken to protect visitors to the Polo Grounds from insults from the said John J. McGraw."

"What sort of times have we fallen on," McGraw roared back, in a statement to the press, "when the president of the league behaves in a way to indicate he can't forget his former role as the paid secretary to Dreyfuss at both Louisville and Pittsburgh. We might as well be in Russia."

McGraw had another trick: He or Brush would send telegrams to the next city on the team's itinerary, asking the chief of police for "protection" when the Giants arrived. The newspapers there would duly report the request, and the Giants could always be certain of appearing before large and hostile crowds—both at the depot and at the ball park.

But they charged through the 1905 season like a flotilla of warships, winning 105 games and losing 48 and sailing to the National League pennant for the second straight year. And, having ascertained this time that the American League would be represented by Connie Mack's Philadelphia Athletics, they graciously consented to enter the World Series "for the baseball championship of the world."

The Giants brought something else to the Series in addition to their fine record: The John T. Brush Rules, drawn by their owner as a code of conduct and operations for the World Series. In fact, Brush drew up the "rules" after the Giants had vetoed the idea of playing in the Series in 1904. He then sought to dignify his veto by proposing a set of rules that would endow the Series with the strength and stability that he had just withheld.

Brush's code called for a four-out-of-seven match. Sixty per cent of the receipts from the first four games would form the players' pool of prize money: 75 per cent to the winning team, 25 per cent to the losers. Umpires and official scorers would be appointed by the National Commission, which also would decide the schedule of games. And the site of the first game (and the seventh, if necessary) would be determined by lot.

The new rules were inaugurated when Garry Herrmann, the chairman of the National Commission, tossed a 50-cent piece into the air. It was called by Ben Shibe, the onetime horsecar driver who made baseballs in his spare time, hiring the neighborhood women to hand-stitch the covers. Now, he also owned the Athletics, and he won the toss and elected to open the Series, quite naturally, in Philadelphia.

From the first pitch, they made history. A huge throng of 17,955 persons overflowed the roped-off areas of the outfield in the four-year-old ball park at 29th Street and Columbia Avenue in the section of Philadelphia known for good reason as Brewerytown, an area permeated with the aroma of hops and yeast. They cheered and hooted, and spilled over into the outfield, and they saw a monumental pitching duel between two former college rivals, Eddie Plank (Gettysburg) and Christy Mathewson (Bucknell). The Giants, dressed in new black-knight uniforms, made 10 hits off Plank. The Athletics, in their regular white uniforms, got only four off Mathewson, although three were two-baggers that disappeared into the crowd behind the ropes.

The Giants scored twice in the fifth inning and once in the ninth, and won the opener, 3-0.

This was a baseball war between two prime cities, prime teams and prime managers, and both camps girded for it as though for a war. The Philadelphia North American even erected a huge gong west of City Hall, and pealed the news of the struggle across William Penn's city. One gong meant a two-base hit, two gongs a three-base hit, three gongs a home run— by the Athletics, of course. But, except for those three doubles in the opening game, the mammoth gong tolled only two other times in a week as the Giants and A's threw some of the strongest pitching in baseball history against each other.

For Game 2, everybody shifted 90 miles north to New York the following afternoon, and a crowd of 24,992 fans raised the roof of the Polo Grounds while McGinnity pitched against Chief Bender. This time, the A's made six hits, the Giants made four hits and two key errors, and Philadelphia evened the Series, 3-0.

Nobody knew it at the time, but they were the last runs, and the only runs, that Mack's team would score during the entire Series.

After a one-day rainout, they resumed things in Philadelphia's Columbia Park, and Mathewson pitched with two days of rest. The result was a four-hitter, and a 9-0 victory for New York. Then, back to New York, and McGinnity again: He gave up five hits to Philadelphia, Plank gave only four to New York. But the A's made two errors, and the Giants won the game, 1-0.

McGraw now held the lead, three games to one, so he wasted no time wheeling in his ace one more time. And Mathewson, working on one day of rest and pitching before 24,187 spectators at the Polo Grounds, outdueled

The great Christy Mathewson, who pitched three shutouts in one week in the 1905 World Series, won 20 or more games 13 times in his illustrious career with the New York Giants.

Chief Bender, 2-0. He gave six hits, Bender gave five. The winning run was scored on two walks, a bunt and a fly ball.

Five games, five shutouts. The great Matty had pitched three complete games in six days: 14 hits, one walk and no runs in 27 innings, and he struck out 18 batters. He was, McGraw observed, "pretty much the perfect type of pitching machine."

New York erupted into an orgy of celebrating and of lionizing the Giants, world champions after five games of incredible pitching and after three years of building the team under John McGraw.

Philadelphia erupted, too. When Connie Mack took his boys home, they were greeted like conquering heroes. Six Philadelphia newspapers staged a tremendous baseball parade for both the Athletics and the Giants. Amateur and semipro teams from Pennsylvania, New Jersey and Delaware marched the length of Broad Street with bands playing and fireworks arching overhead. Open carriages transported the players of both clubs through the streets, and then to a great banquet that celebrated the first formal World Series in baseball history, and in some ways the most remarkable.

Huge caricatures of the players were carted along Broad Street, too, and an elephant from the Philadelphia Zoo plodded along in circus fashion to symbolize Mr. Mack's White Elephants, the Athletics. In the city that lost, it was a joyous celebration of the event itself, and of the people who had performed so nobly in it.

At the peak of the celebrating, a white sheet was draped over the elephant to make the symbol perfect. They really wanted to whitewash him to make the day absolutely memorable, but the people at the zoo drew the line there.

Giants
in the earth

Honus Wagner (left) in the National League and Ty Cobb (right) in the American League accounted for 20 batting championships and dominated the hitting charts for the first two decades of the 20th Century.

CHAPTER 7

When Hans Wagner broke into the big leagues, his manager, Fred Clarke, asked him: "Why don't you take batting practice?" Wagner said: "The regulars won't let me into the batting cage." Clarke replied: "Make them. You're big enough. Force your way in."

Wagner forced his way in, and later won the batting championship of the National League eight times.

One day, he was playing against the New York Giants, and one of the Giants hit a home run against Wagner's Pittsburgh Pirates. As the New York player trotted around second base and past shortstop, he heard Wagner mumble: "Nice hit." And the Giant replied: "Go to hell."

"I liked that remark," Wagner remembered years later, recalling the way it was. "He was the first major leaguer ever to speak to me."

"When I was breaking in," Casey Stengel once said, "you'd come to camp with a letter of recommendation from someone. Then you'd say to yourself: 'I think I'll go up to the batting cage and hit.' But some regular would challenge you, and say: 'Whoa, there. Who are you, and who sent you?'

"So, you'd whip out your card and show it to him. If he thought your recommendation was okay, he'd step aside and let you hit—maybe as much as three times."

When Ty Cobb broke in as a rookie in 1905, the year when Christy Mathewson pitched his three shutouts in one week in the World Series, the regulars on the Detroit Tigers immediately nailed his shoes to the clubhouse floor. It was the accepted first step in hazing a rookie, except that Cobb didn't accept it very gracefully.

"I was just a mild-mannered Sunday School boy," he later said, giving himself the better of it. "But those old-timers turned me into a snarling wildcat."

Some people believed that Cobb had been turned into a snarling wildcat by a family tragedy. His mother fired a shotgun through a bedroom window at a shadowy figure on the porch roof outside, and fatally wounded her own husband. At the time, Ty Cobb was an 18-year-old baseball player from Georgia who was leading the South Atlantic League in hitting. He was notified by telegram that his father had been shot, and promptly went home to the town of Royston, where he learned that his mother had done the shooting. She was indicted on a charge of voluntary manslaughter, was released on $7,000 bail and later was acquitted.

Her son, meanwhile, rejoined his Augusta club and soon received another piece of news: He was being called up to the big leagues by the Tigers. So, he took a much longer train trip this time, arrived in Detroit late one night and reported the next day to the locker room, where his vagabond shoes were soon nailed to the floor. His reaction was savage and direct, and it remained that way. And people suggested later that his personality had been warped by the family tragedy involving his mother and father. But not everyone agreed.

"The trouble with this theory," said Frederick G. Lieb, the longtime baseball writer, "is that Cobb was like that before the tragedy occurred."

"He came up with an antagonistic attitude," said Sam Crawford, who played the outfield alongside Cobb for a dozen years. "He was still fighting the Civil War."

Whatever war he was fighting, Tyrus Raymond Cobb did most of his fighting between the lines of the ball parks he embroiled from 1905, when he arrived, until 1928, when he left. Not all of his fighting, but most of it. He got into a brawl in a hotel room in 1917 with Buck Herzog of the Giants, and he got into another in 1921 with the umpire Billy Evans—under the grandstand. But he did his hellbent best, or worst, during 24 summers on ball fields. And he did it while playing in 3,033 big-league games during which he went to bat 11,429 times and made 4,191 hits.

He won the batting title of the American League in his first full season, 1907, and he won it for the next eight seasons as well. Then he finished second, but came back and won it three more times. Fifteen times in 16 years (1907 through 1922), he was first or second in hitting in the American League. Three times, he hit over .400. Four times, he led the league in driving in runs. Five times, in runs scored. Eight times, in slugging percentage. And he ended his 24 seasons with a batting average of .367.

He was a lefthanded batter with slashing speed, and he also stole 892 bases, many with spikes flying. He was the angriest ball player of his time, and the best.

He signed for $1,800 a season when the Tigers called, he stayed in $10-a-week hotels, carried a pancake glove made by Spalding and even walked to his first game with the Tigers at Bennett Field, which, he recalled later, was "like a cow pasture."

"If any player learned I could be scared," Cobb said years later, offering a rationale for his rousing style, "I would have lasted two years in the big leagues, not 24."

His first afternoon in a big-league uniform was August 30, 1905, and his name was not even listed on the score card at Bennett Field. He was an angry-looking rookie of 18 and he was scared of nobody, including Jack Chesbro, the renowned spitball pitcher for New York, who had won 41 games the year before. Cobb went to bat in the first inning, faced the great Chesbro with a few words of insult and then made his debut a ringing one by hitting a run-scoring double.

Several years later, Cobb was playing in New York one day, and he was trotting out to his position when he suddenly opened his stride and started racing toward the stands. He vaulted the railing, shoved his way through the crowd and went straight for a spectator who had persistently and loudly heckled him every time the Tigers appeared. Without ceremony or warning, Cobb attacked his heckler with both fists, and then fought his way back onto the playing field, where his teammates had formed a protective shield with massed baseball bats.

He was suspended, as he might have expected, but his Tiger teammates rallied round once more and announced that they would go on strike rather than play without Cobb and his .400 batting average. So, on May 18, 1912, they went on strike when Cobb was suspended and they refused to play in Philadelphia. The Tigers' manager was Hughey Jennings, the old Baltimore Oriole crony of John McGraw, and he hired a bunch of sandlot and college players from Philadelphia to represent the Detroit club (and to save it from forfeiting $5,000 for not showing up). While Cobb and his allies sat, the Tigers pro tem went out and lost to the Athletics, 24-2. The Athletics got 26 hits off a pitcher named Aloysius Travers, who later became a Jesuit priest.

"I have been roughed up in print possibly more than any man who ever played at sport," Cobb said, beating his breast long after he had quit beating his enemies. "In legend, I am a sadistic, slashing, swashbuckling despot who waged war in the guise of sport. The truth is that I believe, and always have believed, that no man, in any walk of life, can attain success who holds in his heart malice, spite or bitterness toward his opponent."

"But," he went on, getting closer to the truth, "I did retaliate. If any player took unfair advantage of me, my first thought was to strike back as quickly and effectively as I could.

"When you're on those basepaths, you've got to protect yourself. I had sharp spikes on my shoes. If the baseman stood where he had no business to be, and got hurt, that was his fault. I was their enemy."

"He played," Fred Lieb wrote, "under the law of survival of the fittest."

Even within your own team in those days, you played for the survival of the fittest. The players waited in line for the one shower that might be available in the chicken coop that served as the clubhouse. Their uniforms were seldom laundered. Their gloves had no webbing. Nobody wore sunglasses. The outfield was often crisscrossed by cinder paths. Rookies automatically got the upper berth on the railroad cars. Pitchers cut, wet and otherwise doctored baseballs until the balls turned brown with licorice or slippery elm. On festive occasions, the players might even queue up after games to use the bathtub reserved with a certain splendor for the manager.

Even with all these hardships, though, the old-timers guarded their jobs violently. They ostracized rookies who might snatch their livelihood. They forced Cobb to room by himself. The other outfielders sometimes managed to avoid backing him up on balls hit into his area.

The prevailing view, he was advised, was: "We're going to run Cobb off this club." They didn't. But one Detroit regular died 15 years later, Cobb said, without ever having shaken his hand.

He once developed an infected wound from persistent sliding while stealing bases. He went to the hospital for extended treatment, he said, and paid his own bill. He recalled that the owner of the team, Frank Navin, "visited me just once while I was invalided, and kept both hands in his pockets."

Some of Cobb's greatest battles were fought in his early summers in the big leagues, when teams like his Tigers and the Chicago Cubs made strenuous attempts to dislodge the Philadelphia Athletics and the New York Giants from the pinnacle they had shared in the remarkable World Series of 1905, the first "formal" Series in history and in many ways the foremost.

It was a time when baseball was fastening its grip on the imagination and the pocketbook of the public. And it was later remembered this way by James T. Farrell, the sage of Chicago and the creator of Studs Lonigan:

"The Cubs dominated the National League from 1906 to 1910. They won the pennant every year except in 1909 when their great catcher, Johnny Kling, one of the first Jewish baseball stars, did not play because of a salary difference.

"The Cubs had a small park on the West Side of Chicago with wooden stands. The White Sox park was located at 39th and Wentworth Avenue. The ride to the Cubs' park from the South Side could take from one to two hours. It was the same for West Siders who wanted to see the White Sox play. I might add that Chicago is like three cities—the South Side, the West Side and the North Side. At that time, there was no team on the North Side. From the start of the two modern leagues, the Chicago teams seemed to be in different cities so far as their fans were concerned."

And the rivalry, Farrell observed, seemed to intensify with "the legendary victory of the Hitless Wonders in 1906."

The White Sox that summer were indeed hitless. They had a collective batting average of .230, the lowest in the American League and 49 points lower than Cleveland's team average. They hit only six home runs, the fewest for any of the 16 clubs in the big leagues and 25 fewer than the Philadelphia A's hit. Two of Chicago's home runs were hit by Fielder Jones, the manager, who played the outfield and batted .230. The best batting average on the team belonged to the second baseman, Frank Isbell, who hit .279.

They were hitless, all right. Also, wonders. They were in fourth place on August 2, then won 19 straight games and beat out the New York Highlanders by three games for the pennant.

As a reward, they won the right to play in the World Series against their crosstown rivals, the Cubs, and they were a frightening study in contrasts. The Cubs led the National League in hitting. They had a celebrated pitching front line consisting of Mordecai (Three-Finger) Brown, Ed Reulbach, Orval Overall and Jack Pfiester. They had the brainy Kling catching. And they had a double-play combination that became famous, at least in verse, as Tinker to Evers to Chance.

Joe Tinker was a third baseman from Muscotah, Kan., who also could play shortstop. Johnny Evers was a shortstop from Troy, N.Y., who also could play second base, and did for most of his 1,776 games in the big leagues. Frank Chance was a catcher from Fresno, Calif., who joined the Cubs in 1898. He became a first baseman in 1902 and the manager in 1905, the "Peerless Leader." He was pretty peerless in 1906: The Cubs won 116 games, lost 36 and roared home 20 games in front of McGraw's defending champions, the Giants.

Tinker, Evers and Chance made their first double play on September 15, 1902. While hardly record-setters as a double-play unit, they helped make Chicago a baseball power for a decade with their all-around play. They were so temperamental that Tinker and Evers ignored each other off the field for two years. But they were so cohesive on the field that they were voted into baseball's Hall of Fame as a unit. They also moved Franklin P. Adams to these lines:

These are the saddest of possible words,
    Tinker to Evers to Chance.
Trio of bear Cubs and fleeter than birds,
    Tinker to Evers to Chance.
Pricking our gonfalon bubble,
Making a Giant hit into a double,
Words that are weighty with nothing but trouble,
    Tinker to Evers to Chance.

In the Series, the Hitless Wonders were somewhat hitless through four games. They managed only one hit off Ed Reulbach in the second game. They got only 11 hits in 113 times at bat in the four games. And yet, with a team batting average of .097, they still won two of those first four games and were ready to bust out. And they did. They whacked out 12 hits in the fifth game and they added 14 hits in the sixth game. They won both, they won the Series and they won permanent possession of the title, "Hitless Wonders."

Charles Comiskey, the owner of the White Sox, was so enraptured that he tossed the club's share of the first four games into the players' pool. That was $15,000, and it was enough to give the White Sox players $1,874 apiece in prize money, which was close to a season's salary for some of them. The Cubs, who had set a record by winning 116 games in the regular season, collected $437.50 apiece. The contrast in rewards was so startling that the split provided under the Brush Rules, 75 percent for the winners and 25 for the losers, was changed to a 60-40 split that set the payoff pattern for generations.

One year later, the Cubs ended with 107 victories and barreled to their second straight pennant while McGraw's team fell all the way to fourth. But McGraw at least had the perverse satisfaction of seeing Connie Mack's Athletics do some suffering, too, as the American League race went down the homestretch.

It happened on September 30 during the first game of a scheduled doubleheader in Philadelphia between the Athletics and the Detroit Tigers. In the opening game of the series, Detroit had broken a first-place tie with the A's by winning, 5-4. Now, it was day two.

Trolley cars deposited thousands of fans at the ball park for the Monday doubleheader, and hundreds scaled the walls after the gates had been shut. Then, with Rube Waddell pitching in relief of Jim Dygert and Eddie Plank being held in reserve for the second game, the Athletics took a 7-1 lead in the opener.

But the Tigers rallied with four runs off Waddell in the seventh inning. And, in the ninth, trailing now 8-6, they tied the game when Ty Cobb, 20 years old and already fighting to win a batting title, hit a two-run home run over the right-field fence, and Connie Mack literally fell off the bench. He got up, and forthwith waved Plank into the game, letting the chips fall where they may in the second game. And the teams fought on.

Each club scored a run in the 11th inning, then Philadelphia's Harry Davis hit one into the crowd in left-center for an apparent ground-rule double in the 14th. Sam Crawford, playing center field for Detroit, ran to the edge of the roped-off mob as a Philadelphia policeman, sitting on a soft-drink box, jumped up and lunged for the ball. Or, as some people later contended, he had merely tried to get out of the way of the ball.

The umpire at home plate was Silk O'Loughlin, who said that he hadn't seen anybody interfere with Crawford. But the umpire at first base, Tom Connolly, said that he had seen interference by the policeman who had been sitting on the soft-drink box. So, O'Loughlin ruled that Davis was indeed out, and Philadelphia exploded.

Monte Cross of the Athletics, who wasn't playing in the game, and Claude Rossman of the Tigers got into a fist fight. Players on both sides shouted that it was too dark to see what the hell had been happening, anyway. One player wrestled the baseball away from umpire Connolly, called him "you Irish immigrant" and heaved the ball over the grandstand. And the outraged Connie Mack began rounding up affidavits from policemen and fans testifying that nobody had interfered with anybody on Davis' expunged two-bagger.

Danny Murphy, who followed Davis to the plate, hit a single that surely would have scored Davis and given the A's a crucial victory.

The game finally ended in a 9-9 tie, with darkness halting it after 17 innings and rubbing out the nightcap as well. The A's had wasted a six-run lead, and the Tigers never relinquished their grip on first place. Mack, normally a serene man, never forgave O'Loughlin, and feuded with him for the rest of their lives. He also didn't forgive Waddell for losing the lead. After watching the Cubs beat the Tigers in the World Series, four games to none, with one tie, he promptly sold Waddell to the St. Louis Browns.

But, if September 30, 1907, was a day that lived in infamy for Connie Mack, then September 23, 1908, was a day that lived in treachery for his old rival, John McGraw. It was nearly a year since Mack's team had been embroiled by Ty Cobb and the Tigers, and now it was McGraw's turn to be embroiled by Frank Chance and the Cubs, with the teams battling for the National League pennant and tied in the ninth inning, 1-1.

The Giants were batting with two out; Moose McCormick waited on third base, Fred Merkle led off first base. The batter was Al Bridwell, a young shortstop who had joined the Giants that season as part of a massive housecleaning trade by McGraw. And, when he lined a single to center field at the Polo Grounds, the stage was set for one of the most memorable and maddening moments in baseball history.

McCormick trotted home from third base with the "winning run" as the crowd swarmed onto the field and the players threaded their way through the fans into the locker room. But the Cubs' second baseman, Johnny Evers, didn't think the game was quite over. At least, he didn't *want* it to be quite over, so he disappeared into the swirl of fans on the field, surfaced again with a baseball in his hand, stepped on second base and touched off one of the most clamorous controversies in a sport that thrived on clamor and controversy.

Johnny Evers was an unbelievably slight man in stature, standing about 5 feet, 9 inches and weighing only 105 pounds or so when he came up to the big leagues six years earlier from his hometown team, the Troy Cheer-Ups in Upstate New York. That's right, the Troy Cheer-Ups. He was also unbelievably testy in nature, probably because he was so slight in stature, and he reportedly went to bed at night with a copy of the baseball rules and the latest issue of The Sporting News, the idea being to acquire every possible edge.

He was so crabby in spirit and even in movement across the infield that he became known as "The Crab." And one of his favorite targets was Bill Klem, the umpire, who came to the National League in 1905 at the standard salary of $1,500 a year and became so commanding that he called balls and strikes for 16 years before joining his fellow umpires in rotating around the bases. After one of their arguments, Evers challenged Klem to join him the following day at the National League office to settle the dispute. He went further than that, too. He bet Klem the lordly sum of $5 that he would not show up. And, sure enough, the next day Evers appeared at the league office, but not Klem.

For months afterward, Evers hounded Klem to pay up. He would hold up five fingers; sometimes he even would draw a large and unmistakable "5" with his bat in the front end of the batter's box. And he kept hounding

Klem until the umpire finally paid him the five-spot when they were traveling one day on the same train.

Evers reminded some people of Cobb: aloof, combative, spikes high. His own teammate, Frank Chance, the man on the receiving end of the double plays, once admitted that he would have rather seen Evers playing the outfield. And when he and Joe Tinker got into their celebrated snit, and stopped speaking to each other, the issue was whether Evers had failed to share a taxi with his buddy en route to an exhibition game.

So, completely in character, Evers now hustled across the grass at the Polo Grounds on the fateful afternoon of September 23, 1908, and touched second base, ostensibly forcing out Merkle, who had turned away from the base path and run to the clubhouse. And, if he did force out Merkle, then the inning was over, and McCormick's run did not count. In fact, Evers insisted for years that he had called for the ball after Bridwell's single, and that it had been thrown to him from center field, and through the crowd flocking onto the field. The Giants insisted that Joe McGinnity had actually retrieved the ball, and had flung it into the crowd in the joy of the Giants' victory.

The newspaper writers had already flashed the score of the game by telegraph: 2-1, Giants. But Evers kept screaming at the base umpire, who ignored him and ran into the umpires' room. So, Evers pursued the home-plate umpire, Hank O'Day, who finally ruled that Merkle was out.

Enter John McGraw, roaring: "If Merkle was out, the game was a tie and O'Day should have cleared the field and resumed the game. If not, we won the game, and they can't take it away from us."

But they did. Harry Pulliam, the league president whom McGraw once had baited as "the paid secretary" to Barney Dreyfuss, pronounced the game a tie. If it was needed to decide the pennant, it would be replayed. And, sure enough, the Cubs and Giants ended the season in a mathematical dead heat and the game was needed to decide the pennant.

The replay was staged at the Polo Grounds because the Giants won the toss of the coin. But that was the only thing they won. A howling mob besieged the ball park that afternoon, October 8, smashed through the right-field fence and overran the stadium until city firemen turned streams of water on them. Then the fans pelted the Chicago players with cushions and bottles. But, when Joe Tinker's three-bagger off Christy Mathewson touched off a four-run third inning, the Cubs were on their way to a 4-2 victory and the pennant.

Fred Merkle already had lost 15 pounds brooding about his celebrated "boner" that led to the tied game and the tiebreaker makeup game. Eventually, he recovered his poise and his confidence, and became a fine first baseman. But he was a marked man: "Merkle's boner" became part of the language.

"It is criminal," McGraw said, going to his defense, "to say that Merkle is stupid and to blame the loss of the pennant on him. In the first place, he is one of the smartest and best players on this ball club. In the second place, he didn't cost us the pennant. We lost a dozen games we should have won. Besides, we were robbed of it, and you can't say Merkle did that."

While he may have forgiven Merkle, McGraw never forgave Harry Pulliam. Their relations had been tempestuous throughout. Pulliam was re-elected president of the league, though, with the Giants casting the only vote against him. Then, in February 1909, Pulliam was granted a leave of absence from his desk "for reasons of illness." He stayed away from baseball that spring and early summer, and in July, while at the New York Athletic Club, fatally shot himself in the head. He was 40 years old.

Meanwhile, the Cubs were back in the World Series again, thanks to their October 8 victory, and they were still winning the arguments as well as the money games.

The big blowout of the 1908 Series came in Game 2 and was caused by ropes that had been stretched in front of the bleachers and across a large section of the outfield to hold back an overflow crowd that never materialized. So, naturally, Joe Tinker hit a wind-blown fly ball to right field in the eighth inning with one man on base for Chicago in a 0-0 game, and the ball drifted across the foul line into fair territory and fell into a small bleacher behind the rope. And, at the pregame conference, it had been agreed that any ball hit behind the rope would be a ground-rule double.

But Bill Klem, presiding behind the plate, called it a home run. Cobb came hurtling in from right field yelling that he might have caught the ball if the rope hadn't been there. And the rest of the Tigers came hurtling in to yell that it was only a double, anyway. But Klem drew himself up to full stance, and said:

"That ground rule doesn't cover the bleachers when there is no overflow crowd. I've been calling balls that land in that bleacher home runs all season. And that rope out there don't change it."

Nothing changed it (Chicago went on to win, 6-1), and the Tigers never revived. For the second year in a row, they lost the World Series to the Cubs in five games; and, for the third year in a row, the Cubs had the best record in baseball.

The Series was notable for cold weather and cold interest in Detroit, where the final game was watched by only 6,210 people, the smallest crowd in Series history. For all five games, attendance was only 62,232; and total receipts were $94,975.

It was also the first time that four umpires were assigned to a Series, but the four didn't all work at the same time. They were paired: Bill Klem and Tommy Connolly, and Hank O'Day and Jack Sheridan, and they alternated from day to day, one pair at a time.

The Series also produced the Baseball Writers' Association of America, which became the most influential of the press associations in sports. The Series produced it out of sheer necessity, actually. Many of the writers at the makeup game between the Giants and Cubs in the Polo Grounds became outraged when the press box filled with actors, politicians, barbers and other interlopers or friends of friends. The last straw may have come when Hugh Fullerton found his chair occupied by the actor Louis Mann, who refused to give it up. So, Fullerton sat in his lap, and dictated 5,000 words.

Things weren't much better in the World Series. In Chicago, visiting writers were assigned to the last row of the grandstand. In Detroit, they all were forced to climb a rickety ladder to reach a loft on top of the first-base pavilion.

On the morning of the final game, the writers finally rebelled. They held a meeting at the Ponchartrain Hotel in Detroit on October 14, expressed their indignation and created their association. The baseball writers later became the keepers of the press boxes of baseball, the electors of the principal postseason award winners and also of the Hall of Fame, and writers no longer dictated their World Series pieces while sitting on the laps of actors or anybody else.

The Chicago Cubs and Detroit Tigers now were supreme in baseball, but the New York Giants and Philadelphia A's were clawing their way back. Still, there were some moments of sheer riot before they did. And none was more riotous than a series the Tigers played in Philadelphia in September 1909, when they arrived with a lead of four games. Mr. Mack's Athletics had to sweep the series to tie for the lead, and they almost did.

The series was played before crowds that totaled 120,000, featuring a huge outpouring of 35,409 for the third game. Eddie Plank pitched the Athletics to a 2-1 victory in the opener, played September 16. The next day, seven different Detroit players stole seven bases, and the Tigers evened the series. Then Mack's team won the third game, 2-0, behind the pitching of Chief Bender. And the fourth game, 4-3, behind Plank.

The public passion, naturally, centered on Cobb, who hit .377 that season and who was accorded a welcome befitting an armed enemy. He responded by crashing into two hometown heroes, Jack Barry and Frank (Home Run) Baker, spiking both and splitting their uniforms. The crowds went wild, and then came the letters and telephone calls threatening his life, and some threatening to shoot him if he dared show up at the ball park.

Cobb's manager, Hughey Jennings, who had been McGraw's ally on the Baltimore Orioles 15 years earlier, called Mack for police protection. And, as a result, Cobb was convoyed to the ball park behind a platoon of motorcycle policemen. And, at the ball park, a solid line of bluecoats stood in the outfield between him and the angry, threatening mob that overflowed the foul lines and pressed against the ropes in right field.

The Tigers survived the series and the mobs, left town with their health and a lead of two games and won the pennant two weeks later. But the following year, 1910, they slipped into third place while the Athletics made their comeback after three years of American League domination by Detroit. The Philadelphia players, pennant winners by 14½ games, flashed their loyalty. They chipped in and bought Mr. Mack his first automobile, which chugged up to home plate for the presentation ceremony.

The A's later showed their loyalty in an even gaudier way, winning the World Series against the Cubs, who had won the astounding total of 530 games in five seasons (including 104 in the 1909 season, when they ran second in the National League to the Pittsburgh Pirates). The two leagues were not exactly synchronized in 1910: The American League finished its schedule a week earlier than the National League, mainly because Charles Ebbets of the Brooklyn Dodgers favored holidays and insisted that the season continue at least until Columbus Day. The league obliged, the Cubs were scheduled through October 15 and the World Series didn't open until two days later.

While they were waiting around, the Athletics kept themselves in shape and in gravy by playing daily exhibition games against an all-star team drawn from their league. The all-stars included Ty Cobb, Tris Speaker, Walter Johnson and Ed Walsh, and the competition apparently primed the Athletics for the Series—they hit .316 as a team and upset the older and more established Cubs in five games.

It was a remarkable thing for a young team to do, but times were changing. The domination of baseball by the Cubs was ending, and the return of the Athletics and the Giants was beginning. And the Athletics came with stunning bats. Their young second baseman, Eddie Collins, hit .429 in the Series. The third baseman, Frank Baker, hit .409 (but "Home Run" Baker hit no home runs). Even Jack Coombs, who pitched three victories in six days, hit .385.

It was sort of a coup for the American League, too, because it had lost three World Series in a row and badly needed something to cherish. The Athletics supplied it. And, in the fourth inning of the final game, Coombs supplied something for Connie Mack to cherish: With the bases loaded, he struck out Joe Tinker and Jimmy Archer.

As he did, all hell broke loose on the Philadelphia bench. The young reserve players in the dugout jumped up, flapping their arms and yelling, not far from the small box alongside the bench where Connie Mack was sitting and watching. In the excitement, they flapped so jubilantly that they knocked their manager off his seat and sent him sprawling into the dirt in his starched collar and prim business suit. They were just as suddenly horrified. But Mr. Mack got up, brushed himself off and said:

"It's all right, boys. I'm pretty excited myself, and I have another suit at the hotel."

Ty Cobb, maybe the best player of his time or anybody's time, dashed and slashed his way through a career epitomized by his 1909 high-spikes slide into third baseman Frank (Home Run) Baker.

Honey Fitz

8

A nattily dressed, overflow crowd helped the Philadelphia A's celebrate the 1909 Shibe Park opener as horses and buggies rattled their way down the street behind the new stadium.

CHAPTER 8

T he first steel and concrete baseball park was built at 21st Street and Lehigh Avenue in Philadelphia, and Connie Mack moved his Athletics into it on April 12, 1909, the day after Easter Sunday. It was a spacious place, and you had to give the ball a pretty good wallop to reach the fences: 360 feet down the foul lines, 393 feet in the power alleys and 420 to center field.

It also had 30,000 seats, but many more people overflowed the stadium on opening day, and they were still packing them in when the Athletics knocked off the Chicago Cubs in the World Series the following year and regained the rank they had enjoyed five years earlier, when they played their memorable "shutout Series" against the New York Giants. And now that the Athletics were back on top, they stayed there a while, winning four pennants and three World Series in their first six seasons in their modern new stadium.

The park was named for Ben Shibe, who had been a minority stockholder of the club years before, and a close friend of A.J. Reach, longtime Phillies owner, sporting goods manufacturer and baseball-guide publisher. Shibe also was a manufacturer of baseballs. And he was given the distinct impression that the American League would use his baseballs exclusively if Shibe invested in the club again. He did, and the league did.

The second stadium to use steel and concrete instead of wood was built in Pittsburgh just about the same time that Shibe Park was rising in Philadelphia. The Pirates, in fact, opened it on June 30, 1909, less than three months after Philadelphia opened its new park. And a crowd of 30,338 overflowed its 25,000 seats and spilled into the outfield, where ropes marked the outer limits. The first pitch ever thrown in the new park, which was named Forbes Field, was hit for a single by Johnny Evers of the Cubs, who beat the home team, 3-2.

A baseball park was a badge of civic honor in those days, something like a university or at least a library, and Pittsburgh got its new park when Barney Dreyfuss decided that his ball club and his city deserved better baseball quarters than old Exposition Park. You know, Ben Shibe and Connie Mack were building this fancy new ball park in Philadelphia, so why not us?

There wasn't much doubt that Exposition Park had certain disadvantages—such as the Allegheny River. When the river reached flood tide, the outfield in Exposition Park often went under water. It happened on the Fourth of July in 1902, when 10,000 fans arrived for the morning half of a holiday doubleheader and found a foot of water across the outfield. So, the Pirates consulted the visiting team, the Brooklyn Superbas, and they decided to go ahead and play. The only stipulation was that any ball hit into the lake in the outfield would be a ground-rule single. The Pirates won, 3-0.

By the time they were ready for the afternoon game, the water had reached within 20 feet of second base. But a corps of small boys was recruited to keep wiping off the baseballs, the Pirates won again and the home team swept a high-tide doubleheader.

One year later, the Pirates won their third straight National League pennant and played in the first World Series against Boston's American League champions. In the next five years (1904 though 1908), they finished second three times but did not win another pennant, although their shortstop Honus Wagner was winning batting titles almost every year. He won eight before he finished his career, and he was widely regarded as the best player in the National League and perhaps in either league.

His only serious rival was Ty Cobb, the whiz of the American League. And they had only one hand-to-hand confrontation—in the World Series of 1909, the very year that Barney Dreyfuss bought a pastoral parcel of property from Schenley Farms, with the guidance of his friend Andrew Carnegie, and built his new ball park. The Pirates won the Series in seven games over the Detroit Tigers, and the confrontation of the superstars was one-sided: Cobb hit .231 and stole two bases, Wagner hit .333 and stole six bases. And nobody stole more bases in a Series until Lou Brock of the St. Louis Cardinals stole seven, nearly 60 years later.

"There was nothing there but a livery stable and a hot house, with a few cows grazing over the countryside," Dreyfuss remembered years later. "A ravine ran through the property, and I knew that the first thing necessary to make it suitable for baseball was to level off the entire field."

It cost $2,000,000, and it was so splendid by the standards of the day that the 1910 "Reach Baseball Guide" was at a loss for words in trying to portray it for posterity:

"The formal opening of Forbes Field . . . was an historic event, the full significance of which could be better felt than described.

"Words must also fail to picture to the mind's eye adequately the splendors of the magnificent pile President Dreyfuss erected as a tribute to the national game, a beneficence to Pittsburgh and an enduring moment to himself. For architectural beauty, imposing size, solid construction and for public comfort and convenience, it has not its superior in the world."

The splendors of the *magnificent pile,* and of the similarly magnificent one in Philadelphia, were the envy of baseball. And especially of John T. Brush, the owner of the New York Giants, who was soon forced to build the third steel-and-concrete stadium.

Brush was an orphan who became a clothing salesman in Boston, Troy and Indianapolis, and who enlisted in the First New York Artillery in the Civil War. Later, he more or less drifted into baseball, and eventually supplied the bankroll for John McGraw to build his empire. He also suffered from rheumatism and locomotor ataxia, and as a result he surveyed the empire from a wheelchair. But he was a man with flair.

His daughter, Natalie Brush de Gendron, later recalled that her father "was definitely stage-struck," and added:

"He married an actress and joined the Lambs Club. Almost every actor in New York had a pass to the Polo Grounds, and the big stars had boxes. There was some method, of course, in his generosity. The public was well-advised that, every afternoon when there was no matinee, Julia Sanderson, DeWolfe Hopper, Donald Brian, Frank Craven, William Collier, David Warfield and many others could be seen at the Polo Grounds.

"The passes were another distinctive feature of the era. They were made for my father by Lambert Brothers, the jeweler. They were different each year. One year, a pack of playing cards with an autographed picture of an actor on each card. Another year, a pen-knife with a magnified peep-hole picture of the Polo Gounds in the handle."

But the world of John Brush took a sad turn in April 1911, when the wooden grandstand of his Polo Grounds burned. The fire occurred early in the morning, so nobody was injured. But, after five years of pursuing teams like the Chicago Cubs and Pittsburgh Pirates, the Giants were now primed for a comeback—and suddenly, one morning in April, they were homeless.

Brush was 65 and handicapped, but he drove through Broadway to his ball park, sat in his wheelchair among the ruins and then turned to his wife, the former actress, and said: "Elsie, I want to build a concrete stand, the finest that can be constructed. It will mean economy for a time. Are you willing to stand by me?"

Elsie was, and the next day Brush started work on plans for the major leagues' third stadium of steel and concrete. It was a grand design and it was flavored with some grand touches, like the series of ornamental coats-of-arms for each city in the National League, which were installed and spaced around the summit of the grandstand. Until their own ball park was rebuilt and revived with such elegant touches, the Giants shared the Highlanders' field. But the Polo Grounds was sufficiently rebuilt to welcome them back home in late June, and the Giants went on to appear in their first World Series in six years.

It was a festive event because it turned the clock back to the heroic Series of 1905 when the Giants and Philadelphia Athletics aimed shutouts at each other, and Connie Mack and John McGraw directed armies of players of great magnitude. And everybody seemed caught up in the spirit of the memory. John Brush dressed the Giants in the famous black uniforms of '05 with the white trim. McGraw, Mathewson, Rube Marquard and Chief Meyers "wrote" daily reports on the games for the New York newspapers. Mack, Eddie Collins and Chief Bender wrote rebuttals for the Philadelphia papers. And the Series was played in two bright new stadiums.

The opening game was played before an immense crowd of 38,281 in Brush's reconstructed ball park, but so much commotion and ballyhoo surrounded the Series that even the size of the crowd became an issue. The players, who were being paid on the basis of attendance, had been enraptured by predictions that 50,000 would attend. And they were just as suddenly disabused of their rapture when the official count was reported. In fact, they wondered out loud if they were being short-changed.

They wasted no time sending a delegation to the club owners to find out exactly how many customers had gone through the turnstiles. But the delegation, headed by Chief Jack Meyers, the California mission Indian, came streaming back in retreat when the owners and league presidents berated them for having questioned the integrity of the game.

On the field, the players shook down World Series memories. There was Mathewson on the mound pitching against Chief Charles Albert Bender, the Minnesota reservation Indian, rivals from the teams' great confrontations of 1905, and in this Series the Philadelphia club got the better of the New York club, four games to two. But in Game 1, at least, the Giants prevailed in their newly rebuilt stadium as their old hero Christy Mathewson outpitched Bender, 2-1.

There was no Sunday baseball in the East, so the teams sat out the next day, and then took the train to Philadelphia to resume the Series on Monday. Frank Baker hit a two-run home run off Rube Marquard and the Athletics won, 3-1, with Eddie Plank pitching. And now the ghost-writers had their most gleeful moments.

After Baker cleared the fence against Marquard, the ghost-writer for Mathewson promptly wrote a column chiding Marquard for having pitched the ball where Baker could hit it. The Athletics saw the delicious mischief in that—one New York pitcher criticizing another—so they clipped the review to the bulletin board in the clubhouse. Then they went out and achieved a milestone: They beat the great Mathewson, 3-2, while Jack Coombs was freezing the Giants on three hits. The Athletics won the game in 11 innings after Baker had tied it, 1-1, in the ninth by hitting a home run off Mathewson. So, this time, Marquard's ghost-writer knocked off a review that chided Mathewson for having pitched the ball where Baker could hit it.

Then came one of the natural imponderables of the Series—six days of rain. It rained almost steadily from October 18 through October 23, and by then people were even trying to dry out the field by burning cans of gasoline around the grass. On the 24th, they resumed the Series and McGraw understandably pitched his main man, Mathewson, who had just had six days of rest. He may have had too much rest. In the fourth inning, the A's tagged him for three doubles in a row, including one by the irrepressible Baker, and they got 10 hits in seven innings before McGraw replaced him.

It took the Athletics six games to avenge their defeat of 1905, and they did it with a flourish by overwhelming the Giants in the final game, 13-2. Baker, who had become a national hero as "Home Run Baker," ended the Series with a .375 batting average and two home runs. The Athletics went home as conquerors. McGraw took his team to Cuba for some exhibition games, and was surprised to find that the sporting public in Havana still remembered him as *el mono amarillo* from his visit there as a 17-year-old country boy 21 years earlier with Al Lawson's American All-Stars. His players, after losing two games to the Havana Reds, were just as surprised when *el mono amarillo* ordered them out for morning practice.

There was a reunion the next year, too. The Giants won the pennant again in the National League, and the Boston Red Sox won it in the American. It was the first pennant for the Red Sox since 1904, when Brush and McGraw refused to play the World Series against any team representing a "bush" league.

But there was nothing "bush" about the American League or its No. 1 team of 1912. The Red Sox not only had outperformed Connie Mack and his A's and their $100,000 infield, but also had outperformed everybody else by rising from fifth place to the pennant by the simple device of winning 105 games and playing .691 baseball.

They did it with some exceptional performances: Smokey Joe Wood, whose fastball smoked, won 34 games and lost five, and during his hottest streak won 16 straight. Hugh Bedient won 20 games as a rookie. And the outfield had star quality from left to right: Duffy Lewis, Tris Speaker and Harry Hooper.

The Red Sox also arrived at the World Series with a new ball park, another in the series of steel-and-concrete stadiums that were changing the profiles of some heavily traveled neighborhoods in the big cities along the East Coast. This was Fenway Park, an angled and irregularly shaped park at Lansdowne and Jersey streets in a marshy area of the city known as "The Fens." It had a peculiar and intriguing shape because it was built on a peculiar and intriguingly shaped plot of land, and it also had a 10-foot incline in front of the fence in left field, an embankment that promptly became "Duffy's Cliff" because Duffy Lewis spent long afternoons charging up and down the hill chasing fly balls.

Fenway Park, like its sister stadiums in New York, Philadelphia and Pittsburgh, was a quantum leap forward for people determined to spend their leisure time and their leisure money on a ball game. It replaced the Huntington Avenue Grounds, a 9,000-seat ball park of primitive nature that had been built on an old carnival site in 1901 when Boston was awarded a franchise in the American League. The first World Series game was played on the Huntington field on October 1, 1903. And the first Series championship was won there by the home team, which defeated Pittsburgh 12 days later in the eighth and final game.

The Boston club and its public also arrived at the 1912 Series with a memory: A memory of the day in 1904 when McGraw and Brush refused to play the World Series against a "bush" league and its pennant-winning team, which just happened to be from Boston. They arrived en masse, too, led and commanded and goaded by the mayor of Boston himself: John F. (Honey Fitz) Fitzgerald, a tenor with a fine voice, a compulsion to raise it in song and a stovepipe hat and greatcoat—clad for war against New York and its haughty Giants. This was nearly half a century before the mayor's grandson, John Fitzgerald Kennedy, threw out a "first ball" as President of the United States, and Honey Fitz was the reigning ruler of Boston life.

But the Giants came with no apologies for past sins or slights. They had taken first place in the second week of May and stayed there. And Rube Marquard, their ace lefthander, opened the season by winning 19 straight games. In fact, he didn't lose until July 8.

Marquard was a kind of extension to Christy Mathewson as a quality person and quality pitcher. He was intelligent and sober, and he made the big leagues in a swirl of news and wonder because the Giants paid $11,000 to get him—a record amount for a minor leaguer, and an 18-year-old minor leaguer, at that. They got him in 1908 after a bidding war with other teams, and the bidding reached a peak one day in September that year when the competing scouts gathered to watch their prize pitch for Indianapolis in the American Association. Marquard rose to the occasion with a neat sense of timing. He pitched a no-hitter against Columbus, and the Giants wasted no time paying.

Now, in 1912, Marquard was a 26-game winner and the new ace of McGraw's staff. He also was the husband of the vaudeville actress Blossom Seely, and they spent three winters touring as a dance act before the act and the marriage got canceled.

The Giants also owned a world-class athletic celebrity, Jim Thorpe, who had gone from the Carlisle Indian School to the Olympic Games that summer in Stockholm, where he was saluted by the King of Sweden as "the greatest athlete in the world." Unfortunately, he wasn't the greatest out-fielder in the world. McGraw wasn't even sure he could play baseball. But he was absolutely sure that people would pay to find out, so he signed Thorpe (who first played in the majors in 1913) and let human nature take its course.

"The World Series," wrote Frederick G. Lieb, the baseball writer and historian, who saw his first Series in 1910, "had developed from a postseason event—of concern largely to the interested cities—to something like the great national spectacle that it is today. The country virtually shut up shop to await the results. The queue of fans started at the ticket windows to the Polo Grounds on Eighth Avenue and 157th Street, extended south on Eighth Avenue to 145th Street, where the police turned the line westward to Broadway. It was a line stretching from the Polo Grounds over a mile distant.

"Many started this long vigil the night before, and after standing in line 10 hours and upward, they were rewarded by hearing the heart-rending cry: 'All sold out. No more seats or standing room for sale.' "

The countdown to the Series was a momentous and at times furious thing for the newspapers, too. They ran pictures and stories and matchups comparing the teams, position by position. They ran personal predictions by writers like Hugh Fullerton, who had amazed people by calling the outcome of each game in the 1906 Series between the two Chicago teams, the Cubs and White Sox. Even his own city editor on the Chicago Tribune hesitated to print his prediction that the White Sox, the "hitless wonders," would upset the Cubs. They did, and Fullerton was anointed as a seer of mystic vision.

His mystic vision worked perfectly for a while. He called the next three World Series, and by 1912 his analyses were being published in papers like The New York Times under headlines that said: "Hugh Fullerton Favors Gardner Over Herzog," in the matchup between the rival third basemen. The Times also ran letters from skeptical and irate readers denouncing Fullerton's vision. But the public passion kept building as the Series drew close.

Great events outside the sports pages even seemed to fade in the face of such clamor. Less than six months earlier, the British liner Titanic had struck an iceberg in the North Atlantic during her maiden voyage from Southampton to New York, and sank with a loss of more than 1,500 lives. China became a republic that year, and elected its first president. Capt. Robert F. Scott and four companions reached the South Pole, only to perish while attempting to return to civilization. Teddy Roosevelt broke away from the Republican Party, saying "I feel like a bull moose," and he charged like a bull moose against both President William Howard Taft and Woodrow Wilson in a three-way fight for the White House. Lieut. Charles Becker of the New York Police Department was going on trial for complicity in the murder of Herman Rosenthal, a gambler who had been gunned down at 2 o'clock one morning as he left the Hotel Metropole by four trigger men— "Gyp the Blood" Horowitz, "Lefty Louie" Rosenberg, "Whitey" Lewis and "Dago Frank" Cirosici. A citizen noticed the license plate of the getaway car, and one of the great crime-and-politics dramas of the day began to unfold.

And, as the World Series crowded these events from the top of the front page, an immense naval armada of 123 ships approached New York on a visit and The Times, on the morning of October 7, put it all into historical perspective by observing in an editorial:

"This is to be a week of notable incidents. As the third from the last week of the most bewildering presidential campaign of recent memory, it should be full of political excitement. The greatest naval pageant in the history of this country will begin at the city's gates. A criminal trial of larger significance than any in late years will begin.

"Yet, who will doubt that public interest will center on none of these, but on the games of baseball at our Polo Grounds and in Boston?"

Mayor Fitzgerald certainly didn't doubt it. He staged a semipro game in Fenway Park to raise money to buy a car for the manager of the Red

Sox, Garland (Jake) Stahl, a first baseman who could hit as well as manage and who also worked in the off-season as a banker in Chicago. Then Honey Fitz, on the eve of the Series, gave a public reading to a telegram he had just received from William Gaynor, the mayor of New York, inviting him to share the municipal box at the Polo Grounds the next day "to witness the defeat of the Red Sox by the Giants."

Honey Fitz then dashed off the following reply: "It will give me pleasure to be your guest as the Red Sox begin their onward march to the world championship and to congratulate you upon the fact that your city, the greatest in the country and possessing the best ball team in the National League, is to have the distinguished honor of adding to the glory of the best city in the world and to the laurels of the finest ball team ever organized."

Having delivered the challenge, the mayor of Boston then went to the front rank of the marching army known as the Royal Rooters, several hundred strong, and with two brass bands and hordes of other fans, they all boarded four special trains and headed for New York.

Upon arriving, they announced that they had come with "unlimited money to bet on the Red Sox," and they began to flash it as soon as they checked into the Bretton Hall Hotel at Broadway and 86th Street. They flashed it in the lobbies of hotels along the main stem, they swept through bars and restaurants, they looked blankly when a New Yorker in one taproom shouted: "I am ready to pay $100 right now for a pair of tickets to tomorrow's game."

William Pink, a wholesale liquor dealer from Boston who was in charge of the Royal Rooters' invasion, said there was $100,000 in Sox money aboard the caravan. But, he added with chagrin, it was going begging along Broadway.

That night, the sky over Manhattan was glowing with a torchlight parade down Broadway, the Royal Rooters crossing Manhattan in one long and loud body behind the imposing figure of Honey Fitz. They stopped at street corners to serenade the multitudes with their theme song, "Tessie," and with songs of the day like "When I Get You Alone Tonight." And, every couple of blocks, Honey Fitz would render the solo in his Irish tenor to salute the finest ball club in the world.

On the front page the next day, The Times reported: "If the air around Times Square was surcharged with suspense of the approaching contest, there was no word to describe the cumulative excitement in the atmosphere around the Polo Grounds, where the general admission line began to form at 9 o'clock last night."

When the great moment arrived on Tuesday, October 8, there were nearly 36,000 persons crammed inside the gates, and the first salutes were fired by the Royal Rooters. They entered from the Eighth Avenue side and marched onto the field like an army at full tilt, 300 of them in the line of march with a 30-piece band. And they crossed and recrossed the diamond with no apparent intention of leaving so the ball game could begin. They finally were herded to their block of seats, where they kept singing and roaring, and where they wore out their favorite war song to the tune of "Tammany," with paeans to the Red Sox:

> Carrigan, Carrigan,
>   Speaker, Lewis, Wood and Stahl.
> Bradley, Engle, Pape and Hall.
>   Wagner, Gardner, Hooper, too.
> Hit them! Hit them! Hit them! Hit them!
>   Do, boys, do.

Downtown, the center of Manhattan was clogged by thousands of people packed into Times Square to follow the game on an electric scoreboard that had been hoisted on the north side of the Times Building, and the press reported: "There have been vast crowds in Times Square before, but never one as large as that which congregated there yesterday."

The scoreboard was 16 feet long and 7 feet high, and it was operated by direct wire from the ball park to The Times, where an operator flashed the play-by-play information to the board itself. Separate tables on the board showed the balls and strikes, the number of outs and so on. White lights depicted the baserunners as they advanced toward home plate. The crowd started gathering one hour before Jeff Tesreau's first pitch, and traffic was diverted from the Square by dozens of policemen.

In the Polo Grounds uptown, bedlam. Honey Fitz was resplendent in black silk hat and white collar, posing for pictures with a police commissioner, a governor, several mayors and an admiral. He kept up a running stream of encouragement for the Red Sox, who scored one run in the sixth inning after Josh Devore crossed in front of Fred Snodgrass on Speaker's long drive, and the misplayed ball went for a triple. Then they scored three more in the seventh, and won the game, 4-3, while the Royal Rooters tore the place apart.

The next afternoon, the cavalcade swept into Boston, where Mayor Fitzgerald made several speeches, presented the new car to Manager Stahl, presented another to Tris Speaker, took the first ride in it, and then presented a silver bat to the shortstop, Heinie Wagner. It was an impressive performance, and one New York fan was quoted in the press as saying: "If Barnum had lived in the same town with the mayor, P.T. would have had a look-in."

The teams played 11 long innings to the accompaniment of two brass bands, and the blaring reached a peak in the first inning when the Red Sox nicked Christy Mathewson for three runs. The Giants sabotaged Mathewson by making five errors overall, but they seized a 5-4 lead with a three-run rally of their own in the eighth inning. But Art Fletcher booted a grounder at shortstop in the bottom of the eighth that enabled the Red Sox to tie the score, and then they were grappling in extra innings.

The Giants went ahead again in the top of the 10th. But in the last half of the 10th, Mathewson gave it back when Speaker tripled and kept going, trying to stretch it into an inside-the-park home run. As he rounded third, Speaker got the hip from Buck Herzog, and that slowed him down a bit. In fact, he would have been nailed at the plate because of a perfect relay from Tillie Shafer (who had replaced Fletcher), but the catcher dropped the ball and Speaker was safe—and the game was tied again.

Speaker then got up and ran back to third base, where he settled the score with Herzog. They threw punches, both teams joined in and a long and loud afternoon grew longer and louder. Then, after 11 innings, they were still tied at 6-6, and the game was called because of darkness.

There wasn't much precedent for this, since only one other World Series game had ended in a tie. The National Commission whipped into executive session and decided that the tie should be replayed in Boston the next day before everybody got aboard the night-owl express and bucketed back to New York.

So, the two clubs and the two brass bands and the 300 Royal Rooters and Honey Fitz did it one more time. And this time, Rube Marquard pitched the New Yorkers to a 2-1 victory in a game that ended with even more confusion than the tie of the day before.

The reason was the weather: A heavy mist seeped into the Boston ball park from the sea at sundown and wrapped everybody in darkness and fog. As it did, Forrest Cady hit a long line drive with two Red Sox on base in the last half of the ninth inning. Josh Devore of the Giants apparently made a running catch, and kept on running into the Giants' clubhouse. But many of the Boston faithful left the ball park thinking the ball had carried past Devore and that the Red Sox had won it at the final bell, 3-2. The hassling went on far into the night and accompanied the caravans on the night-owl to New York.

The Red Sox got their revenge the next afternoon in the Polo Grounds when Joe Wood outpitched Jeff Tesreau, 3-1, and now Boston took the lead again in the Series. Then, back to Fenway, where 34,683 fans packed the park on Columbus Day and watched 22-year-old Hugh Bedient outpitch Mathewson, 2-1, and the Red Sox were one game away.

But, back in the Polo Grounds on the merry-go-round, the Giants did it McGraw's way and scored five runs in the first inning. It was vintage McGraw—two infield singles, two outfield singles, a pair of doubles, a balk, a wild throw and a double steal. Not bad for one inning, especially the first, and Marquard had no trouble holding the lead and sending the commuters back to Boston. The Red Sox now led by three games to two, with one tie.

Game 7 was memorable, in the best and most clamorous manner of these two teams and these two cities. President Taft was aboard the yacht Mayflower off Newport, and he inquired how the ball game was going. So, the details were supplied through naval wireless at Torpedo Station—the running details, as the Giants and Red Sox and their partisans raged at each other.

The trouble started early, after the Royal Rooters did their marching numbers on the field with full brass accompaniment. When they started to file off, they found their special section in the grandstand had been filled by intruders. So, the Royal Rooters did the only sensible thing: They marched back onto the field and refused to leave, even as Smokey Joe Wood went to the mound to pitch.

For 30 minutes, they fought off waves of policemen on foot and on horseback, until they were driven back toward the outfield fence. Then they charged the bleacher fence like the Light Brigade, knocked it down and poured into the crowd, brass bands playing and all hell breaking loose while Joe Wood stood on the mound waiting to throw his first pitch.

Wood waited so long in a cold and blustery wind that he was thoroughly chilled and stiff when the game finally began. And the Giants took full advantage of the Boston chaos by scoring six runs in the first inning off a man who had won 34 games in the regular season. And when they went on to win, 11-4, they had tied the Series after trailing by three games to one.

So, everything came down to Game 8, winner take all, and it was played in Fenway Park because the Red Sox won the toss of the coin that was used to fix the site of the game. The Royal Rooters weren't there, having been angered and alienated by the evident resale of their seats the day before. But the game was a classic.

The pitchers were the great Mathewson, who had started twice without winning, and young Bedient, who had won his only start and allowed just one run in 11 innings overall (he also had made two relief appearances). And they did their work nobly. The Giants got one run in the third inning, but the Red Sox came back with one in the seventh. Nobody got anything in the eighth or ninth, and by now Joe Wood was pitching for Boston in relief against Mathewson. But, in the top of the 10th, Red Murray doubled, Fred Merkle singled and the Giants suddenly were back in front, 2-1, with Mathewson still pitching and three outs from winning the World Series.

Bottom of the 10th, and Clyde Engle lifted a soft fly to center. Fred Snodgrass moved 10 feet, raised his glove, seemed to catch the ball—and then let it trickle to the grass. Engle kept running, and was standing on second base.

Then Hooper lined a mean one to center and the same Snodgrass made a tremendous catch. Unfortunately, people remembered his muff longer than his catch because Mathewson walked Steve Yerkes and gave the Red Sox a late shot. The batter was Tris Speaker, their best hitter, and John McGraw watched in satisfaction as Mathewson got him to lift a foul ball alongside first base. But then McGraw watched in horror as Chief Meyers, the catcher, and Fred Merkle, the first baseman, stopped short and let it drop between them. Reprieved, Speaker lined a single to right field, tying the game and sending Yerkes to third base.

McGraw then ordered Mathewson to walk Duffy Lewis intentionally: Load the bases and look for a forceout at the plate or maybe even a double play. He got neither. Larry Gardner hit a long fly to right field, Yerkes tagged up and scored, and the Red Sox beat the team that had refused to play them in the Series eight years before.

As the game ended and the crowd flooded onto the field, McGraw ran over and shook Stahl's hand in the customary beau geste by the losing manager. As he did, he was tripped from behind by a celebrating (and foolhardy) young fan, at whom he immediately took a roundhouse swing.

The next day, reported The Times' man in Boston, after the Giants had carried their wounded back home: "Mayor Fitzgerald, clad in his greatcoat in which he romped so joyously about the Polo Grounds, was at the ball grounds early to congratulate the players. There was a tremendous rush of people at Faneuil Hall, where Mayor Fitzgerald and Speaker Walker of the Massachusetts House spoke."

Honey Fitz doffed his stovepipe hat toward the enemy, saying: "I am going to write to Muggsy McGraw—I believe that is what he's called—and tell him that any man like Matty who can give this team such a run must be the best in the world."

The crowd cheered, and Speaker Walker shook the mayor's hand. Then, tipping his stovepipe hat toward the home team, Honey Fitz promised silver cups to all the Red Sox, extolled them in superlatives, and ended his speech with a ringing plea for cheaper seats in the ball park.

Shoeless Joe and the khedive of Egypt

9

Chicago's Shoeless Joe Jackson, "the natural," confessed that he had helped to throw the 1919 World Series—though he collected 12 hits and batted .375.

CHAPTER 9

"**U**ntil 1912," James T. Farrell once wrote, fixing his memory on great events in American life, "I had not seen a major league game in which the catcher used shin guards. These were invented by the Hall of Fame catcher Roger Bresnahan. In the 1912 season, one of the White Sox catchers was a young player named Walter Kuhn, who appeared in 75 games. He was the first White Sox catcher to wear shin guards."

As a youngster growing up in Chicago in the days before he fashioned Studs Lonigan and his times, Jim Farrell played second base frequently and imagined that he was playing second base the rest of the time. The city, the neighborhood, the team blended into one frame of reference, and he or any other kid in the early years of the century looked at the world through that frame of reference. And ball players were often the most visible heroes of the neighborhood and the defenders of the city.

"Before World War I, Chicago was a great baseball town," Farrell remembered. "It remained so after the war, but I am speaking here of the time when I was a little boy and first became aware of baseball. In those days, pictures of baseball players, both major league and minor league players, came with certain brand packages of cigarettes—Piedmonts, Sweet Caporals and Sovereigns. Not just the stars, but practically entire teams would be included in these pictures. My brother and I collected these, and even before I started and could read, I could name the players on every picture. We used to stand in front of cigar stores and ask men as they came out to give us the baseball pictures in their cigarette packages."

There was nothing wrong with Jim Farrell's memory of Roger Bresnahan, the best and certainly the best protected catcher of his time. He was a versatile and inventive ball player who started his career as an 18-year-old pitcher in the majors (he tossed a six-hit shutout in his big-league debut) and who ended it as a 36-year-old catcher. He was this versatile: In 1903, his first full season with McGraw's Giants, he stole 34 bases, batted .350 and often played center field. He saw service as a leadoff hitter, even after he became a full-time catcher in 1905. And that was the year when he caught Christy Mathewson and Joe McGinnity in the only World Series in which every game was a shutout.

Two years later, Bresnahan decided that cricket players did things with more sense than ball players. Catchers had been known to wear some protective covering over their shins, but they placed the covering under their heavy woolen stockings. Bresnahan put his shin guards *outside*.

Was he lionized for his vision and hailed as one of the visionaries of sports? Of course not. He was ridiculed by some other teams and by the fans, and Fred Clarke, the manager of the Pittsburgh Pirates, even said that the shin guards were unsafe to sliding baserunners. But Bresnahan kept them on. He also made some modifications in the basic catcher's mask, and tried wearing a leather "helmet" over his baseball cap after he was beaned by Andy Coakley and missed 30 days of the season. He eventually gave up the batting helmet, although he was half a century ahead of his time. But the shin guards became part of every catcher's battle gear.

That was "the Duke," the man in the iron mask. "The Duke of Tralee," he was called during his entire career, because he had people believing that he and his family had come to this country from Tralee in Ireland. That was vaguely true for his parents, who came from other parts of Ireland. But after Roger Bresnahan retired from baseball, the genealogy was straightened out. He had actually been born in Toledo.

Where you came from, what equipment you wore, which way you threw the ball and swung the bat, where you ate and drank and spent your evenings after you spent your afternoons in the ball park—mattered very much to a public captivated by the game and its performers. And no group was more passionate about it all than the performers downtown. In New York and every other city along the railroad right-of-way where actors rode the circuit, stage players and ball players reigned as the demigods of sporting society.

The newspapers regularly reported the names of celebrities who attended World Series games, and even split them into categories, such as "the theatrical profession," which was represented at the 1913 Series between the Giants and Athletics by George M. Cohan, Samuel Harris, James J. Corbett, Miss Catherine Calvert, Miss Louise B. Johnson, Al Jolson, Wilson Mizner, Harry Bulger, Eddie Foy, DeWolfe Hopper, Jake Shubert, Lee Shubert, Willie Collier, Frank Fogarty, Billy Jerome, Gus Edwards, A.L. Erlanger, Marc Klaw, William A. Morris, Felix Isman, Paul Keith and William Hammerstein.

This was a marriage of true minds, the ball park and the theater, and many actors spent their afternoons in the ball park as relentlessly as some of the baseball people spent their evenings in the theater—or, at least, in the restaurants, clubs and bars near the theater. Even the terrible-tempered John McGraw spent 15 weeks in the winter of 1912-13 touring the vaudeville circuit, rendering a stand-up monologue from material written by Boseman Bulger of the New York Evening World and using a stage technique bestowed by his theater cronies at the Lambs.

His rival manager of long standing, the erect and austere Connie Mack, made an even longer leap into the public arena. Stiff white collar and all, he could be seen beaming from newspaper advertisements beneath his straw hat, a smile on his long face and these words supposedly on his lips: "I drink Coca-Cola myself, and advise all the team to drink it. I think it is good for them." (At five cents a glass, it couldn't hurt.)

The appeal was national now, and it was about to become international. Baseball teams had taken tours abroad before, but not with John McGraw running the show.

Now, in the winter after the 1913 World Series, which the Giants lost to the Athletics, the most extensive trip of all was planned by McGraw and Charles Comiskey. They recruited players from their own teams, the Giants and the White Sox, and signed up players from other teams, too. They even signed up Bill Klem, the umpire who never missed one; or, at least, who never admitted that he missed one.

They started in Cincinnati on October 18, and played ball games to raise money as they headed west to Chicago, Missouri, Kansas, Oklahoma, Texas, California, Oregon and Vancouver. They played in the snow in Springfield, Ill., and they played in front of hundreds of Indians from the reservations near Sioux City, Iowa, who had come to cheer Chief Meyers and Jim Thorpe. They played just about every place they stopped, crossing the continent with an entourage of 50 players, officials and friends of McGraw, traveling in an eight-car special train and then embarking on the Empress of Japan on November 19 for 23 days at sea, and stormy days they turned out to be.

They traveled to Yokohama, Kobe, Nagasaki, Shanghai, Hong Kong, Manila, Brisbane on New Year's Day of 1914, then on to Colombo in January, through the Suez Canal to Cairo, Alexandria, Nice, Marseille, Paris, Rome on February 8, then London and finally home aboard a liner named the Lusitania.

McGraw dispatched a diary on his adventures to The New York Times, and he depicted the tour as a kind of monument to baseball as an international messenger.

"When I was a kid," he said, "I traveled with some teams whose members were very bad actors. After I joined the Baltimore club in 1891, there were more notorious bad actors on the club than on any team in the world. The old Orioles were champions of the world when it came to rough stuff. From the park to the nearest saloon, there was a beaten path that these players took as soon as they could get dressed.

"But in spite of the great improvement in the class of men who play the game, the bad name has clung to the sport, and lots of folks expect the professional ball player to be rough and are surprised when he talks English which can be understood."

In his dispatches, he told how "a great crowd" had appeared at Brisbane when the tour reached Australia. Then, after a rough sea voyage to Japan, he described a "most cordial reception in the Mikado's country," where he also discovered with some wonder a Japanese pitcher with good control and some "stuff," and "a pair of heavy, gold-rimmed spectacles."

Jim Thorpe and his bride climbed into a rickshaw and took a tumble when their weight crushed it and they were dumped onto the ground. And in Tokyo, some of the Giants got into a misunderstanding with a pair of policemen, and it nearly blossomed into an old-fasioned ball-park fight until they boarded a steamer for Nagasaki while throngs of Japanese stood on the pier and in the streets shouting "banzai, banzai."

But McGraw saw it all as a sign of times to come, and he predicted: "Someday, the streets of Japan will have signs reading: 'Baseball today, Japan vs. United States.' You'd be surprised how quickly they pick up the tricks of the game."

They met the khedive of Egypt and the Pope of Rome, and they met the King of England after a brief comedy of protocol in which the Giants switched hurriedly from high hats to bowlers and frock coats. Then they played a ball game before 35,000 Englismen, and stood before George V, who said:

"I am glad to meet you, Mr. McGraw. Your game is very interesting, and I would like to know more about it."

Bowing as he retreated toward his team's bench, McGraw replied: "We certainly hope that you will have a chance to see more of it."

By the time they reached home, it was March 6 and they had traveled 30,000 miles in 4½ months and had built McGraw's "monument" to baseball from Cincinnati to Australia to the pyramids.

They didn't know it when they stepped down the gangway in New York, where they were greeted by Ban Johnson and Charles Ebbets, but they were stepping from an international hayride into a domestic thicket. Another baseball war had broken out: The Federal League, a minor league, had rounded up a bunch of major league bankrolls and was mounting a serious challenge to the American and National Leagues for their talent and their customers.

The bankrolls belonged to people like Harry Sinclair, the oil baron, who controlled $60 million and was willing to spend some of it for ball players. Sinclair later won the Kentucky Derby with the colt Zev, and still later went to prison after the Teapot Dome oil scandal. He made a monumental bid for the No. 1 player in the game, Ty Cobb, offering him a three-year deal for $100,000. If the league failed, Cobb remembered later, he would fall back on a guaranteed business arrangement that would make him the highest-priced oil-lease man in the history of the Sinclair Co. Cobb declined the offer, but used it to win a 50 percent raise from the Detroit Tigers and became the highest-paid player of his time.

The man behind the Federal League's invasion was James A. Gilmore, a coal and paper executive who had been named president of the league in the summer of 1913 after it had opened for business with six clubs. They were placed in Chicago, St. Louis, Cleveland, Pittsburgh, Indianapolis and Covington, Ky. (Covington's franchise, which represented the Cincinnati area, was moved to Kansas City in June.)

The Federal League teams were facing collective bankruptcy when Gilmore was talked into taking charge. He did, and promptly went hunting for bankrolls.

He bagged some imposing ones, at that. Besides Sinclair, he came up with Charles Weeghman, a Chicago restaurant man; Philip deCatesby Ball, the "ice king of St. Louis," who manufactured ice-making machinery; and Robert Ward and his brother George, who owned Ward's Bakery in Brooklyn.

Gilmore eventually rearranged the geography of the Federal League, dropping Cleveland and adding Newark, Buffalo, Brooklyn and Baltimore. And he announced that the Feds did not intend to honor anybody else's "reserve clause," which meant they were declaring open season on talent in the two established big leagues.

Their first prize was Joe Tinker, the shortstop and manager of the Cincinnati Reds. He was offered three years at $12,000 a year plus some shares of Weeghman stock if he would jump to the Chicago Whales of the new league, and he did. Tinker became playing manager of the Whales, and his old double-play partner, Johnny Evers, was offered $30,000 in cash and $15,000 a year for five years to abandon the Chicago Cubs and switch to the Whales, and he did not. But it was a little more complicated than that. Evers actually gave the Cubs a chance to match the offer, and they took it to be a notice of resignation, so they released him. However, the president of the National League quickly stepped in, arranged for the Cubs to trade him to Boston, cut Evers in for a bonus of $25,000 and saved one star player for the league.

But the Federal League raiders were not striking out. They signed Mordecai (Three-Finger) Brown, longtime Cubs star, as manager of the St. Louis Feds. They signed Leonard Leslie (King) Cole, a pitcher owned by the Yankees. They signed Bill Killefer, the catcher for the Phillies, for three years at a total of $17,500. But, when the Phillies matched that a few days later, Killefer jumped back.

At the height of the war, 221 players jumped from various levels of baseball to the Federal League (which claimed "major league" status in 1914 and 1915), and 81 of them were major leaguers. For a brief time, one of them was the great Walter Johnson, who pitched 32 victories in 1912, then 36 the following year and 28 the year after that, and who struck out 771 batters during those three summers.

Johnson had not yet signed his contract for 1915 when he jumped to the Federal League, although he was still presumably bound to the Washington Senators by the reserve clause. But the reserve clause had been coming under attack from time to time, and it did not always escape without some challenge. So, Clark Griffith, the owner of the Senators, hustled to see Ban Johnson in some fright over the loss of his ace pitcher.

"I told him," the president of the American League said later, "to get Johnson back by offering him as much as the Feds had—or beat their top price. Griffith explained that the club did not have that much money in the treasury. So I advanced the money to Griffith."

The owner of the Senators took it, traveled to Kansas and made his pitch. It worked. Walter Johnson returned to the team for $12,500 a year, which reportedly matched the Federal League offer, and won 27 games for the Senators in 1915.

Things were getting a bit sticky now for the Federal League, especially after the loss of an Olympian name like Walter Johnson. So, early in 1915, the league sued the 16 presidents of the big-league clubs and the three members of the National Commission, accusing them of conspiracy to restrain trade in violation of the antitrust laws.

The suit was heard in Northern Illinois federal district court, and the presiding judge was a spare and even gaunt 48-year-old Ohioan named for the Georgia battlefield where his father had been seriously wounded in the Civil War: Kenesaw Mountain Landis.

The judge had come to public attention 10 years earlier when he fined John D. Rockefeller's Standard Oil Co. more than $29 million in a freight-rebate case. His action was later overturned by the Supreme Court, but the shock of Landis' ruling remained. He was also a fairly regular visitor to the home games of both the Cubs and the White Sox, and his affinity for baseball showed through his early observations during the Federal League hearing.

"Do you realize," he said, "that a decision in this case may tear down the very foundations of this game, so loved by thousands, and do you realize that the decision must seriously affect both parties?"

Landis apparently realized it, and he accordingly entered a prolonged period of deliberation without rendering any decision. He deliberated from January into the spring, and from the spring into the summer. Strictly speaking, he didn't really deliberate all that time. Rather, he waited all that time, fully believing that a settlement out of court would be better for baseball and fully expecting that one would be reached without any judicial lightning from his bench.

Landis was right, but it took a great deal of maneuvering on both sides for the war to end. The end was hastened when the 1915 season proved ruinously expensive to both sides, the established leagues and the Federal League. Then, on October 18 that year, the Federals lost one of their most important bankrolls when Robert Ward died. He reportedly had lost $1 million on his investment.

Ward's passing, The Sporting News predicted, would lead to the collapse of the Federal League. But then, the prediction itself was part of a war within the war. The Federal League had been opposed by The Sporting News editorially and embraced by Sporting Life, a Philadelphia-based rival.

John George Taylor Spink, who had succeeded his father, Charles C. Spink, as publisher of The Sporting News upon Charles' death in the spring of 1914, aimed his first major editorial crusade at the Federal League, and events were finally hastening its departure.

The out-of-court settlement that Landis had envisioned began to take shape when the National and American Leagues held their winter meetings after the 1915 season. One month later, the National Commission met and worked out the treaty: The two major leagues agreed to restore all the Federal League players to the eligibility list, but made no commitment to sign any of them, and specificially refused to take any liability for the $385,000 still owed on their contracts. Charles Weeghman bought the Cubs and moved them into his ball park on the North Side of Chicago, later to be known as Wrigley Field. Philip deCatesby Ball bought the Browns in St. Louis, and he and Weeghman now paid their way into the major leagues. And, as the final term in the treaty, all lawsuits were to be dropped.

"I thought there was plenty of room for three major leagues," James Gilmore reflected. "I admit I had the wrong perspective. There is no room for three major leagues."

So, the war between the leagues was ended. But the world was already locked in a real war, a catastrophic "war to end all wars," and it was changing the face of nations and the fate of millions of people in Europe. It also was changing the outlook and style of life in America, where the war finally came home in the first week of April in 1917.

The baseball season was played, and it was somewhat leaner and more solemn, but it did not lack drama. The Giants completed a remarkable comeback from last place to first place in two years, and won the National League pennant. The White Sox won 100 games, beat out the Boston Red Sox by nine games and swept to the American League pennant. They knocked off the Giants in six games in the World Series, which was marked by the customary fights and by one more legend: Heinie Zimmerman, playing third base for New York, chased Eddie Collins across home plate with the ball in his hand when the Giants' catcher and pitcher left the plate unguarded. It was the last game of the Series, and Zimmerman was assaulted on all sides for his supposed "boner." To which the Great Zim replied with considerable logic: "Who the hell was I going to throw the ball to? Bill Klem?"

John McGraw, crotchety in the extreme, proved not very gracious in defeat. As he left the field, Pants Rowland, the manager of the White Sox, ran past and said: "Mr. McGraw, I'm sorry you had to be the one to lose." McGraw looked up, and snarled: "Get away from me, you damned busher."

The big show, though, was happening someplace else. The newspapers were running columns of names of "Men Enrolled in the National Army," along with the number of those needed "to fill the quota." About 20,000 draftees were paraded along Fifth Avenue. The American Army organized its first camouflage company, and appealed for volunteers to learn "the art of military concealment, to spread the magic veil of invisibility—camoufleur is to the modern soldier what the handiest bush was to the American Indian."

Songsheets of "Slide, Kelly, Slide" and "Our National Game" took on a patriotic fervor. The Washington Senators became the Washington Statesmen. Sarah Bernhardt, appearing in "L'Aiglon" at the age of 72, said the great hope of her life was "to be in Paris when victory is won and France is restored." Col. Theodore Roosevelt became the war columnist for the Kansas City Star, and the paper announced that his dispatches would make Kansas City "the center of a momentous discussion of events of transcendent importance."

The magnificently named Colonel Tillinghast l'Hommedieu Huston, who bought the New York Yankees in early 1915 along with Colonel Jacob Ruppert, showed the colors by leading his Reserve engineering unit abroad. But, before he did, he suggested that every club conduct military drills in spring training. Ban Johnson adopted the idea for the American League, which imported regular Army sergeants to instruct the players in close-order drill. Some players thought it was laughable, and the National League in particular thought it was laughable. But Johnson persisted, and even held a competition among his clubs late in the season, with a colonel brought in from Washington to judge the military drills.

The St. Louis Browns finished first in the competition, which was six places higher than they finished in the American League.

At the ball parks, soliders and sailors were passed through the turnstiles free. Announcements were made at the games to stimulate recruiting. Sometimes, troops in uniform staged marches on the field before games. The 10 percent federal tax applied to entertainment was applied to baseball tickets. And, after the Selective Service Act was voted by Congress on May 18, 1917, ball players began to head for the ranks in steadily increasing numbers.

Because the first draft of men between the ages of 21 and 30 did not take place until July 20 that summer, only 40 ball players were taken that season. But the trickle turned into a torrent in 1918 after Gen. Enoch B. Crowder, the Provost Marshal and director of the draft, issued the "work-or-fight order," and went on to explain that the order was aimed at "sturdy idlers and loafers standing at the street corners and contemplating placidly their own immunity." To clinch the point, he listed a number of "non-essential occupations" that would not carry any exemption from the draft. They included "persons engaged and occupied in and in connection with games, sports and amusements."

For perfectly proper reasons, many people began to stream into essential occupations, and some ball players followed a kind of exodus into shipyards. But they were not always given the benefit of the doubt on motive, and some were criticized as "shipyard slackers" whose main duty was to pitch the company baseball team to celebrity status. And, despite the temper of the times, some shipyards and steel mills began to induce ball players to leave their clubs and find a haven playing ball in "an essential occupation."

Very few people did it with the humor or mischief of Casey Stengel, who was then an outfielder for the Pittsburgh Pirates and the ringleader of a clubhouse gang of hell-raisers. He was known, with good reason, as "the king of the Grumblers."

One afternoon in 1918, Stengel insulted an umpire by removing his Pittsburgh uniform shirt and offering it to the umpire with the remark: "You try playing on our side for a while." For this irreverence, he was fined $50 by the president of the National League with the full approval of Barney Dreyfuss, the harassed owner of the Pirates. So, the next day, Stengel found a rather drastic way out.

"I went down and enlisted in the Navy," he said. "I beat the league out of 50 bucks, but it wound up costing me $750 in pay. They put me to work in the Navy Yard in Brooklyn, not far from the ball park; I was supposed to paint ships, they found out I could paint. But one day this lieutenant commander walked in and said, 'You're the manager of the ball team.' "

"I used to board them ships," Stengel said, explaining his *modus operandi*, "as soon as they got in, and make a date for a game the next day. I found if they'd been on land too long, we couldn't beat them."

Baseball's relations with the draft took a sharp turn in the summer of 1918 when a federal order put things succinctly: End the season by Labor Day. The Secretary of War, Newton D. Baker, gave the two pennant winners time to play the World Series in early September, and they did. The Boston Red Sox defeated the Chicago Cubs, four games to two, and won the Series for the third time in four years.

Much of the success of the Red Sox was centered in the exceptional talent and versatility of their 23-year-old prodigy, Babe Ruth, a lefthanded pitcher of distinction who won 78 regular-season games in those four years, one in the 1916 World Series and two more in the 1918 Series. He also ran his string of Series shutout innings to 29⅔.

But Ruth was already a hitter of distinction, and his pitching career was about to be surpassed by his hitting career. He hit 11 home runs in the shortened season of 1918, playing the outfield frequently when he wasn't pitching. In the Series, he pitched a six-hit shutout against the Cubs in Game 1 and then pitched into the ninth inning in Game 4—a game in which he batted sixth in the lineup and tripled home two runs for a 3-2 victory.

By winning, the Red Sox continued a domination of the Series by the American League, which now had taken eight of the last nine. In fact, the only National League team that won one was the "miracle" Boston Braves team of 1914. Their miracle, though, was getting there. They had finished in last place for four straight years beginning in 1909, then edged up to fifth place in 1913. But the following season, they were back to their old tricks: last on the Fourth of July, last as late as July 18.

Then the Braves began the most remarkable climb in history. With

George Stallings running the team as manager, they climbed past teams behind some of the best pitching in the league. Bill James won 26 games that season. Dick Rudolph won 27, George Tyler 16. By September 8, they were crowding their way into first place past the Giants, who were trying for their fourth straight pennant. By closing day, Boston was 10½ games in front of the Giants and headed into the World Series against the Philadelphia A's, who were solid 3-1 favorites.

That's when the Braves produced their second miracle. Hank Gowdy, the catcher, a .243 hitter during the season, hit .545 in the Series. Their pitchers stopped the A's on one run in two games and no runs in another, and held them to a .172 batting average. And they swept four games from a team that had won four American League pennants in five years, and had won three World Series in four years.

Afterward, Connie Mack blamed the Athletics' collapse on the Federal League, which was raiding talent in those days.

"The Federal League wrecked our team spirit and undermined us with their persistent offers," he said. "I knew Chief Bender and Eddie Plank had already jumped. We tore up two, and in some cases three, contracts with other discontented stars that season, trying to keep up with Federal demands. The wonder is that we won the pennant."

★ ★ ★

After the "miracle" of the 1914 Braves, it was five years before the National League won another World Series—and it would have been better for baseball if it hadn't won that one.

It should have been a joyous time, the first full season after the Armistice and the end of World War I. It should have been a rousing World Series, with the Cincinnati Reds winning their first National League pennant and facing the Chicago White Sox, powerful and highly favored to win—until rumors and warnings began to fly on the morning of the opening game, October 1, in Cincinnati.

"The most sensational happening to occur during my term of office as president of the American League," Ban Johnson said later, "was the successful attempt of eight members of the Chicago White Sox team to throw the World Series of 1919."

The eight were Eddie Cicotte, the leading pitcher in the league that year with a record of 29-7; Claude Williams, another pitcher, who won 23 games and lost 11; Joe Jackson, the "natural" in left field, who hit .351 that season, fourth best in the league; Happy Felsch, the center fielder, who hit .275 and drove in 86 runs; Swede Risberg, the shortstop, who had played only his third major league season in 1919; Chick Gandil, the first baseman, a .290 hitter; Buck Weaver, the third baseman, who hit .296 in the regular season, and Fred McMullin, a reserve infielder.

Two groups of gamblers were involved in separate transactions to fix the Series, but the main effort was made by Arnold Rothstein of New York, who reportedly put up $100,000. The other bunch, led by Abe Attell of Philadelphia, supposedly came up with $10,000 after a lot of slipping around.

The president of the Reds was Garry Herrmann, who also was chairman of baseball's National Commission, and that became a bit of a problem when Herrmann was confronted with the bad news and hated to believe it. After all, his team ostensibly scored a tremendous upset by winning the Series. Not only that, but he also had issued a ruling that year as chairman of the commission, extending the Series to a five-of-nine format, instead of four-of-seven. The idea was that all first-division players were voted a share of the prize money that year, so Herrmann extended the Series to produce more prize money.

Cincinnati went wild, along with Garry Herrmann, when the Reds roughed up Cicotte for five runs in the fourth inning and went on to open the Series with a 9-1 rout.

"There was much rejoicing in the Redland camp," Fred Lieb recalled, "but only bitterness in the White Sox clubhouse. Reports drifted out of some hot words between Eddie Cicotte and Ray Schalk, the great Chicago catcher, who accused Eddie of repeatedly crossing his signals. Reporters also remembered how gamblers had made the Reds strong favorites just before game time. At the Metropolis Hotel, gamblers with fistfuls of bills were in the lobby frantically trying to place money on the Reds on the morning of the contest."

The Reds won the second game, too. They were outhit, 10 to four, but the White Sox apparently made sure that they weren't outscored. Claude Williams pitched the four-hitter for the White Sox, but walked three batters in the fourth inning, gave up a single and triple and three runs, and lost the game, 4-2.

On the train headed for Chicago that night, Charles Comiskey of the White Sox went to John Heydler, the president of the National League, and reported that "something fishy" was going on. He quoted the manager of the team, Kid Gleason, and said: "The Kid can't put his finger on it, but he knows there has been some funny business on his team."

Comiskey told his tale to Heydler because he was feuding at the time with the president of his own league, Ban Johnson, and he didn't think he could complain to Garry Herrmann, chairman of the commission, since Herrmann also was the owner of the Reds. But Heydler got dressed and went to the compartment of Ban Johnson, who replied: "That's the yelp of a beaten cur."

In the third game, little Dickie Kerr pitched three-hit ball for the White Sox, who won for the first time, 3-0. But, the next day, Cicotte made two bad fielding plays that undermined a fine pitching performance on his part, and the Reds won it, 2-0.

They went to the fifth game, and Felsch made a bad throw and misplayed a fly ball in one inning in center field. The Reds won, 5-0, and now led in the Series, four games to one.

Then the teams took their strange Series back to Cincinnati, where the White Sox put on a respectable show and won the next two games, 5-4 and 4-1. And now Chicago was right back in the Series, it seemed, even though Cincinnati still needed only one more victory to win it all. That was no problem: In one-third of an inning the next day, the Reds hammered Claude Williams for four hits and four runs and barreled on to win the game, 10-5, and the Series, five games to three.

Some strange performances: Shoeless Joe Jackson, whom many people were inclined to forgive or even to exonerate, got 12 hits, knocked in six runs and batted .375 for the best average on his club. Buck Weaver, also a marked man, was next with .324. Eddie Collins, the captain of the White Sox and an innocent victim of the fix, played his heart out—and hit .226.

As soon as the Series ended, Comiskey offered $10,000 to anyone who could supply any evidence that it hadn't been on the level. Nobody did. But the rumors followed the White Sox into the next season, and right into the homestretch of a three-way race for the pennant with the Yankees and Cleveland Indians. On September 27, in the final week, the Philadelphia North American ran an interview with one of the local gamblers that reportedly "caused a panic in the ranks of the players." The next day, Cicotte and Jackson went before the Cook County Grand Jury in Illinois and confessed, and Felsch and Williams followed.

All eight were indicted for "conspiracy to commit an illegal act," but these were only preliminary indictments. They were enough, though, to spring the trap. Comiskey immediately addressed a letter to the players who had betrayed his team, and got right to the point:

"You and each of you are hereby notified of your indefinite suspension as a member of the Chicago American League Baseball Club.

"Your suspension is brought about by information which has just come to me directly involving you and each of you in the baseball scandal resulting from the World Series of 1919.

"If you are innocent of any wrongdoing, you and each of you will be reinstated; if you are guilty, you will be retired from organized baseball for the rest of your lives, if I can accomplish it.

"Until there is a finality to this investigation, it is due to the public that I take this action, even though it costs Chicago the pennant."

Something cost Chicago the pennant in 1920, but it was close. It was also remarkable that the White Sox ran so well, under the circumstances. They won 96 games and finished two behind the Indians and one in front of the Yankees. Cicotte won 21 games, Williams won 22 and Joe Jackson hit .382.

The great fix came unraveled after Cicotte had gone before the jury and broke down, saying:

"My God! Think of my children, I never did anything I regretted so much in my life. I would give anything in the world if I could undo my acts in the last World Series. I've played a crooked game and lost, and I am here to tell the whole truth.

"I've lived a thousand years in the last year."

Then he told how he had played his hand in throwing two games:

"In the first game in Cincinnati, I was knocked out of the box. I wasn't putting a thing on the ball. You could have read the trademark on it when I lobbed the ball up to the plate.

"In the fourth game, played at Chicago, I deliberately intercepted a throw from the outfield to the plate which might have cut off a run. I muffed the ball on purpose.

"At another time in the same game, I purposely made a wild throw. All the runs scored against me were due to my own deliberate errors. I did not try to win."

Cicotte also related that he had first confessed to Comiskey earlier that morning. He went to the owner's office and said: "I don't know what you'll think of me, but I got to tell you how I double-crossed you, Mr. Comiskey. I did double-cross you. I'm a crook, and I got $10,000 for being a crook."

To which Comiskey replied: "Don't tell it to me. Tell it to the judge."

Cicotte did tell it to the judge, and in remarkable detail. He said that Risberg, Gandil and McMullin had been pressuring him for a week before the Series to join the plot.

"I needed the money," he said. "I had the wife and kids. I bought a farm. There was a $4,000 mortgage on it. There isn't any mortgage on it now. I paid it off with the crooked money.

"The eight of us got together in my room three or four days before the games started. Gandil was the master of ceremonies. We talked about throwing the Series. Decided we could get away with it. We agreed to do it.

"We all talked quite a while about it, I and the seven others. Yes, all of us decided to do our best to throw the games in Cincinnati.

"When Gandil and McMullin took us all, one by one, away from the others, and we talked 'turkey,' they asked me my price. I told them $10,000. And I told them that $10,000 was to be paid in advance. 'Cash in advance,' I said. 'Cash in advance, and nothing else.' "

There was some talk about paying some of the money up front and the rest later, after the White Sox had lost. But Cicotte told Gandil, as though they were arranging a sale: "Cash in advance, and not C.O.D."

Then, in perhaps the most ironic statement of all, Cicotte told Gandil: "If you can't trust me, I can't trust you. Pay or I play ball."

The haggling subsided, and Cicotte won his point: He found the $10,000 under his pillow, and later said:

"I don't know who put it there, but it was there. It was my price. I had sold out 'Commy.' I had sold out the other boys, sold them for $10,000 to pay

*Kenesaw Mountain Landis, the federal judge who became the first com-
missioner of baseball, restored the integrity of the game after the Black
Sox scandal by throwing thunderbolts as well as baseballs.*

off a mortgage on a farm, and for the wife and kids."

When Joe Jackson was called, it struck many people as the downfall of innocence—or maybe ignorance. He was a country boy from Brandon Mills, S.C., now 32 years old and apparently stunned by the enormity of what had happened. He hung his head and covered his face with his hands as he walked to the grand jury room through a massed horde of newspaper cameramen.

Inside the jury room, he told how he had been promised $20,000 but got only $5,000, which was handed to him in Cincinnati by Lefty Williams. When Jackson threatened to spill the beans, he was told: "You poor simp, go ahead and squawk. We'll all say you're a liar, and every honest baseball player in the world will say you're a liar."

Jackson testified that, despite his solid batting average in the Series, he had either struck out or hit easy balls when hits would have meant significant runs. He testified nearly two hours, then came out of the room walking erect and even smiling, and said:

"I got a big load off my chest. I'm feeling better."

The grand jury returned full indictments against all eight players late in October 1920, but nothing happened for months because the jury's records and the players' confessions were stolen from the prosecutor's office. By then, the players had repudiated their confessions; and, in February, the indictments were dismissed. But Ban Johnson was determined not to let it go at that. He traveled thousands of miles, rebuilt the case and submitted his evidence to the grand jury again. On March 26, 1921, new indictments were handed down.

After all that, it was ironic that the eight players were found not guilty by a Cook County jury on August 2. But on August 3, all eight were banned from baseball for life by the new commissioner of baseball—Judge Kenesaw Mountain Landis, who had been offered the job nine months earlier during the upheaval created in baseball by "the Black Sox scandal." And Landis, who replaced the three-man National Commission, wasted no time setting the tone for his term of office.

In a statement issued immediately after the eight were acquitted, he said: "Regardless of the verdict of juries, no player that throws a ball game, no player that entertains proposals or promises to throw a game, no player that sits in a conference with a bunch of crooked players and gamblers where the ways and means of throwing games are discussed, and does not promptly tell his club about it, will ever again play professional baseball."

The era of wonderful nonsense 10

Among the great American heroes of the 1920s were Gen. John J. Pershing, who led the armies in World War I, and Babe Ruth, who temporarily traded in his Yankee uniform during a trip to Washington.

CHAPTER 10

In the spring of 1921, the United States was cheerfully spiraling into the decade of wonderful nonsense.

The boys were finally back from Over There, the "reparations problem" was left to grayer heads like Lloyd George, and the great tide of Prohibition was causing very little public inconvenience—except in the new "rum courts," which were struggling to handle a landslide business in bootleg cases.

It was a time of suffragettes, heroes, heavyweights and hoopla. Of Suzanne Lenglen in flowing white dress, socking a backhand on the court at Cannes. Of Mary Garden, the "directrix" of the Chicago Opera Company, burrowing through papers on her desk in the midst of "the New York season." Of Man O' War making his final appearance on the course of the Kentucky Association in Lexington.

Ethel and John Barrymore were performing at the Empire Theatre in Michael Strange's new play, "Clair de Lune." Ziegfeld was offering Marilynn Miller and Leon Errol at the New Amsterdam in "Sally." Jackie Coogan was "Peck's Bad Boy" at the Brooklyn Strand.

The Lyric was unfolding "the world's greatest motion picture, 'The Queen of Sheba,' the most sensational and thrilling spectacle ever shown on the screen." (Its chariot scene, commented the critic of the New York Evening Telegram, was "the last word in thrills.") And at the Capitol, D.W. Griffith was opening his revival of "The Birth of a Nation," modestly described as being "to the screen what Hamlet is to drama, Faust to opera, Mikado to comic opera." All that plus an orchestra of 80 pieces in the pit.

In its gentler moments, American society might applaud "Madame Curie's genius," attend Sunday afternoon tea dances at roadside places like the Pelham Heath Inn, or warm to rotogravure photographs of Billie Burke as Mrs. Florenz Ziegfeld walking with her daughter Patricia at Palm Beach.

In its frenzied moments, which seemed more numerous, it might rail at the Bolshevik threat, issue ultimatums on occupying the Ruhr Valley, or rush to get cash down on the Dempsey-Carpentier fight.

Getting there was not only faster than ever before but more splendid, besides. By air from Paris to Brussels to Amsterdam, for instance: Leave Paris at 11 a.m., arrive in Amsterdam at 3:30 p.m.—"thus, the journey consumes only 4½ hours, one-third of the time formerly required by railway."

Overland, the going was even sportier. A 1920 Chandler, "a chummy roadster," went for $1,275. A 1917 Amesbury Berlin sedan—"with Westinghouse shock absorbers, bumper, two spare tires and other extras; just overhauled, painted and reupholstered"—could be viewed "on inspection by appointment."

It was a time of idols, and sometimes idols stacked on other idols. Douglas Fairbanks posed with Jack Dempsey perched comfortably on his right shoulder, and insisted airily that it was "just as easy as holding up the Woolworth Building."

A time of "McGrawmen," who shared America's biggest ball yard with the homeless Yankees and their new hero, Babe Ruth, who had moved into the Polo Grounds because they needed a bigger ball park. And, after they bought Ruth from the Boston Red Sox in the winter before the 1920 season, the Yankees richly needed a bigger ball park than that.

It was a time when a "little country estate" of four acres in Dobbs Ferry, N.Y., 12 rooms, four baths, could be had for $175 a month (unfurnished).

It was a time when a war-weary public snapped up almost any pronouncement from the actors who paraded across this clamorous stage, and then treated itself to the full range of emotional responses.

People were impressed when Marshal Foch announced grandly that Napoleon himself had been the "teacher" of the Allies in 1918. They were not dismayed that Napoleon had failed to teach the Allies how to collect for the lesson—eight-column headlines told almost every day of the Allies' frustration in forcing reparations from the Germans, despite warnings by Prime Minister George, Premier Briand and President Harding that Napoleon's pupils would march again if Berlin failed to reply in six days.

In London, the House was taken aback when Lady Astor "delivered another of her Friday afternoon sermonettes to the enlivenment of an otherwise dull sitting of Commons." Her theme: The duty of parents toward their children. A chorus of masculine "ohs" greeted her feminine assault on "rotters."

New York was elated when Madame Curie arrived from Paris and announced that radium could cure even most deep-seated cancers. Two days later, it was deflated when her secretary announced that Madame Curie had meant only that radium could cure *some* types of cancer.

The public conscience was appeased when John D. Rockefeller Jr. contributed $1 million "to the starving children of Central Europe." And it was exalted when he helped to dramatize China's "wretched harvest" by eating a luncheon of dried corn and tanbark from a bowl.

It was further redeemed when Henry Ford began to grow wheat on thousands of acres adjoining his estate in Dearborn, Mich., ground it into flour and sold it to his workers for $7.80 a barrel instead of the $10 that retail stores commanded. Henry Ford, the press reported, "has turned miller for the benefit of his employees."

Broadway listened gravely when Tex Rickard, the impresario of box-ing, disclosed that he had received formal "assurances" that Georges Car-pentier would head for America aboard the S.S. Savote for the big fight at Boyle's Thirty Acres in Jersey City. And it swayed with anticipation at reports that the Frenchman had thereupon set sail "with dozens of sports-men from England and the Continent intent on witnessing the battle, in which Carpentier will attempt to wrest the world's heavyweight champion-ship from Dempsey."

From the ridiculous, the public could soar splendidly to the sublime. Prof. Michael I. Pupin of Columbia declared in a lecture that great ad-vances in nuclear studies showed that the electron of 1921 was not the "final unit" in the structure of the atom. (He was right.) Then it could plunge back to the ridiculous. Carpentier, getting more newspaper space than Pupin, reported that "Dempsey is made to order for me." (He was wrong.) Demp-sey's mother, winning bigger headlines than either the professor or Carpen-tier, predicted staunchly that Jack would win. (She was right.)

Still, none of the pronouncements or issues in that spring of 1921 equaled, in public fervor or identification, the controversies that suddenly swirled around two of the most celebrated figures of the day.

They were John J. McGraw, the most famous manager in baseball, and Thomas A. Edison, the wizard of Menlo Park, N.J. They were as different as two men could be. So were their *causes célèbres*. And so were the responses of a passionate public.

McGraw's case challenged the public's capacity to drink, Edison's chal-lenged the public's capacity to think, and therefore—interrupting the flow of wonderful nonsense—was not nearly so open and shut.

McGraw marched before the bar of public justice first. On February 7, he was brought to trial in federal district court in New York City before the distinguished Judge Learned Hand. The charge: "Having in his possession a bottle of whiskey at the Lambs," the theatrical haven in midtown Manhat-tan where the manager of the Giants spent many long evenings with the stars of the Broadway stage, replaying the afternoon's feats of his ball players at the Polo Grounds uptown.

Having a bottle of whiskey in one's possession at the Lambs was consid-ered neither unusual nor illegal by most persons, the Volstead Act notwith-standing. In fact, it would have been considered unusual if McGraw or any of his circle had spent an evening at the Lambs without a bottle of whiskey. But this particular bottle landed the renowned manager into Learned Hand's courtroom because it had been followed by a fight and a mysterious accident.

The fight had taken place in the grill room of the club six months earlier, on August 8, 1920. The principals were McGraw and William Boyd, the actor, who had been the leading man for Ethel Barrymore, Maude

Adams and other prima donnas of the stage. McGraw, a veteran of number-
less brawls on the diamond from his teen-age years with the Baltimore
Orioles in the 1890s, said later that Boyd had objected to his language in the
presence of the cleaning woman at a late hour on a Sunday night, or Monday morning. And so McGraw had simply hit Boyd over the head with a
water carafe.

The mysterious accident took place a short time later after McGraw
had taken a taxi to his apartment on the northwest corner of Broadway and
109th Street. He was accompanied by John C. Slavin, the musical comedy
actor, and Winfield Liggett, who lived at the Lambs. What happened as they
poured one another out of the cab was never made clear. But Slavin was
found unconscious on the sidewalk later with a fractured jaw, and when
detectives rang McGraw's bell, the manager roused himself from sleep and
answered the door with a somewhat battered face and a decidedly black
eye.

The chief Prohibition agent in New York, James S. Shevlin, responded
to the news with a swift sword. He pressed for a federal indictment against
McGraw for "willfully possessing a bottle of whiskey" in violation of the
Volstead Act, and he got it. The Lambs, caught in the act of serving drinks
in the grill room, promptly expelled McGraw in righteous indignation. William J. Fallon, the famous criminal lawyer, just as promptly leaped to the
defense, took over as McGraw's counsel and clamored for a grand jury
investigation to clear the name of the Little Napoleon of New York.

McGraw's defense had one bad moment before the case was called to
trial. One month after the fight, the manager received a visit from William
Lackaye, another actor-friend and member of the Lambs. He went to
McGraw's home "to give him some friendly advice," and came out with a
broken ankle.

Despite incriminating setbacks like this, though, Fallon managed to
win a one-month postponement when the trial opened in New York on
February 7. Everybody realized that one month later McGraw would be in
spring training with his Giants, thereby making another postponement inev-
itable. But in 1921, neither James S. Shevlin, Learned Hand nor the Volstead
Act would likely come between New York and the Giants as they primed for
another baseball season.

As a lull settled over the case, a distraction was immediately presented
from a laboratory in Orange, N.J., by Thomas Edison—who was every bit as
combative in the public eye as McGraw, but not nearly so lucky in his
choice of causes.

Three days after McGraw was granted his postponement, the inventor
heralded the approach of his 74th birthday by expressing his ideas on mankind.

This had been a favorite pastime of Edison's for years. And while
McGraw had been provoking people with his fists and tricks with baseball

bats, Edison had been tweaking them with mental gymnastics for decades.

When he was 12 years old, he had been the most precocious railroad newsboy and candy butcher in the Midwest, a little hustler selling newspapers, apples, sandwiches, molasses and peanuts on the dawn run from Port Huron to Detroit.

When a stationmaster taught him telegraphy, he promptly invented an automatic repeater that relayed messages from one wire to another without the intervention of another operator.

When he decided to manufacture printing-telegraph equipment on his own, he opened workshops in Menlo Park and West Orange and revolutionized life in spasms of inventing that produced the megaphone, phonograph, motion picture camera, electric light and hundreds of other devices.

When he ended his long research on the electric light, he started the dynamos in his central station at 257 Pearl Street in downtown Manhattan, threw the switches at 3 p.m. on September 4, 1882, and declared majestically: "They will go on forever unless stopped by an earthquake."

When he began to offend educators with sweeping denunciations of formal schooling and college training, he touched off a running battle that irritated learned persons around the world. He once invited Prof. John Dewey and some Columbia colleagues to the Edison Laboratory to view motion pictures as a teaching device. They shook their heads, and when one educator rashly asked how algebra could be taught on film, Edison replied that algebra was of little practical use and, besides, "I can hire mathematicians at $15 a week, but they can't hire me."

"I like the Montessori method," he said on another occasion. "It makes learning a pleasure. The present system casts the brain into a mold. What we need are men capable of doing work. I wouldn't give a penny for the ordinary college graduate, except those from institutes of technology. They aren't filled up with Latin, philosophy and all that ninny stuff. America needs practical, skilled engineers and industrial men. In three or four centuries, when the country is settled [sic] and commercialism is diminished, there will be time for literary men."

So, Edison had long since established himself as a wizard at shocking the public when, in February 1921, he crept into the news by offering his birthday views on the state of mankind.

He outdid himself this time, too, probably because he had been provoked by an interviewer who ventured to ask about reports that illness in his 74th year had undermined Edison's physical vitality. The white-haired inventor sprang from his chair at the suggestion, snapped to ramrod attention like a soldier, and replied: "Do I look it?"

Without waiting for an answer, Edison thereupon launched into a formula for saving the United States: "Adopt Otto Kahn's plan for a tax of one-third of 1 percent on all sales, and place Herbert Hoover in a position in the government where his great executive ability and experience can be utilized best." Besides, he said without transition, there was danger of war with Japan unless that country was given room to accommodate its increasing population. "But," he added quickly in a postscript, "I am absolutely opposed to letting them come over here."

Goaded royally now by the insinuations about his vitality, Edison stayed on the offensive for weeks. He was assured minimum competition from McGraw's celebrated trial, at least, when the trial was predictably postponed again on March 7. McGraw, explained the newspaper accounts, "is at present with the Giants in their Southern training center."

So, the stage was Edison's, and he fired a shot heard 'round the world a few weeks later by revealing his latest invention—which was immediately dubbed the "brainmeter"—and declaring:

"Men who have gone through college I find to be amazingly ignorant. When I find that anyone fails to come up to the standard I set, I give him a week's pay and fire him."

The standard, he disclosed, was contained in an intelligence test he had drawn for job applicants and employees at his plant in West Orange. The results, he said, had "disappointed" him.

The next day, under headlines reporting that "Edison Condemns the Primary School," the battle was joined. "The trouble is," he insisted, "that boys' minds are atrophied before they reach college. I have never seen a boy who liked to go to school, and I don't suppose I ever will, unless they change the method of teaching."

But an intelligence test? Yes, he conceded a bit warily, he had indeed prepared the test himself and had administered it at his laboratory. It contained 163 questions, and only one of the 23 men who tackled it passed with a 100 percent, or "A" rating, in an hour and a half. They all looked "bright and well-dressed," he allowed, but the men who took more than two hours were classified in the "XYZ" group. And, sure enough, he gave them a week's pay and fired them.

The cat now being out of the bag, the wizard of Menlo Park suddenly found himself besieged by disbelief, dismay and howls of protest. It was as though his disk phonograph had gone haywire and was amplifying a screeching babble. The United States Army had stirred interest in intelligence tests in 1917 by administering a million and a half to soldiers. But now, four years later, Edison had triggered an overnight clamor by administering his own homemade tests to prove a homemade theory.

Moreover, although a few of the questions were leaked out by disgruntled test-takers, he shrouded the rest in silence. But people were amazed at the leaked samples. On what day of the week was the Battle of Waterloo fought? Where is Mount Ararat? What is fiat money? Who is Brand Whitlock?

"We hope," editorialized The New York Times, "that Mr. Thomas A. Edison will not despair of the Republic altogether because so many college graduates flunked in the examinations by which he tests the efficiency and intelligence of young men who aspire to high places in his shops and factories. There are eight-score questions on this list. It is not to be wondered at that they are not all answered.

"Besides, is Mr. Edison's questionnaire really a conclusive test? 'What is copra?' Was any man ever kinder to his mother because he knew what copra is? 'What is zinc?' Does Mr. Edison himself know what zinc is? Dante, one of the most learned men of his time, could have answered only one of the six to test general knowledge. 'How did Cleopatra die?' John Milton no better. Even Henry Ford would be stumped by some of these questions. 'Where is Magdalena Bay?' How can anybody answer that question?"

It was May now, and while Edison was suddenly impaled on the hook of public protest, John McGraw was suddenly off it.

"The defendant," said The Times on May 3, reporting the manager's twice-postponed trial, "came into court on crutches due to a sprained ankle which he received while practicing at the Polo Grounds on Sunday. On motion of William J. Fallon, McGraw's counsel, the indictment was dismissed because it failed to specify where the defendant was when the alleged liquor was in his possession. Then McGraw was arraigned on an information which charged him with having the liquor in his possession at the Lambs Club on August 8. He pleaded not guilty."

The prosecution, giving it the old college try, called an assistant district attorney, Albert B. Unger, as a witness. He testified that he had talked with McGraw on August 14 and that McGraw had said he indeed had had a bottle of whiskey at the Lambs. However, Fallon pounced on the witness with a stream of questions designed to show that McGraw had also said he had given all his money to two scrubwomen and therefore couldn't have bought a bottle of whiskey, even if he had wanted one.

The assistant district attorney, now on the defensive, didn't remember that part of the conversation exactly. But he did recall McGraw's saying that he had cashed a check in the grill room at the time. And that statement proved to be the Volstead Act's last time at bat in the case.

McGraw hobbled to the witness chair and testified in his own behalf—to the admiring stares of jury and audience alike—that he had been entirely without money that evening. He might have cashed a check; but, if so, he had not cashed one in the grill room.

The jury kept Judge Learned Hand and McGraw—on his crutches—waiting exactly five minutes. Not guilty.

Fresh from this triumph, the public resumed its pursuit of the wizard of Menlo Park, who had neither William J. Fallon nor a sprained ankle to temper the opposition.

Jack Dempsey announced that he was studying French to understand what Carpentier might say in the ring, and New York boggled. The New York Athletic Club voted to permit women to smoke, and New York glowed (even though the vote was close, 187 to 134). Carpentier solemnly visited Teddy Roosevelt's grave on a pilgrimage to Long Island, and Oyster Bay was touched. Dempsey was reported stricken with spring fever, and Broadway swooned.

But Edison pontificated, and the United States was rubbed the wrong way.

When the headmaster of the Buckley School said no well-read man could fail to answer 80 percent of Edison's questions, he was rebutted by "victims" of the test who argued that only "a walking encyclopedia could answer the questionnaire."

"Edison Questions Stir Up A Storm," headlined the press. "Not a Tom Edison test, but a Tom Foolery test," complained one letter to the editor. And so it went.

The inventor, now afflicted with a cold (which aroused no such compassion as McGraw's sprained ankle), refused to answer an inquiry for a copy of his test. His secretary, H.W. Meadowcroft, said the questions were being kept secret because future applicants might crib the answers.

Still, 141 questions were mailed to The New York Times on May 11 by Charles Hansen, an unsuccessful candidate for a job at Edison's laboratory. No person taking the test was allowed to copy the questions, the paper noted, but Mr. Hansen had *memorized* them, a feat that impressed Edison less than the fact that he nonetheless had flunked, anyway. Mr. Hansen said they were "silly."

Across the country, the "brainmeter" became a parlor craze. A reporter for the Chicago Tribune bearded 25 students at the University of Chicago and gave them a sample test. He picked 16 men and nine women at random. On the first question (Where do you get shellac from?), seven gave the wrong answer, eight the right answer and the rest didn't know. On "what is a monsoon?" the tally was four right and 21 wrong. The first six who were asked "Where do dried prunes come from?" didn't know. And no one got the answer to "Where do domestic sardines come from?"

Two students thought cork was imported from Ireland. Nobody knew the voltage in a streetcar, or which states produced phosphates, or where the condor was found. One coed said that cast iron was called "pig" because "it's unrefined." That was kind of clever, but it wasn't what Edison had in mind.

The next day, editorial writers sprang to her defense as a heroine of repartee. It would be a mistake, said The New York Times, to mark her wrong on the pig-iron answer. It demonstrated "a quick mind, a sense of humor, the ability to hide ignorance and get along without specific knowledge."

"Edison's Questions Still Puzzle City" roared the headlines. And: "College Men Pore Over Tomes and Maps."

In New York, "much perturbation" was reported among college graduates and students. In one university, the members of a literary club spent hours inspecting the map of West Virginia trying to find the exact boundaries.

In one book-publishing house, an editor gave himself a rating of 90 on a set of "leaked" questions. But "the glory of his performance was dimmed," it was noted, when he was discovered to be a lexicographer and a bit of a ringer.

On the Lexington Avenue subway, two young women became so engrossed in "What is the longest railroad in the world?" that they missed their station in downtown Manhattan and rode all the way to Brooklyn, presumably making the Lexington Avenue subway the longest railroad in the world for them.

In Boston, the great Albert Einstein arrived at South Station en route to Harvard. He had just received an honorary degree from Princeton and was about to get another from Harvard. But the only thing the throng at the station wanted to talk about was the Edison brainmeter. "What is the speed of sound?" the physicist was asked. And through an English-speaking secretary, he replied that he couldn't say offhand.

Finally, on May 13, The Times cracked the case wide open. In headlines, it proclaimed: "Here Is Edison's 4-Column Sheaf of Knowledge. His Most Famous Questions Answered by the Book, the Specialist and the Man in the Street." And, in a crossline and subhead: "Something Nobody Knows. That Is, Who Invented Printing?"

As for that last jab, the Times delved into arguments about printing and recited the history of Korean, Japanese and Gutenberg printing. But, wasting no time on side issues, it declared that "advocates of specializaton hold that the ability to achieve a high mark in the tests is a sign of a misspent youth," and then proceeded to shake the skeletons from Edison's closet.

It listed 146 questions that had been "remembered" by various applicants for jobs and gave answers by experts, "some of which may be subject to correction and controversy."

No. 1 on the list was: "What countries bound France?" The answer rendered by the panel of experts: "Spain, the tiny independent state of Andorra in the Pyrenees, Monaco, Italy, Switzerland, Germany, Luxembourg and Belgium." And if that didn't discourage job-seekers at Edison's laboratory, nothing would.

No. 2: "What city and country produce the finest China?" Answer: "Some say Limoges, France; some say Dresden, Germany; some say Copenhagen, Denmark."

No. 3: Where is the River Volga? In Russia.

No. 5: What country consumed the most tea before the war? Russia.

No. 6: What city leads the United States in making laundry machines? Chicago.

No. 74: Where are condors found? In the Andes.

For those who stumbled on Cleopatra, the experts reported that she had been Queen of Egypt and (with colossal delicacy) a "contemporary" of Julius Caesar and Mark Antony who had committed suicide by causing an asp to bite her.

For the 25 pioneers at the University of Chicago, they disclosed that domestic sardines came from Maine and California.

For Albert Einstein, they noted that the speed of sound was about 1,091 feet a second in dry air at freezing; about 4,680 feet a second in water; and 11,463 feet a second through an iron bar 3,000 feet long.

As for Magdalena Bay, three were located—in Lower California, in Spitsbergen and in Colombia. And as for "in what part of the world does it never rain?"—the United States Weather Bureau replied that nobody was ever in one place long enough to say, but that natives of the Sahara Desert had expressed amazement when told that water *ever* fell from the sky. Let the wizard of Menlo Park chew that one over!

However, if anybody thought that the inventor of the disk phonograph would be shattered by the pirating of his intelligence test, they underestimated him. The next day, Edison sat down and dashed off a new questionnaire. His ever-present secretary, Mr. Meadowcroft, reported that Mr. Edison had been "following" the controversy and had decided at once to draw up a completely new set of questions to preserve the integrity of his job-testing.

"Mr. Edison," said Meadowcroft, rising to the occasion, "is a man of extremely varied reading. He does not seem to forget anything."

Each week, he said, the inventor received 40 or 60 pounds of periodicals at his home, kept 62 periodicals on file, and also read three books every seven days. His field of reading extended, Meadowcroft added, from the Police Gazette to the Journal of Experimental Medicine—and included The New York Times.

But, in spite of this insight into the habits of the father of the brain-meter, the tide had turned against him.

Prof. William Shepher of Columbia supported the formation of a National Women's Club in a speech at the university's Faculty Club, but said in a bon mot that "we will not make membership dependent on Mr. Edison's 300 questions."

The Times, in another editorial, said that the list of questions (sticking to 163) showed that the Freudian belief that nobody ever forgets anything was true only in a special Freudian sense. And if Edison took a test of similar questions, he, too, would be "convicted" of ignorance.

A youth in Holyoke, Mass., appeared at the police station and said he had written the answers to the Edison test in a book that now was worth millions. He wanted police protection. "The police," the press reported, "believe he has become temporarily demented as a result of studying the Edison test."

A professor of educational psychology at Teachers College in Columbia, Dr. E. L. Thorndike, said the test was only one-tenth effective, anyway. "I wouldn't take an engineer," Dr. Thorndike said, "and cross-examine him on what he knows about Amy Lowell."

At Harvard, now receiving his second honorary degree of the week, Einstein said under pressure that, yes, he thought a college education was a good thing. And under heavier pressure from the mob at Edison's heels, he said he had "heard of" Edison—as the inventor of the phonograph.

"More Slams At Edison," the headlines cried. And, as May turned into June, the sniping turned into a sweeping offensive. The brainmeter and its founder became the chief topics, mostly the chief targets, at college commencements, and even Lloyd George, the reparations problem and Georges Carpentier took back seats.

Edison got in one or two licks, but they were not haymakers.

He piqued the commencement speakers by declaring that numerous college professors still didn't know where Korea was, or the chief ingredients of white paint, or what voltage was used in streetcars.

Some people suggested in his behalf that perhaps he had been putting them on, in a kind of gigantic bit of trivia-game mischief. After all, they noted, one of his favorite questions was "If you were desirous of obtaining an order from a manufacturer with a jealous wife, and you saw him with a chorus girl, what would you do?"

He also said, on another occasion, that he really didn't care if a man knew the location of Timbuktu. But he did care "if he ever knew any of these things and doesn't know them now."

Whereupon, flexing his mental muscles for the last time in the great debate, the old wizard rattled off the answers to a long series of questions in all fields—and scored 95 percent.

At the Haverford College graduation, some doubts about the public "victory" over the old man's arrogance also were expressed by Dr. John Alexander MacIntosh, professor of philosophy, religion and ethics at the McCormick Theological Seminary in Chicago. He told the Haverford graduates that "this is a serious charge, coming from a scientific man," and suggested that the colleges prove Edison wrong.

At the Johns Hopkins commencement, the president of the school, Dr. Frank J. Goodnow, told the graduating class that "a man of eminence in the world of practical affairs" had caused a furor by questioning the purposes of education. "If you have learned in your courses how to work," Dr. Goodnow said, sounding vaguely like Edison, "your education may be regarded as complete—so far as you can complete it in any institution."

Even Sears, Roebuck and Co. inadvertently cast a shadow over the debate. It advertised the Encyclopaedia Britannica for $1 down and "the balance in small monthly payments"—29 volumes, 44 million words, printed on the famous India paper. "It answers questions like: How shall America readjust her industrial conditions? Is the present League of Nations likely to succeed? Is the fall of the Bolshevik regime in Russia imminent? Will Germany fulfill her treaty obligations?"

If the Britannica had supplied the correct answer to the last two or three of those questions, it would have been a bargain at twice the price. But the decade of wonderful nonsense rolled on, certain that "yes" was just as good an answer as "no," and impatient with any questions that ruffled the public's feathers.

It was much happier with provocateurs like McGraw, who was leading his Giants that summer to the glory of another National League pennant—the first of four straight and a monumental series of confrontations with the Yankees and their new star, Babe Ruth.

The public also cheered when McGraw, exonerated in his moment of trial, retaliated against his critics at the Lambs Club by retracting the free passes given to members the next time they appeared at the Polo Grounds press gate. Three years later, he was to be vindicated completely. He was readmitted to the Lambs after 300 members had signed a petition of forgiveness.

Edison, though, emerged from his part in the battles of 1921 with far less redemption. Still, he managed to give his pursuers a touching moment as the din reached a peak and then subsided.

On the same afternoon that Dr. Goodnow was cautioning the Johns Hopkins class about its future, The Times provided a final, poignant glimpse of the embroiled wizard. In a brief story headlined "Edison In The Box," it reported from West Orange that "Thomas A. Edison took part in his first baseball game today."

The inventor, who had been virtually deaf since childhood and who once said that "the happiest time of my life was when I was 12 years old," pitched five balls in a game between the Disk Record Department and the Laboratory staff of the Edison plant—all of whom presumably had passed his much-maligned intelligence test.

After winding up, Edison pitched the first ball, "which the batter avoided by ducking." The second, third and fourth pitches also went astray, but the fifth ball finally was pitched near enough to the plate to produce a foul.

Then the 74-year-old genius retired to the sidelines.

"I was always too busy a boy to indulge in baseball," the Father of the Brainmeter said a little sadly.

Among the legendary teams of baseball's formative years were the Boston Red Stockings, who won four straight National Association pennants and had a great team in 1874 (above), and the 1885 New York Giants (below), who finished second in the National League.

Detroit's Ty Cobb ranked among the greatest baseball stars of all time, though his rugged style and high-flying spikes (above in 1912) never failed to create hostility and controversy.

Even as a youngster at St. Mary's Industrial School in Baltimore, George Herman Ruth (above and right) could pitch, catch and hit better than anybody in town. The incomparable Grover Cleveland Alexander (left) was pitching better than just about anybody in baseball when his career was interrupted for duty with the 89th Infantry Division during World War I.

Judge Kenesaw Mountain Landis (above), baseball's first commission-er, waved in a much-needed era of discipline and tough-minded deci-sions. The venerable Connie Mack (right), the longest running show in baseball, waved his celebrated score card to signal strategy throughout his half century as manager of the Philadelphia Athletics.

Joe DiMaggio arrived in New York in 1936 while Ted Williams made it with the Boston Red Sox in 1939. For the next generation, they were the consummate professionals and ruling superstars of the American League.

Satchel Paige, legendary star of the Kansas City Monarchs of the Negro leagues, and Bob Feller, superstar of the Cleveland Indians, met in November 1945 before matching fastballs in an exhibition game in Los Angeles. Less than three years later, they were teammates.

As a player, Casey Stengel usually raised a rumpus, as he did in 1920 as King of the Grumblers on the Philadelphia Phillies. To Stengel's right are Cliff (Gavvy) Cravath and Fred Luderus.

Jackie Robinson, basestealer deluxe for the Brooklyn Dodgers after cracking baseball's color barrier, steals home against the Boston Braves in 1948 as the front end of a triple steal that moved teammates Gene Hermanski to third base and Pee Wee Reese to second.

It became known as the shot heard 'round the world. Ralph Branca of the Brooklyn Dodgers threw the ball, Bobby Thomson of the New York Giants hit it and Andy Pafko of the Dodgers watched it clear the fence (left) in the Polo Grounds. Thomson struggled home (above) to win the 1951 pennant playoff . . . and to complete the Miracle of Coogan's Bluff.

315 FT.

Mickey Mantle (left) and Roger Maris (right) of the New York Yankees and St. Louis star Stan Musial took time to pose at a 1962 spring training session.

Four baseball commissioners and 40 years of baseball converged at the 1969 All-Star Game in Washington. Enjoying the reunion are (above, left to right) Bowie Kuhn, who succeeded William D. Eckert, who succeeded Ford Frick, who succeeded Happy Chandler. By 1968, former Yankee Clipper Joe DiMaggio (below left) had moved into the coaching ranks with the Oakland A's and California Gov. Ronald Reagan was a former movie actor headed for his biggest role.

The great Willie Mays produced 3,283 hits that included 660 home runs, 140 triples and 523 doubles. And, said Casey Stengel, "If a typhoon is blowing, he catches the ball."

One of the great milestones of the modern era was passed by Henry Aaron (above) in 1974 when the Atlanta slugger overtook Babe Ruth as the leading career power hitter in history.

Three of the great arms of the modern era belong to Nolan Ryan (above), who has struck out more batters than anyone in history while producing five no-hitters, Sandy Koufax (below left), who helped pitch the Dodgers to four pennants and threw four no-hitters, and Don Drysdale (below right), who pitched a record 58 consecutive scoreless innings.

Tom Seaver, the man-child star of the 1969 Miracle Mets, has dragged his right knee through 300-plus victories and 3,000-plus strikeouts.

Steve Carlton's style, high leg kick and pitching mastery also produced more than 300 victories and 3,000 strikeouts.

Bambino

The greatest baseball legend of them all was George Herman Ruth, the Bambino, the Babe, the game's awesome symbol of power.

CHAPTER 11

George Herman Ruth was born in Baltimore on February 6, 1895, and life quickly became a series of long shots. When he was 8, he was placed in St. Mary's Industrial School, a reform school for incorrigible boys. When he was 15, his mother died. When he was 23, his father was killed in a scuffle outside the saloon he owned.

But Ruth had one or two things going for him. He had a remarkable physique—6 feet, 2 inches in height and 215 pounds at his best; and later, many more pounds at his worst. Mostly, though, he had the rarest of talents with a baseball: He could throw it, catch it and hit it with Olympian strength. And one of his teachers at St. Mary's School, Brother Matthias, focused on Ruth's talents and created a legend.

But, in the early years of the century, the legend was still a strapping teen-ager in blue overalls. He was also a lefthanded catcher, pitcher and hitter, and he played all three roles better than anybody else in town. He was signed right out of school by Jack Dunn, the president and manager of the local International League team, the Orioles, and Dunn now became on the outside what Brother Matthias had been on the inside—a father figure.

So, when Dunn took his teen-age prodigy to spring training for the first time in 1914, the husky round-faced youngster became Jack's boy, Jack's baby—the Babe.

Dunn wasted no time getting his rookie onto the fast track. He concentrated Ruth's energies on pitching, got good results and sold him to the Boston Red Sox in July. Ruth was in the big leagues at 19. He also was back in the minor leagues at 19, but not for long. The Red Sox sent him to their Providence club in the International League, where he pitched some days and played the outfield on others. Then, with a combined pitching record of 22-9 for Baltimore and Providence that summer, he was recalled by Boston —and stayed.

One year later, Jack Dunn's baby was winning 18 games for the Red Sox. And, one year after that, he was winning 23, defeated the Brooklyn Dodgers in the World Series and came back to win 24 games the year after that.

Then it was 1918, and in the season bobtailed by the wartime decree, Ruth won 13 games for the Red Sox—and hit 11 home runs. Not only that, but he hit his 11 home runs and knocked in 64 runs in only 317 times at bat. He hit .300, which was properly far below Ty Cobb's average of .382, the best in the big leagues. But Ruth's slugging percentage of .555 was the best in the business, he knocked in as many runs as Cobb did (and the Detroit star had 104 more times at bat), and he hit 26 doubles, a figure surpassed in the American League only by Tris Speaker, who hit 33.

By then, Jack Dunn's baby was the hottest hybrid in baseball, the best lefthanded pitcher in the league and the best power hitter in either league, even part-time. So, in the spring of 1919, the manager of the Red Sox, Edward Grant Barrow, made the choice. He could have Ruth every fourth day as a pitcher or every day as a hitter. He elected the long ball, and made history.

Ruth promptly hit .322 in his first season as the full-time left fielder for the Red Sox, batted in 112 runs and whaled 29 home runs—a record for both leagues. The postwar crowds, hungering for pleasure, release and action in one package, began to flock to the ball parks to watch.

So did two other fans home from the wars: the Yankee colonels, Huston and Ruppert. They were operating in a city dominated by John McGraw and his Giants, and they were even playing in a ball park dominated by McGraw and his Giants. Since 1913, the Yankees had been sharing the Polo Grounds because only 15,000 people could fit into their ball field, Hilltop Park, at Broadway between 165th and 168th streets. The Yankees needed a stage, and a star.

They found the star in Boston, where the Red Sox were foundering financially in spite of Ruth's booming bat. They were owned by Harry Frazee, a onetime bill poster from Peoria whose weakness still was the theater. It was a fatal weakness, too. He kept sinking money into shows that flopped.

Frazee turned to New York for help, and asked Ruppert to lend him half a million dollars. The colonel countered in one word: Ruth. That was a tall order, even for someone as strapped as Frazee, so he went back to Boston and put the proposition to Barrow, who pointed out that none of the Yankees, individually or collectively, was worth taking in exchange for Babe Ruth. But he added a postscript: If Frazee was saying he needed the money to stay in business, then he had no choice but to cash his main asset for the highest price.

Frazee agreed, and then accepted $125,000 in cash from Ruppert plus a personal loan of $350,000. The colonel took a mortgage on Fenway Park as collateral—and the Yankees got Babe Ruth.

The size and significance of the deal were lost on no one. On the morning of January 6, 1920, The New York Times reported both under a headline that said: "Yanks Buy Babe Ruth for $125,000." And, below: "Highest Purchase Price in Baseball History Paid For Game's Greatest Slugger."

In words that matched the occasion, the story said:

"Babe Ruth of the Boston Red Sox, baseball's super-slugger, was purchased by the Yankees yesterday for the largest cash sum ever paid for a player. The New York club paid Harry Frazee of Boston $125,000 for the sensational batsman who last season caused such a furor in the national game by batting out twenty-nine home runs, a new record in long-distance clouting."

A few paragraphs farther down, The Times placed Ruth in his world in these words: "Ruth was such a sensation last season that he supplanted the great Ty Cobb as baseball's greatest attraction, and in obtaining the services of Ruth for next season the New York club made a ten-strike which will be received with the greatest enthusiasm by Manhattan baseball fans."

Ruth was making $10,000 at the time from the Red Sox, but he wanted more and the Yankees promptly came across with $10,000 more. After all, this *was* a ten-strike for the Yankees. It was also a record ransom paid for a ball player, more than double the previous record: the $50,000 (plus players) paid by the Cleveland Indians in 1916 to acquire Tris Speaker from the Red Sox. Two years before that, the Chicago White Sox paid $50,000 (without players) to get Eddie Collins from the Philadelphia A's.

Babe Ruth, according to a subhead in The Times, was "The Perfect Hitter." And, with state-of-the-art attention to detail, it told why:

"Ruth's principle of batting is much the same as the principle of the golfer. He comes back slowly, keeps his eye on the ball and follows through. His very position at the bat is intimidating to the pitcher. He places his feet in perfect position. He simply cannot step away from the pitch if he wants to. He can step only one way—in. The weight of Ruth's body when he bats is on his left leg. The forward leg is bent slightly at the knee. As he stands facing the pitcher, more of his hips and back are seen by the pitcher than his chest or side. When he starts to swing, his back is half turned toward the pitcher. He goes as far back as he can reach, never for an instant taking his eye off the ball as it leaves the pitcher's hand.

"The greatest power in his terrific swing comes when the bat is directly in front of his body, just halfway in the swing. He hits the ball with terrific impact and there is no player in the game whose swing is such a masterpiece of batting technique."

Ruth wasted no time paying off on the investment and the tributes, enriching the Yankees beyond their wildest expectations and restoring the image of baseball after the devastation brought by the Black Sox scandal. In 1920, his first season in New York, he hit .376, scored 158 runs, knocked in 137—and hammered out 54 home runs, an unthinkable total that not only set records for power hitting but also inflamed the public's passion as the public turned its passion into the decade of the Roaring Twenties.

In 1921, he hit baseballs with even more stunning effect than that: a .378 average, 177 runs, 171 runs batted in and 59 home runs.

By May 24 that season, the home run was being discerned as the national symbol of baseball, and Babe Ruth was being discerned as the national symbol of the home run. The Times discerned both the symbols that morning under a headline that read: "Home Run Epidemic Hits Major Leagues." And the subhead said: "Spring Slugging Puts Records in Danger."

"An epidemic of home run hitting has broken out in both major leagues," The Times reported, "and if the average maintained to date continues through the season, some new records in circuit drives will be established. In the 1920 campaign, the American League set the remarkable total of 370 circuit drives, while clubs of the other major organization hit a total of 261. Both figures were so far beyond the normal totals for home runs that they occasioned considerable comment. The 1920 figures, however, seem destined for decisive eclipse in the campaign now under way."

About one-fifth of the season had been played by then, and the National League had already hit 94 home runs, more than one-third of the total for all of the season before; the American League accounted for 85. In the National League, the Phillies led with 21; then came the Giants with 17, and the St. Louis Cardinals with 15. In the American, alone at the summit, the Yankees had a total of 25—and Ruth had nearly half of those, 12. And that was as many as hit by the entire Cleveland club, which ranked second in the American League.

"A livelier ball is the only answer that fits the case," The Times suggested. "It is true that the restrictions that were imposed upon pitchers, starting with the opening of the 1920 pennant races and still in force, have made hitting easier, but even this does not explain the great advance in home run hitting. The fact that many players who seldom hit for the circuit have branched out as long distance sluggers is not explained satisfactorily by changes in pitching rules. They are no stronger physically than before, yet their drives are carrying far beyond the former limits.

"The firm that manufactures the baseballs used in the two leagues makes the statement that it is following exactly the same procedure as in the years when the hitting did not attract as much attention. The same amount of cork and wool is used in each ball, but the manufacturers admit that they are getting a better grade of Australian wool. This may be the answer. At any rate, the ball is livelier than in the past and home runs are blooming where they never bloomed before."

One place they were blooming outrageously was the Polo Grounds, because the Yankees were still sharing the park with the Giants and were upstaging them every time Babe Ruth went to bat. This was star quality in a town that cast its stars in gigantic dimensions. It was a quality that may have had something to do with the "restrictions" imposed on pitchers, as The Times surmised: In 1920, the spitball and "other unorthodox deliveries" were declared illegal. Each team was allowed to designate its certified spitball pitchers before the 1920 season, and those pitchers—and only *those* pitchers—could throw the wet one during a transition time of one season. After that: everything dry.

Two months after the 1920 World Series (which featured an unassisted triple play by Cleveland's Bill Wambsganss), the temper of the times prevailed. After all, this was the Prohibition Era, and it was dry in name only. And, in December, baseball relented, too. Eight pitchers in the National League and nine in the American were declared card-carrying spitball pitchers, who apparently were doomed to extinction unless they were allowed to go to their mouths. They were therefore and henceforth granted the right of throwing the wet one for the rest of their careers.

It was a kind of selective dispensation. But nobody could prove that either the absence or the presence of the spitball prompted the "epidemic" of home runs that was now engulfing the game, and revolutionizing it and its appeal.

One better, and much more visible, explanation was Babe Ruth. In 1920, when he reached New York, one in every seven home runs hit in the American League was hit by Ruth. And the Yankees' attendance reflected the power of power: The year before they got Ruth from the Red Sox, the Yankees played before 619,164 fans at home. The year he arrived and hit his big 54, the attendance skyrocketed to 1,289,422. In one fence-busting, record-busting summer, it doubled.

The power of power also was reflected in other ways. After the Black Sox scandal had rocked public confidence in the credibility of baseball, The Sporting News saw its circulation wither to 50,986. And this was after a boom in circulation during World War I. During a baseball meeting in New York in 1917, Taylor Spink heard from Colonel Huston of the Yankees that the doughboys in Europe craved baseball news. Spink turned the information over to Ban Johnson, and suggested that the American League buy 150,000 copies of the paper every week at reduced prices and send them to the American Expeditionary Forces. The club owners agreed, and the presses rolled.

But, within two years, the Black Sox snapped the bloom off the rose, and circulation nosedived. But then, along came Babe Ruth and his magnetic bat, public confidence poured back into the game and public involvement surged. So did Spink's circulation. By 1924, when Ruth was reigning as the most exciting and accomplished figure in the business, The Sporting News went past 90,000 in circulation, the highest figure in its 38 years.

The credit for baseball's comeback from the great "fix" of 1919 probably should be shared by the two most contrasting personalities on the national scene: the rollicking child of nature, Babe Ruth, and the spare, severe and stern swift sword of justice, Kenesaw Mountain Landis. The former supplied the irresistible force of star performance on the field; the latter supplied the immovable object of integrity both on and off the field.

Ruth arrived first, having reached New York in time for the 1920 season. Landis arrived after the close of the season, when the owners of the 16 major league teams decided that they needed a figure of unquestioned probity to recapture the image of their business. The Times reported the judge's arrival on November 13, 1920, under a rather ringing headline that said: "Baseball Peace Declared; Landis Named Dictator."

The story, under a Chicago dateline, described the moment in these words:

"With Judge Kenesaw Mountain Landis of the United States District

Court as arbitrator, a one-man court of last resort, peace will obtain in professional baseball for at least seven years, while the eminent jurist will also continue to strike terror into the hearts of criminals by retaining his position as a federal judge.

"Sixteen club owners of the National and American Leagues reached this happy solution of their difficulties after a three-hour conference at the Congress Hotel today. They then adjourned to wait upon Judge Landis in a body and present their proposition to him. After only a few minutes' talk with the major league magnates, the Judge accepted the highest responsibility that can be conferred by the promoters of the national sport, and in his acceptance made it plain that he was undertaking the task as a public trust, having in mind the millions of fans of all ages who are interested in baseball.

"By this action, the former three-man National Commission was permanently discarded, and the supreme authority over baseball was centralized in the hand of one man."

Landis showed his stern sense of proportion the very moment the baseball owners put their proposition on the table. They offered him $50,000 to take the job of running their business. But he was making $7,500 as a federal judge, and he elected to continue to earn it and to continue "to strike terror into the hearts of criminals." So, he subtracted the $7,500 federal salary from the $50,000 baseball salary, and accepted the job for $42,500.

So, the new era was confirmed. Landis left no doubt who was boss when he disregarded the acquittal of the eight Black Sox players in another court in Chicago and hurled his thunderbolts at them as the "one-man court of last resort" in baseball. And, on the diamonds swept clean by the judge, Babe Ruth was leaving no doubt who was boss, either.

But John McGraw's irritation had been soaring with Ruth's popularity, especially after the third-place Yankees in the American League outdrew the second-place Giants in the National League in 1920 by more than 350,000 admissions. And they did it in the Giants' own ball yard.

"The Yankees," he raged to Charles Stoneham, the owner of the Giants then, "will have to build a park in Queens or some other out-of-the-way place. Let them go away and wither on the vine."

But the Yankees withered on nobody's vine. Early in 1921, they announced instead that they had bought 10 acres in the Bronx from the estate of William Waldorf Astor, and noted that "the running time from 42nd Street by subway will be about 16 minutes." And the new stadium planned for the site would be an oval like the Yale Bowl, and would be made "impenetrable to all human eyes, save those of aviators, by towering embattlements."

They also planned to build it across the Harlem River from the Polo Grounds, and the challenge was delivered: The Yankees and their new superstar and their new stadium would fight the Giants and their superstar manager and their longstanding grip on the public. The Battle of Broadway was joined.

It was 1921, and they could not have picked a busier stage for their showdown, nor a gaudier one.

"The vandals sacking Rome," observed Gene Fowler, describing the time and the tide, "were 10 times as kindly as the spendthrift hordes on Broadway. The Wall Street delirium was reaching the pink-elephant stage. Chambermaids and counter-hoppers had the J.P. Morgan complex. America had the swelled head, and the brand of tourists that went to Europe became ambassadors of ill-will. The World War killed everything that was old Broadway. Prohibition, the mock-turtle soup of purists, provided the *coup de grâce.*

It was a time of swirling stars, in baseball and on Broadway and in politics, and Alexander Woollcott reflected it on May 2, 1921, when he wrote in The New York Times that an Actors Equity review was a "show of strength" at the Metropolitan Opera House.

"Here, for instance," he wrote, "was John Barrymore, a pallid, rose-clad Romeo, looking unutterably romantic to the last as the ruthless elevator withdrew him from sight. Here was Laurette Taylor, all loveliness as Ophelia, and Lionel Atwill, looking twice as melancholy and several times as Danish as the usual Hamlet. Here was Chrystal Herne, allowed just a moment to suggest how enchanting a Viola she might be, and Jane Cowl as the Shrew glaring defiance at the amiable Petruchio of John Drew.

"Here was Doris Keane playing Portia to the evil-looking Shylock of George Arliss, and here was Genevieve Tobin, a most delicate Ariel, dancing before the Prospero of Frank Bacon. There was no fairer vision than that which Peggy Wood presented as Imogen—an hour of 'Cymbeline' after two years of 'Buddies.'

"It was, in a sense, a night of reunions, for here was Lillian Russell resplendent as Queen Katherine and such old favorites as James T. Powers and Rose Coghlan to show that the Equity was no mere enthusiasm of the youngsters. But between these old-timers and such stars of tomorrow as the Duncan sisters, the audience was all affable impartiality. When these frivolous newcomers did their turn, there was wild applause. For their stage-setting they use a three-legged stool. Florence Moore brought it on for them. Herbert Corthell carried it off. The mind of the onlooking manager must have reeled at so idyllic a spectacle of cooperation."

It was the time of roaring drinkers, roaring events and roaring words to describe them all. When the Giants crossed into Brooklyn to play the Dodgers once, a 30-minute trip by taxi, bus or subway, their tribulations were described in The Times as "arduous and fruitless explorations in a region that makes the old stomping grounds of Stanley and Livingstone seem like Maiden Lane by comparison."

Tribulations or not, the Giants were about to meet all challengers in the most direct way possible: They won four National League pennants in a row. But, having opened that streak of success in 1921, they encountered Ruth and the Yankees time and again.

For three straight years, in fact, they would be battling for Broadway in the grandest arena in sports: the World Series. And they opened their running battle in the ball park they had been sharing, the Polo Grounds, with each team serving as the home team on alternate days. It was the first Series played in the "reign" of Landis, and the last one played under the best-of-nine format. After that, the Series reverted to a best-of-seven, and stayed there.

The Yankees didn't take long to fire the challenge. In the first inning of the first game, Babe Ruth singled home a run. It proved enough, as Carl Mays—another Yankee import from Boston—protected the lead by allowing the Giants only five hits, four of which were made by 23-year-old Frank Frisch, the bellicose infielder from Fordham who had made his major league debut two years earlier in a regular-season game by pinch-hitting against Grover Cleveland Alexander (he was safe on an error).

To add insult to injury, Mike McNally stole home against the Giants and, in 98 minutes, the Yankees racked up a 3-0 victory.

The next day, the Giants did even less. They got just two hits off Waite Hoyt, who graduated from the New York sandlots as "Schoolboy Hoyt" and who also became a Yankee as a refugee from the Red Sox. Same score, 3-0, and now the Giants were two games down and boiling.

In the third game, the Yankees kept rolling along. They whacked Fred Toney for four runs in the third inning, and now the Giants were two games and four runs down and still hadn't scored a run in the Series. And no team in the 17 years of World Series history had spotted a rival two games and survived.

But the Giants couldn't be tamed for long. They scored four runs in the home half of the third inning, then eight more in the seventh and stormed on to win, 13-5. And in the next game, they squared the Series by winning, 4-2, despite Ruth's first home run in a World Series—his first of 15 during the next dozen years.

The next day, the Yankees went back in front, 3-1, and Babe Ruth made even bigger news: He beat out a bunt. However, he also developed an abscess on his left elbow and, except for one appearance as a pinch-hitter, his Series was finished. And so, for all practical purposes, were the Yankees. Without their champion, they didn't win another game, as the Giants tied the Series, 8-5, then went ahead, 2-1, and finally won it all, 1-0, with Art Nehf allowing four hits and Waite Hoyt giving up six.

McGraw, who had lost four Series in a row since the all-shutout classic in 1905, won this one with a memorable flourish at the close. It came in the ninth inning: Ruth pinch-hit and grounded out; then Aaron Ward walked, and Home Run Baker lined a pitch toward right field. But Johnny Rawlings, the second baseman whom McGraw had obtained from the Phillies that summer, lunged for the ball and knocked it down on the rim of the outfield grass. Still on his knees, he fired the throw to first base to get Baker. Ward, meanwhile, had rounded second and was headed for third. But George Kelly, the first baseman, relayed Rawlings' throw across the infield to Frisch, who tagged Ward at third base for the out that ended Round One in the Battle of Broadway.

"I signaled every pitch to Ruth," McGraw said while the Giants celebrated in their suite in the Waldorf. "In fact, I gave the sign for practically every ball our pitchers threw. They preferred that I do. It was no secret. We pitched only nine curves and three fastballs to Ruth during the entire Series. All the rest were slowballs, and of the 12 of those, 11 set him on his ear."

Ruth, who struck out eight times in the five games he started, was sulking with his abscessed elbow when he read in Joe Vila's column in the New York Sun that he had been laying down on the job. Not being one to sulk in silence, Ruth went straight to the press box, which was then at ground level behind home plate, and bearded his man through the wire screen that protected the writers from foul balls.

He became so thunderous and menacing that Vila finally picked up his typewriter and held it in front of his face something like a shield while the Giants and Yankees on the field watched the "sick" man storm.

Then Ruth got entangled with an even higher power.

He had signed for a baseball barnstorming tour after the Series, but Judge Landis said the tour was unauthorized and off limits. But, as soon as the Series ended, Ruth embarked on the trip. He didn't even wait to collect his loser's share of $3,510, which Landis impounded, anyway.

Ruth was suspended for 39 days at the beginning of the next season, and did not play until May 20, 1922. Two of his teammates, Bob Meusel and Bill Piercy, also took the forbidden tour and also took the penalty. And, by the time Ruth got back into the lineup the following spring, he had lost some of the golden touch.

He hit only .315 that season and slipped to 35 home runs, a decline of 24, and ended a three-year streak as the big leagues' undisputed home-run leader. Ken Williams of the St. Louis Browns replaced him as the American League kingpin with 39 homers and Rogers Hornsby of the St. Louis Cardinals topped the majors with 42. And the Browns' George Sisler led everybody in hitting with an astronomical average of .420. It was, you might say, a pretty good year for high hitters: Ty Cobb of Detroit and Hornsby each hit .401, but Cobb still lost the batting title by 19 points.

Despite all the muscle at bat, the Browns somehow finished second to the Yankees, who won their second pennant in a row. The Giants, meanwhile, had neither the Yankees' pitching nor the Browns' hitting (Williams had 155 RBIs), and had nobody close to the Cardinals' Hornsby, who not only led the National League in batting and home runs but also knocked in 152 runs.

But McGraw was taking certain precautions. He acquired Heinie Groh from Cincinnati and Jimmy O'Connell from San Francisco, and he signed two young infielders named Travis Jackson and Bill Terry. He lost a little serenity when he got Terry, who already had a good job with Standard Oil and who seemed a bit indifferent. And the impression was confirmed when McGraw offered Terry the chance to go straight to New York from Standard Oil's semipro team in Memphis, and Terry calmly lit a cigar and replied: "For how much?"

Terry didn't go straight to New York, after all. He didn't play his first game there until the following season. But he stayed 14 years, hit .341 for his career and succeeded McGraw as manager in 1932.

Fortified, the Giants pulled clear of Cincinnati and St. Louis, clinched their second straight pennant on September 25 and, nine days later, stood in the Polo Grounds as the curtain rose on Act Two of the war to determine who really owned New York.

With flags flying and money pouring, New York reacted with fury. Wall Street brokerage houses, certain that oil and rail stocks were skyrocketing, were not so certain about the fine edge of distinction separating the two hometown teams. But, in the manner of the day, they quoted prices on the Series and handled bets the way they handled transactions and risks of other kinds. In this case: $3,500 to $2,500 on the Yankees, one broker reported.

Tex Rickard, the impresario of boxing, leaned toward the Yankees. Devereux Milburn, the captain of the "Big Four" of the Meadowbrook polo team, took time out before riding for Lord Louis Mountbatten and said: "The Yankees, of course." Willie Hoppe, the billiard king, rode with the billiard king of baseball and said: "I have a hunch the Giants will win."

When the Series opened on October 4, the front boxes were filled with the stars of public life: J. P. Morgan, Harry Payne Whitney, Harry Sinclair. In a box near the dugout, Mary Roberts Rinehart entertained a group of friends. George M. Cohan, Louis Mann and Jack Dempsey took bows. And when Gen. John J. Pershing made an unexpected appearance, the crowd stood and cheered, as it did for Al Smith and the old brown derby. Two governors, four former governors, two mayors and swarms of actors, politicians and tycoons were there. Christy Mathewson was there, no longer a combatant, but still the old hero of the Giants, and he got headlines just for attending. And so did Babe Ruth, just for striking out twice.

"Truly," The Times said, casting its editorial eye on the scene, "baseball is the national game. From east and west, from north and south, the fans are gathering to see two New York teams battle in the blue-ribbon event of the diamond, the World Series."

For those fans who couldn't squeeze through the gates, creative genius went galloping to the rescue: For the first time, a World Series game was carried to the public by radio, and large bold-faced advertisements in the newspapers lost no time announcing the revolution in drum-beating words:

"Hear the crowd roar at the World Series games with Radiola. Grantland Rice, famous sports editor of the New York Tribune, will describe every game personally, play by play, direct from the Polo Grounds. His story, word by word, as each exciting play is made by the Yankees or Giants, will be *broadcasted* from famous Radio Corporation-Westinghouse Station WJZ."

No argument over what it might cost, either: "There's an R.C.A. set for every home and every purse. As low as $25. Prepare for the big event by buying your R.C.A. set from your nearest dealer and ask him for the Radiola Score Sheet." And a footnote advised the dealers not to block the path of history, either, but to "cut this out and paste in your window."

To explain the mystery of radio, the advertisements went into some detail, to wit: "At 1:45 each day, Grantland Rice will speak into a transmitter which will actuate the radio apparatus in Newark and carry the game play by play to the radio audience. The broadcasting will be done on a wave length of 360 meters."

And, if that didn't dispel the mystery, The Times carried the explanation a few steps beyond when it reported the first game with this nod to the history of it:

"Radio for the first time carried the opening game of the World Series, play by play, direct from the Polo Grounds to great crowds throughout the Eastern section of the country. Through the broadcasting station WJZ at Newark, New Jersey, Grantland Rice, a sportswriter, related his story of the game direct to an invisible audience, estimated to be five million, while WGY at Schenectady and WBZ at Springfield, Massachusetts, relayed every play of the contest.

"In place of the scoreboards and megaphones of the past, amplifiers connected to radio instruments gave all the details and sidelights to thousands of enthusiasts unable to get into the Polo Grounds. Not only could the voice of the official radio observer be heard, but the voice of the umpire on the field announcing the batteries for the day mingled with the voice of a boy selling ice cream cones.

"The clamor of the 40,000 baseball fans inside the Polo Grounds made radio listeners feel as if they were in the grandstand. The cheers which greeted Babe Ruth when he stepped to the plate could be heard throughout the land. And as he struck the ball, the shouts that followed indicated whether the Babe had fanned or got a hit even before the radio announcer could tell what had happened."

What happened was that Ruth knocked in the first run of the Series with a single, as he had done the year before. This time, Ruth delivered in the sixth inning of Game 1, but the Giants rallied to win, 3-2. And, in the second game, the Giants raised the roof: Irish Meusel hit a three-run home run in the top of the first inning, but Wally Pipp singled home a Yankee run in the bottom of the first, Aaron Ward hit a home run for the Yanks in the fourth, Ruth and Bob Meusel doubled in the eighth, and the teams were deadlocked at 3-3 and headed for extra innings.

Behind first base, enthralled, sat Lord Louis Mountbatten, Grand Admiral of the Fleet, illustrious cousin to the Prince of Wales and uncle to an empire. Leaving nothing to chance, the press kept the box score on His Lordship: He ate six ice cream cones and two bags of peanuts, drank four bottles of soda pop and rooted for Babe Ruth until he was hoarse. Lady Mountbatten, one of the reigning beauties of Europe, resplendent in brown, watched through a tortoise-shell lorgnette. When Ruth appeared alongside the Yankee dugout, she leaned over and shouted, "Atta boy, Babe." When the umpire called a strike on Wally Pipp, Her Ladyship was heard to grumble: "Rotten." His Lordship said it was the greatest game he had ever seen.

It was the greatest game a lot of people had ever seen, and it was still going on as the afternoon wore on. They were still tied in the bottom of the 10th when the Yankees batted as the home team: Ruth fouled out, Pipp grounded out, Meusel fouled out. It was 4:40 p.m. and the sun was still shining. But suddenly the home-plate umpire, George Hildebrand, wheeled around, swept his face mask through a wide circle with his hand and announced: "Game called on account of darkness."

Judge Landis, erect and dignified, had just been introduced to Mountbatten and his bride in the box of Colonel Ruppert. For a moment, the crowd didn't quite grasp what Hildebrand meant. But then players began running from the field and suddenly thousands of people stood and growled and raged, and then poured from the stands and headed straight for Landis and his visitors. Landis stood upright in the box, his great white mane shaking, and tried to restore order. But he had no chance of reasoning with the mob, and he was overpowered by shouts of "crook" and "robber," and somebody even yelled: "Where are the White Sox?"

A police escort was finally marshaled, and it escorted Landis and his wife from the park through the howling crowd. Mountbatten, startled by the violent ending to his "greatest game ever," turned to the beleaguered commissioner and said, in a royal understatement: "My goodness, Judge, but they are giving you the bird."

Landis, a diplomat as well as a jurist, finally got the mob off his back by announcing that all the money from the tied game would be turned over to a charity for disabled soldiers. The amount was $120,554, and dozens of organized charities promptly besieged him for a piece of it.

As things turned out, the tie was as close as the Yankees came to winning in the 1922 Series. The next day, they were shut out by Jack Scott, "a baseball derelict picked up by McGraw for the price of a uniform," the press put it. The price really had been a uniform and $50, which McGraw had anted up to give Scott another chance in the big leagues after a sore arm had seemingly ended his career. Scott stifled the Yankee power on four hits, and set off an uproar when he nicked Babe Ruth with a pitched ball. Ruth soon retaliated by barreling into stumpy Heinie Groh in a play at third base, then spent the rest of the afternoon exchanging insults with the Giants' bench. When the game ended, Ruth and Bob Meusel went even further: They stormed into the Giants' locker room and went nose to nose with the enemy.

But, just as players on both sides were rolling up their sleeves, McGraw came into the clubhouse with his old Baltimore Orioles' crony and coach, Hughey Jennings, and told Ruth and Meusel to "get out and stay out." And they did.

After that, the Yankees turned tame. They lost the next game, 4-3. They lost the game after that, 5-3. They lost the Series in four straight, minus the much-maligned tie. Babe Ruth had been stopped with two hits in 17 times at bat. And, as predicted, the cheers could be heard throughout the land on a wave length of 360 meters.

"Behind these latest triumphs of the Giants," said The Times, "the directing genius of John McGraw shone more brilliantly than ever before. There is none to dispute his right to the title of greatest manager in baseball history. His record stands alone and unchallenged. He is the outstanding figure among all the managers in the history of the game."

Since McGraw's arrival in 1902, the Giants had won eight pennants and had beaten back the Yankees two years in a row in the World Series. And, in 1923, they went shooting for a record: three in a row.

But the Yankees were no longer the poor tenants. They opened the '23 season by opening their new stadium and moving into it with all the pomp of potentates, and they did nothing to hide the facts of its splendor: 45,000 cubic yards of earth just to rough-grade the property; 950,000 board feet of Pacific Coast fir, shipped to New York through the Panama Canal, to build the bleachers; 20,000 cubic yards of concrete; 800 tons of reinforcing steel, and 2,200 tons of structural steel for the stadium proper. And, for the seats in the grandstand in three tiers: 135,000 individual steel castings; 400,000 pieces of maple lumber; one million brass screws, and more than 90,000 holes drilled into the concrete to bolt the seats to the decks.

It was so splendid a monument and so grand a landmark that McGraw had no trouble hating the Yankees as the most upstart of the nouveau riche. He even refused to let his team dress in Yankee Stadium for the World Series, ordering them instead to change into their uniforms in the Polo Grounds and take fleets of taxicabs over the Central Bridge across the Harlem River to the Yankees' park.

McGraw also refused to allow the Yankees to use the rookie Lou Gehrig at first base during the Series in place of the veteran Wally Pipp, who had broken several ribs during September. The Yankees filled in for Pipp late in the season by recalling Gehrig from Hartford, Conn., and he went 10 for 21 at the plate in six games (after breaking into the majors earlier in the season with a 1-for-5 performance in seven games).

Gehrig's late-season recall came after the roster deadline of September 1, so he wasn't eligible for the Series. Citing precedents, Ruppert asked for a waiver of the roster rule on the ground that the Yankees had a legitimate emergency. Landis told him: "It's all right with me, but McGraw must give his consent." And McGraw, giving no quarter and no consent, said: "The rule is there and, if the Yankees have an injury to a regular, it's their hard luck."

So, the Yankee trainer, Doc Woods, bandaged Pipp's ribs, and he went out and played a solid Series.

"I like the Giants," said Wilbert Robinson, the manager of the Dodgers, "for their smartness, hitting and team play."

"Pitching will decide," said Connie Mack, "and I look for the Giants to hold up their end in this respect. McGraw has good pitchers, make no mistake about it. But so have the Yankees. It's a tossup, and I can't honestly predict a winner."

"You know the old wheeze," said George M. Cohan, the Yankee Doodle Dandy of the Broadway stage. "New York will win the World Series. But honest to goodness, I think the Giants will win it."

"Nothing to it," replied Leon Errol, "but the Yankees. The team has been going too good all year to be stopped now."

Walter Catlett said: "John McGraw and the Giants will surely win." But Fanny Brice said: "I pick the Yanks. Babe Ruth should be at his best, and I believe he will show that he can still make home runs." Florenz Ziegfeld, one impresario to another, said: "McGraw has demonstrated that he is the greatest manager in baseball, and his team this year is as great as any he ever directed." But Marilynn Miller, one prima donna to another, said: "The Yankees will win, but I think it will be a hard-fought Series. I am certain Ruth will be the big factor."

She was right on all counts. And most of the money on Wall Street agreed. The books quoted 11 to 10, Yankees. One brokerage house reported Yankee money of $17,000 against Giant money of $15,000. J.S. Fried & Co., which handled risks of all kinds, put $4,400 against $4,000—on the Yankees. But at 20 Broad Street, the house of G.B. de Chadenedes & Co. announced the biggest bet in town—$23,000 against $20,000, Yankees.

The teams whirled into the ninth inning of the opening game at Yankee Stadium, inseparable at 4-4, and then the Giants took their shot. It was an unlikely shot, at that: 33-year-old Casey Stengel delivered it against Bullet Joe Bush, who had relieved Waite Hoyt. Stengel, a lefthanded batter, hit a line drive over the head of the Yankee shortstop Ernie Johnson. The ball, remembered Fred Lieb in the press box, "wasn't hit too hard—it looked like a single to me."

But it carried between Meusel in left field and Whitey Witt in center, both of whom had been overshifted toward right field. It carried into the gap, and it skipped on the hard ground all the way to the fence 450 feet from home plate, and it reminded everybody how spacious the new ball park really was—especially Meusel and Witt, who were chasing the ball.

But their ordeal was nothing compared to Stengel's. As he circled the bases, Casey realized that he represented the tie-breaking run. But he also realized that his gimpy old legs might not carry him all the way home. And, he recalled years later, as the crowd of 55,307 roared and he ran, he said to himself: "Go, legs, go. Drive this boy around the bases."

Rounding third, Stengel half lost a shoe, but he staggered along anyway. Then, with the relay throw headed home, Casey pitched himself toward the plate, one shoe flapping, both feet dragging. And high over the scene, Damon Runyon watched and later wrote his highly stylized description of one aging ball player and his race against time and the ball:

This is the way old Casey Stengel ran yesterday afternoon running his home run home.

This is the way old Casey Stengel ran running his home run home to a Giant victory by a score of 5 to 4 in the first game of the World Series of 1923.

This is the way old Casey Stengel ran running his home run home when two were out in the ninth inning and the ball still bounding inside the Yankee yard.

This is the way—

His mouth wide open.

His warped old legs bending beneath him at every stride.

His arms flying back and forth like those of a man swimming with a crawl stroke.

His flanks heaving, his breath whistling, his head far back. Yankee infielders, passed by Old Casey Stengel as he was running his home run home, say Casey was muttering to himself, adjuring himself to greater speed as a jockey mutters to his horse in a race, saying: "Go on, Casey, go on."

The warped old legs, twisted and bent by many a year of baseball campaigning, just barely held out under Casey until he reached the plate, running his home run home.

Then they collapsed.

★　　　★　　　★

The Giants now had won eight straight games, with one tie, over the Yankees in their three-year postseason feud. But the die was cast, especially for any team that relied on Casey Stengel's bat to overpower Babe Ruth's, as the teams moved to the Polo Grounds for Game 2.

"Why shouldn't we pitch to Ruth?" McGraw said, tempting fate. "I've said it before, and I'll say it again, we pitch to better hitters than Ruth in the National League."

"Ere the sun had set on McGraw's rash and impetuous words," wrote Heywood Broun in the New York Sun, "the Babe had flashed across the sky fiery portents which should have been sufficient to strike terror and conviction into the hearts of all infidels. But John McGraw clung to his heresy with a courage worthy of a better cause.

"In the fourth inning, after lunging at a fastball with almost comic ferocity and ineptitude, the Bambino hit the next pitch over the stands in right. In the fifth, Ruth was up again and by this time Jack Bentley was pitching. Snyder the catcher sneaked a look at the little logician in the dugout. McGraw blinked twice, pulled up his trousers, and thrust the forefinger of his right hand into his left eye. Snyder knew that he meant: 'Try the Big Bozo on a slow curve around the knees, and don't forget to throw to first if you happen to drop the third strike.' Ruth promptly poled the slow curve around the knees into the right-field seats.

"For the first time since coming to New York, Babe achieved his full brilliance in a World Series game. Before this, he has varied between pretty good and simply awful, and yesterday he was magnificent."

He was magnificent, all right: two home runs in consecutive innings, and his first shot even cleared the Polo Grounds roof and dropped into the parking lot outside, where a policeman picked it up and examined it like some astounding fragment from space. And, in the top of the ninth inning, McGraw again stood on the dugout step and held up three fingers to signal his catcher, Frank Snyder.

Well, at least they were pitching to him, as McGraw had boasted. But Ruth forthwith hit a gigantic drive that almost became his third home run of the game. It was run down and caught on a spectacular play by Bill Cunningham, who raced to the center-field bleachers to keep this one from going in.

The next day, back in Yankee Stadium as the teams alternated ball parks day by day, old Casey Stengel hit another home run, this one over the fence, and it was the only run of the game. Now, the Giants had the lead in the Series again, two games to one, but not for long.

The Yankees, swinging the big bats again, bombed six runs over the plate in the second inning of the next game and won it, 8-4. Then, before 62,817 fans back in the Bronx in the fifth game, they demolished the Giants again, 8-1. And, by now, McGraw was walking Babe Ruth. (He drew eight walks overall in the Series.)

But, with the Series on the line in the sixth game, Ruth did it again. He hit a home run the first time he went to bat, his third homer of the Series.

The gods were not kind to McGraw on this October afternoon. His team weathered Ruth's first-inning shot, came back to build a 4-1 lead and then blew it when the Yankees scored five times in the eighth inning. It was even more cruel than that. With the bases loaded, Ruth batting and the Giants clinging to the lead by one run, McGraw signaled three times to his pitcher,

The immortal one-two punch of Lou Gehrig and Babe Ruth put the New York Yankees of the late 1920s and early '30s among the greatest teams of all time.

Rosy Ryan, to fire the ball low.

"Ruth was so anxious to hit," McGraw said, "that I knew he didn't have a chance. So I ordered Ryan to throw him three pitches right in the dirt."

It worked, but it was only a skirmish in a war that the Giants soon lost. Miller Huggins, the manager of the Yankees, had sent in two pinch-runners to get maximum mileage out of anything that might be hit. And that's what he got. Meusel bounced a single over the mound into center field, both pinch-runners scored, another run scored when the throw from the outfield went past third base, the Yankees wiped out the lead and, one inning later, wiped out the Giants and their dominant grip on old Broadway.

It was the first million-dollar Series, the first gate of 300,000, the first "network" broadcast of a Series, the first time a player would pocket as much as $6,143 for winning or $4,112 for losing. But mostly, it was the first time that Babe Ruth had knocked John McGraw off the peak. He hit .368 with three home runs, and he owned New York.

"Ruth showed that the Giant supremacy could be broken down," The Times observed, in a kind of social commentary on the issue of the day. "Leading the way himself, he showed that the Giants were not invincible, that their pitchers could be hit, and that John J. McGraw's strategy, while superb, was not invincible."

"The Ruth," wrote Heywood Broun, putting it all into one short sentence, "is mighty and shall prevail."

Score-card Harry **12**

Harry M. Stevens started feeding the multitudes in the 1880s and later became the confidant and caterer to such club owners as Jacob Ruppert of the New York Yankees.

CHAPTER 12

In the decade of the Twenties, you got $3 a day as an allowance if you were serving on a federal court jury, and that wasn't enough to hold young Graham McNamee during his lunch-time recess from the court in lower Manhattan. He frequently skipped lunch, saved 50 cents on the spot and took himself for a stroll up Broadway.

McNamee was a practicing baritone from the Northwest, where his father was a lawyer for the Union Pacific Railroad, and he already owned a short stack of favorable reviews to prove it. He made his professional debut in 1921 at Aeolian Hall, when he was 22 years old, and he shook down some fine adjectives from the critic for the New York Sun, who wrote: "He sang with a justness, a care and style."

Within a couple of years, McNamee was singing 150 times in one recital season, and he was commanding notices like this one in The New York Times:

"Anyone who sings the air 'O Ruddier Than The Cherry' from Handel's 'Acis and Galatea' with such admirably flexible command over the 'divisions,' with such finished phrasing and such excellent enunciation as McNamee showed, is doing a difficult thing very well indeed."

Now it was 1923, and McNamee was getting hungry to try that excellent enunciation on something more rewarding than "O Ruddier Than The Cherry." So, he walked purposefully up lower Broadway during his lunch break from the jury one day in May, turned into the building at 195 Broadway, glanced at the sign that read "Radio Station WEAF," rode the elevator to the little two-room studio on the fourth floor and stepped out into a new life.

The station was a sideshow subsidiary of the American Telephone and Telegraph Co., and it was a novelty. So, after McNamee introduced himself to Sam Ross, the program director, he was permitted to spend his lunch hour looking over the shoulders of a few of the pioneers of commercial radio. Before he returned to the jury box that afternoon, he had been hired to join them as a jack of all trades—at $30 a week.

Three months later, McNamee got his first big assignment as the baritone of WEAF radio. He sat at ringside while Harry Greb was winning the world middleweight championship from Johnny Wilson, and described it, blow by blow, elbow by elbow.

Then it was September, and one day Sam Ross called McNamee in and rewarded him with another assignment that would test his vocal powers and that would thrust him into the center of the greatest show on earth: the third and climactic World Series between the Yankees and Giants, Round Three of the Battle of Broadway, the greatest in money and fans and interest, and the final confrontation between the titans John McGraw and Babe Ruth.

Surrounded by the biggest crowds in baseball history, McNamee was seated behind a saucer-shaped microphone in a seat in the open. He had an engineer, but no guidelines and no precedent for the job of describing one of the spectacles of the day. And he was doing it across a network of telephone lines that carried his voice to cities along the Eastern Seaboard, north to WMAF in South Dartmouth, Mass., and south to WCAP in Washington, D.C.

The program listing for WEAF that day, opening day of the Series, suggested that daytime radio took a mighty leap upward at 1:30 o'clock in the afternoon:

11 a.m.—Playing the Health Game, by Clara Tebutt.
11:20—Writing for the Movies, by Mrs. Frances Patterson.
11:50—Market reports.
 1:30—World Series, play by play.

Two and a half hours later, allowing little time for a slow game or extra innings, WEAF said it would return to the home studio for "Milton F. Rehg, baritone, with piano and soprano." That was a switch. Now McNamee was being *followed* by a baritone recital. However, station WJZ in New York, which also carried WEAF's baseball broadcast, gave plenty of room on its program schedule for the game to end. It listed no other program until 5:30 p.m., when it threatened to go back to reality with "Closing Report of the New York State Department of Farms."

Like Grantland Rice the year before, McNamee was a pioneer; unlike Grantland Rice, he was a pioneer whose early work in the business carried him to the heights of the business as a performer. And this was only five months after he had taken his stroll up lower Broadway during the lunchtime recess in the federal court.

This was also only 10 years since the earliest experiments in transmitting sports events from arena to studio, and they were chiefly laboratory experiments at universities. In one of the first of those experiments, pioneers at the University of Minnesota had attempted to carry football games by radio using a spark transmitter and telegraph signals. And, as late as 1922, Texas A&M was testing play-by-play of its Thanksgiving Day football game against Texas.

The most imaginative sports broadcasting was being performed by people at KDKA in Pittsburgh and at a few stations in other cities. In April 1921, with the postwar frenzy for entertainment starting to build, KDKA carried a description of the fight between Johnny Dundee and Johnny Ray. In July, WJY, the sister station to WJZ, did even better by carrying the Dempsey-Carpentier title fight from the wooden bowl at Boyle's Thirty Acres in Jersey City.

At the microphone sat Major Andrew White; at his elbow sat David

Sarnoff. Across the metropolitan area of New York, crystal sets and one-tube receivers were tuned in. But this was a time when "remotes" were almost unknown, and certainly undeveloped. So, White's play-by-play account of the fight was transmitted by wire to the studio, where it was reconstructed by another announcer, J. O. Smith. It was actually a team job: White was the reporter at ringside, the eyes and ears; Smith was the voice in the home studio, and it was his voice that was heard by an audience estimated at 300,000 persons.

When the World Series arrived in October that year, KDKA was already handling baseball scores in a bolder way than before. Scores were normally read on the air at fixed intervals, like the weather forecast. Now, though, KDKA was giving the scores as soon as the runs crossed home plate.

Actually, it took a little ingenuity and a lot of nickels to accomplish this. A staff member of KDKA was positioned in the top row of the bleachers at Forbes Field in Pittsburgh for the regular-season games of the Pirates. As each inning ended, he wrote the results on a piece of paper, leaned over and dropped the message outside the fence to an accomplice, who ran to the nearest coin telephone and relayed the score to the studio announcer.

The Series that year was the first between the Giants and Yankees, and a public event of high drama, so the people at KDKA went even further. They installed a wire between New York and Pittsburgh, and Grantland Rice used it to report details of the game at irregular times. Another twist was created by WJZ in New York, which telephoned the plays from the ball park to the studio, where an announcer named Thomas H. Cowan sat at a microphone and recreated a game he never saw.

By the next year, 1922, the middlemen and their nickels were being replaced by progress. Grantland Rice made his pioneering broadcast of the World Series from the ball park direct to WJZ, and from there to those "great crowds throughout the Eastern section of the country" that the advertisements had envisioned. And the following year in May, a Harvard baseball game was carried live over WNAC in Boston.

It was the age of the radio and the motorcar, and life was being rapidly widened by both. A precise and pontifical newspaperman named H.V. Kaltenborn had already broken ground in public affairs by discussing the coal strike in 1922, and offering an editorial analysis over WVP at the Fort Wood Signal Corps. A year later, he turned up at WEAF, just as Graham McNamee did, and he began to broadcast a weekly news report. Kaltenborn, then an editor of the Brooklyn Daily Eagle, had an intellectual range almost as broad as McNamee's vocal range. And in no time, he was covering topics of the day like Lloyd George, conditions in the Rhineland and the old devil Prohibition.

On New Year's Day, 1923, WGY in Schenectady described the inauguration of Al Smith as governor from nearby Albany. On August 2, half an hour after the Associated Press had flashed word of President Harding's death, John Daggett was on the air at KHJ in Los Angeles with a memorial broadcast—20 minutes of extemporaneous talk over "suitable piano music" supplied by Claire Forbes Crane.

But sports and stunts thrived the most. The following year, WJZ began carrying baseball scores every 15 minutes every afternoon, and WGN regaled Chicago with a nonstop description of the Indianapolis Speedway Classic as the racing cars whipped past the microphone at close to 100 miles an hour. By 1925, all home baseball games—not just the scores—were being broadcast by WMAQ, Chicago, and by KHJ, Los Angeles, which wasn't even in the major leagues.

In 1926, radio really scaled the heights. Station WJAS in Pittsburgh carried an interview between an announcer and a lady flagpole-sitter on top of the Fort Pitt Hotel. In Cleveland, WTAM rigged up a three-way talk between the roof of the Allerton Hotel, the Goodyear plant in Akron and the crew of a dirigible overhead. In Philadelphia, no stunt but a true beachhead on history: WCAU established one of the enduring institutions of American life on the air, the "Amateur Hour."

It was all new and strange, and even mysterious. John McCormack, the renowned tenor, arrived to give his first concert from a radio studio and complained: "My, oh my. This is dead. I can never sing here." And Lucrezia Bori, arriving for her first studio recital, said: "Why, I can't even hear myself or tell what I'm doing. Does it sound that way outside?"

But this was no business, and no time, for the faint of heart. And McNamee plunged ahead as the voice of the World Series. He immediately became part of the event, too. When it rained during the 1923 Series and his suit became soaked, he made the newspapers. When he dropped a thermos of coffee and soaked his suit again, he got letters. In fact, after the Series, he got 1,700 letters. And, two years later, after the 1925 Series, he received 50,000 letters.

"When Ruth batted," McNamee said, remembering his World Series debut and Game 6 of the 1923 classic in particular, "I was almost too engrossed to speak."

He overcame that problem in a hurry, though, and quickly became eloquent and even rapturous, to the point of overlooking the strategic nuances of a bases-loaded situation. Here is how he described the melodramatic peak of the eighth inning of the final game, when the Yankees rallied to win, even though the mighty Ruth struck out:

"Then came the thrill of all time, all World Series and all sports. Babe Ruth stepped up to bat. One hit would mean victory for the Yanks, and for them the Series. It was another 'Casey at the Bat,' and the stands rocked with terrific excitement.

"John McGraw took the biggest chance of his historic life. He ordered Ryan to pitch to Ruth. The crowd faded into a blurred background. Cheering became silence. Ruth lashed out at the first ball. Ruth hurled his bat and weight against the second. Ruth spun at the third. Ruth shuffled back to the dugout, head hung low. A picture of dejection."

The Yankees survived the eighth-inning strikeout—they scored five runs in the inning to win the Series—and the Babe was redeemed. But McNamee later remembered the emotions of the moment this way:

"The biggest thrill passed when the great Babe fanned. Time's phantom flits into oblivion in moments like this. I was a dripping rag draped over the microphone when the 1923 diamond laurel finally graced the Yankee brow."

How's that for eloquent? It was eloquent, indeed, and McNamee succeeded mightily by expressing rhapsody some of the time and adventure all of the time. He became a celebrity himself at historic events like the 1924 Republican National Convention in Cleveland, which he broadcast alone, and at which he introduced Calvin Coolidge on the air and even teased a few words from the silent one.

After the National Broadcasting Company was organized in 1926, he was heard in parlors, living rooms and dens from coast to coast. He always opened his broadcasts with "Good afternoon, ladies and gentlemen of the radio audience." And he always closed with "Good night, all."

On the eve of his World Series debut in 1923, the wonders of radio were being heaped onto the public. The American Radio Exposition opened that week at Grand Central Palace, and more than 100 manufacturers displayed radio sets, from simple crystal types to "super-receivers" devised by the Radio Club of America.

The point of it all, Graham McNamee said, was this:

"You must make each of your listeners, though miles away from the spot, feel that he or she, too, is there with you in that press stand, watching the pop bottles thrown in the air; Gloria Swanson arriving in her new ermine coat; McGraw in his dugout, apparently motionless, but giving signals all the time."

★   ★   ★

If any pop bottles were thrown in the ball park, they were later collected with care by an employee of the company that sold all the soda pop in the stadium, the concessionaire, Harry M. Stevens Inc. If Gloria Swanson arrived in her ermine and wanted a hot dog, it was forked over by a vendor for Harry M. Stevens Inc. When Lord Louis Mountbatten ate his way through that disputed tie game in the 1922 World Series, feasting on six ice-cream cones and two bags of peanuts and four bottles of pop, all duly reported in the press in a kind of gastronomic box score, it was all supplied by Harry M. Stevens Inc.

This was part of the life inside the ball park that Graham McNamee was intent on portraying to the radio audience, the sights and sounds and almost the smells of life inside. From the earliest days, many ball parks were market places—places where crowds might be drawn and where they might be sold large quantities of the beer brewed by the man who owned the ball park. And the team that played in the ball park was the thing that drew the crowds inside. But even when baseball and beer were not part of the same business at the same address, a baseball team could always draw the biggest crowd in town, and you didn't have to be a business genius to see the possibilities.

Harry M. Stevens saw the possibilities almost the first time he laid eyes on a stadium crowd. He got his view of the Promised Land in 1887, just five years after he had arrived from Derby, England, with his wife Mary and their three children. They settled in Niles, Ohio, a small town in the Mahoning Valley Steel district not far from Youngstown, where Harry got a job as a puddler in the steel mill. A puddler was somebody who helped to make steel by puddling molten iron, and he was not to be confused with a *peddler*, which is what Harry Stevens soon became when the mills were shut by a series of strikes.

Now he was really in a bind, an immigrant with a wife and three kids and no job. And the strikes were part of widespread labor trouble that even led to the Haymarket riot of 1886 in Chicago. That's when the puddler became a peddler, taking to the road across Ohio trying to sell copies of the biography of John A. Logan, the onetime Civil War general who established the Grand Army of the Republic and later became a popular politician in Ohio.

Loaded with stacks of the "Life of General Logan," and selling them literally door to door, Harry Stevens trouped around the state and eventually landed in Columbus. He headed for the local ball park one afternoon for a break in his travels, and immediately got the picture: There was no way for a stranger, or anybody else, for that matter, to identify the players.

Stevens promptly made his pitch, and offered to take charge of printing and selling score cards. The owners of the club said it could be done for a fee of $500, and Harry said no, that was out of his league. There weren't that many copies of the "Life of General Logan," anyway. But he made a counter-offer: He would solicit advertising for the program. Two days later, he handed the club a check for $700, and the hardest-working and farthest-traveling book agent in Ohio became the concessions man at the Columbus baseball park.

"Few fans had been educated to the score-card habit up to the time I started in the business," he remembered later. "Score cards had been gotten up carelessly, and had been merely printed slips with the names of the players. Often they were incorrect, no attention being paid to changes in the batting order. I made it a business to find out just how the teams batted, and gave fans a card on which they could keep score.

"It was a selling campaign. I had to convince them that a game could not be really enjoyed without a score card. I made it a point to know the people who came regularly, and spoke to them by name. I introduced selling methods that had never been thought of in connection with selling score cards."

His grandson, Joseph B. Stevens Jr., class of '38 at Yale and chairman and chief executive officer of the company one century after "Score-Card Harry" made his debut, saw him in family memories and legends as a spectacularly visible one-man concessions army, working his way through the grandstand in red coat and straw hat, quoting Byron and Shakespeare and enthralling the crowd while he supplied it with his printed programs and lineup cards.

"I went through the stands shouting at the top of my voice," Harry Stevens said. "I'd shout, 'They all look alike on the field. Buy 5 cents worth of independence, gents, 5 cents, five pennies, a nickel only, and get the names of all the players. It's cheap for the price.'

"I just roared at them. They never had score cards before."

The score cards were studded with local advertising, and were sold by Stevens with such energy and success that the business quickly expanded to ball parks in Wheeling, Pittsburgh, Toledo and Milwaukee, where his son Frank added a dimension by printing score cards in English and German for the pleasure (and nickels) of the large immigrant population there.

They hit a public relations jackpot when Detroit won the National League pennant in 1887 and St. Louis won the American Association pennant, and Stevens was invited to bring his score card to their postseason series by Chris Von der Ahe, the saloon baron who owned the St. Louis club.

"My real hit was made in that series," Harry Stevens remembered. "Year after year, I added to my circuit. When the Brotherhood League opened [1890], I got the privilege in Boston. In the meantime, I added Brooklyn, Pittsburgh, Washington. And one day, it was the latter part of the season of '93, when the Giants and Pittsburgh were playing, the Giants winning, I met John Ward just as he was leaving in the bus for the hotel. I told him I'd like to sell score cards in New York. 'Sure, come along,' he said. 'I'd like to hear you.'

"I landed in New York broke. Just had $8.40 in my pockets when I came in, but I got the contract."

In the winter, Harry would tour the area selling advertising on the curtains of vaudeville theaters, then a popular and profitable business. But he made the giant stride after landing in New York in 1894. He decided it was time to supply the customers with something more filling and more rewarding than lineup cards: food.

He won the right to operate the dining rooms at Madison Square Garden during the six-day bicycle races and the first automobile show, as well as the Garden's original perennial, the Westminster Kennel Show. This kept him busy during the winter months until the baseball season, and then the business turned outdoors again with peanuts, soda pop and hot dogs.

They even operated a resort hotel on Staten Island, The Richmond, in the days when Midland Beach was a weekend and summertime resort across the harbor from Manhattan. And they opened new horizons in 1901 after H.K. Knapp signed Harry to cater aboard his yacht North Star during the America's Cup races. Knapp owned a steamship line, but also served as secretary of the Saratoga Racing Association in Upstate New York, the crossroads of society every summer.

Nobody knew it, but Knapp was shopping for a new caterer for the racetrack. The president of the racing association, William C. Whitney, suspected that they were being clipped by the caterer on the price of champagne, and told Knapp to start looking. But, after Harry Stevens wined and dined him aboard the North Star, he looked no further. Stevens now was catering at racetracks, fed the multitudes at Saratoga for the next 79 years and eventually catered at 20 tracks around the country.

At Churchill Downs, where the Kentucky Derby gives the Stevens company its busiest day every year, crowds of 125,000 and more are customary and mint juleps are mandatory. To handle the demand, Stevens buys the entire mint crop of one supplier near Louisville, and then creates juleps in five "julep houses" that keep the vendors stocked. For years, the company was required to take out a rectifier's license from the federal government to prepare the bourbon whiskey mix, and agents were on hand at the close of the day to make certain that any mix still left on the premises was poured down the drain.

"The food phase of the business in the ball parks grew slowly," said C. Homer Rose Jr., the senior vice president and historian of the company. "At first, it was peanuts, ice-cream cones, lemonade and bottled soft drink. We have a contract copy in our files dated 1895 from Cavagnaro Inc. for an advertisement in the New York Giants' score card to be paid for with bags of peanuts and the stipulation that only Cavagnaro's peanuts would be sold in the ball park. Such was the nature of Harry M. Stevens that the company did all its peanut business with Cavagnaro until the firm went out of business sometime in the late 1920s."

The Stevens people bagged their own peanuts, and gathered in their own soft-drink bottles after games—each bottle carried a 2-cent deposit. Some people believed that Harry M. Stevens also pioneered in the use of straws in bottles, so that the fans could sip their drinks and watch the ball game at the same time.

The hot dog, though, is one institution still shrouded in the clouded claims of history. H.L. Mencken gave full credit to Baltimore, his hearty hometown, where he extolled the prime hard crabs, blue in color and eight inches long, with snow-white meat, hawked in Hollins Street at 10 cents a dozen in the waning years of the 19th Century. Soft crabs, of course, cost more—two and one-twelfth cents each. And Mencken recalled his mother's anger when the fishmongers began to sell shad roe instead of tossing it in with the fish. When a 20-inch shad went from 40 cents to 50 cents, his father predicted that the Republic would not survive the century.

But the most enduring landmark was probably the "Wecker," or, freely transcribed from the German, the common hot dog. To Mencken and his contemporaries, it was as indigenous to Baltimore as the old Orioles.

"I devoured hot dogs in Baltimore way back in 1886," Mencken said, "and they were then very far from newfangled. They contained precisely the same rubbery, indigestible pseudo-sausages that millions of Americans now eat, and they leaked the same flabby, puerile mustard. Their single point of difference lay in the fact that their covers were honest German *Wecke* (or *Wecken)* made of wheat-flour baked to crispness, and not the soggy rolls prevailing today."

Lest anybody take that as a cheap shot at the role of the hot dog and the stature of the sport it spiced, Mencken reported at another time in his reminiscences: "The one sport my father was really interested in was baseball, and for that he was a fanatic."

He was a fanatic, all right. The center of baseball in Washington in the old days was a cigar store at Seventh and G streets owned by Mencken's father, August, as a branch of his store in Baltimore. His father even became vice president of the Washington ball club, and soon found himself in a running series of fights with the railroads over their rates for transporting ball players. He considered it outrageous when they charged $30 apiece for 13 players on a trip from Baltimore to Cincinnati to Columbus to Louisville to St. Louis and back to Baltimore.

Be that as it may, and with due respect to the hot dogs of old Baltimore, the Harry M. Stevens family remembers the arrival of the frankfurter in a somewhat different way:

"The German frankfurter sausage," Homer Rose said, "taking its name from Frankfurt-am-Main, where it was reputed to have originated, was well known in the German meat markets at the turn of the century. It was the same red-colored, blandly flavored sausage product that it is today. Whatever its earlier history may have been, on a cool day at the Polo Grounds in New York in the early 1900s, the ice cream and soda pop were not selling.

"Harry M. had an idea. The Polo Grounds at that time was in a German neighborhood. He sent out for the red frankfurters, known locally as dachshund sausages, and the long pointed Vienna rolls. He heated the red sausages in hot water, put them into the split rolls (so a person could hold the hot sausage) and sent them out into the crowd, telling his hawkers to call out, 'Get your red hots, get 'em while they're hot.'

"They were a success. History says that on that chilly day, Thomas A. (TAD) Dorgan, a famous sports cartoonist of the era, was searching for an idea. He drew a cartoon of the frankfurters and the hawkers and patrons, animating the frankfurters. Not being sure of the spelling of dachshund, he coined the name 'hot dog.' "

Harry M., giving the subject the respect it seemed to deserve, tried to reconcile the conflicting views by taking a modest stance in the chronicle of the hot dog.

"I have been given credit for introducing the hot dog to America," he once said. "Well, I don't deserve it. In fact, at first I couldn't see the idea. It was my son Frank who first got the idea, and wanted to try it on one of the early six-day bicycle crowds at Madison Square Garden.

" 'Pop, we can sell those people frankfurters, and they'll welcome them for a change,' Frank told me. At the time, we had been selling mostly beer and sandwiches, and I told Frank that the bike fans preferred ham and cheese. He insisted that we try it out for a few days, and at last I concurred.

"When I first got the contract in New York, no one ever had heard of ice-cream cones or 'hot dogs,' and soft drinks were considered effeminate. We used to sell beer through the bleachers. We had big-handled glasses, and sometimes a thirsty fan would empty three or four of them.

"Then we used to sell pies and hardboiled eggs. The latter were very popular, and we sold lots of them. We also used to get rid of a lot of pies. I remember DeWolfe Hopper was especially fond of cocoanut pies. He would eat several of them during the course of a game. What soft stuff we sold was sold in the glass. The vendor would go out with a tray of glasses full of ginger ale and sarsaparilla, just as another would leave with a tray of beer.

"Fans in different cities have different tastes. In New York and Boston, our patrons are confirmed peanut eaters. In the Middle West, they go in more for popcorn."

It was no small thing. In the 1920s, when hot dogs went from 10 cents to 15, Paul Gallico wrote a column in New York berating the Stevens clan. When the New York Racing Association years later switched caterers after more than three-quarters of a century, Red Smith wrote a column extolling the Stevens clan as the symbol of decency and intelligent caring. When the baseball season opened in San Francisco every year, Prescott Sullivan customarily wrote a column "reporting" on the comparative size and merit of the new season's "goobers."

It became impossible to separate the sport or the team from the concessionaire. In the early years of this century, Harry M. was exceptionally close to Stanford White in Madison Square Garden, and kept an office in the tower of the Garden, where White kept an apartment. Joe Stevens surmises that his grandfather also may have been the last person to speak to Stanford White on that evening in 1906 when Harry K. Thaw pulled the trigger on the architect in the roof cabaret.

"Frank Stevens and Babe Ruth were great hunting and fishing friends," Joe Stevens said, referring to his uncle. "They would go off to the Caribbean or Newfoundland, all over. And Babe Ruth would stop by the office for a drink after games.

"There were no hospitality rooms for the press at the track or in the stadium in those days. They'd hang out at the Stevens office. It was customary. The writers would come by after the game and stand around the office while the Stevens people were counting the day's receipts. They'd have the money stacked neatly on the desk, right out in the open. And Walter Winchell once came in and looked at the scene, and said: 'They have all the money on the table—and all the whiskey locked in the safe.' "

Harry M. died in 1934, the same year John McGraw died. But the Stevens family was so close to the Giants from the very beginning that, when the team moved to San Francisco in 1958, the Horace Stoneham family pleaded with Stevens to go along and serve the Bay Area fans. It was a long way down the turnpike, but the Stevens company made the trip.

The company grosses around $100 million these days, from Boston to Miami and Puerto Rico, and west through Churchill Downs and San Francisco. For years, the heart of the operation was centered in the East, chiefly the three New York ball parks in the heyday of the Giants, Dodgers and Yankees; Madison Square Garden; in Fenway Park, Boston, and something like 20 racetracks.

It's a family business still. Harry M. had four sons, and three of them joined him in the business: Frank, Hal and Joe. The fourth, Will, became president of a bank back home in Niles. He also had one daughter, Annie, who married Homer Rose, and her side of the family also joined the business in force.

Next came the grandsons, to a remarkable degree. There was Harry M. Stevens II, the son of Frank. And Homer Rose Jr., the son of Annie. Also, Joseph B. Stevens Jr., the son of Joe, and William H. Stevens Jr., the son of Will. Later, James G. Titus came in, the husband of Frank's daughter Alice. And later still, the great-grandsons: Frank Stevens Rose, the son of Annie's son Harry; Joseph Brewster Stevens, the son of Joe Jr.; Harry M. Stevens III, the son of Harry II; Billy Potter, the son of granddaughter Mary; Hector Griswold, son of Jane; Hal Stevens Rose and Homer Rose III, sons of Homer; James Titus Jr., son of Alice; Robert Thomas Stevens, the son of Bill, who was killed in a tragic industrial accident at Belmont Park; and his brother and sister, William III and Pamela. And, finally, the first great-great-granddaughter, Margaret, the daughter of Frank Rose.

With all this remarkably biblical genealogy, it was amazing to people in 1982 when the Stevenses elected William Koras president. He became the first president of the company who was not a member of this endless and supremely well-knit line of succession. Many of them seem to have gone to Yale, and all of them seem to be known by their first names around the office at 521 Fifth Avenue or in the stadiums. Or, with the civility that marks their relationships, the senior members of the clan are often addressed as "Mr. Joe" or "Mr. Homer." From Shea Stadium in New York, where John Morley runs the show with a mixture of precision and cheer, to San Francis-

Graham McNamee, the concert baritone who became the voice of base-ball, calls the 1931 World Series while the sportswriter and columnist Westbrook Pegler (left) glowers beneath his fedora.

co, they feed about half a million souls each day.

But the symbol of the show is "Score-Card Harry," hawking his programs in the grandstand, resplendent in red coat and straw hat, feeding the multitudes from DeWolfe Hopper to Lord Louis Mountbatten. Selling his three-ounce bags of peanuts, and quoting Byron: "You'd best begin with truth." Or, perhaps sensing the human comedy and human tragedy on all sides in all arenas, spicing his hot dogs with a dash of Shakespeare: "Frail we are all—the best of us, the fewer faults we have."

Men to match my mountains

One of the great arms of the era belonged to Walter Johnson, who struck out 3,508 batters for the Washington Senators in a career that produced 416 victories.

CHAPTER 13

Walter Perry Johnson was digging post holes for the Idaho Telephone Co. in 1907 when the Washington Senators sent an injured catcher to scout him in a baseball game. Johnson was the son of Swedish farmers who had migrated to Kansas by wagon train, and now he was 19 years old and digging the post holes in Idaho and he could pitch a baseball like the Furies.

The Washington ball club heard about him from a liquor salesman who happened to be traveling across the Rocky Mountain states and caught his act. The salesman promptly fired off a telegram to the manager of the Washington club, which had lost 95 games the year before and needed all the help it could get.

The scout, Cliff Blankenship, watched Johnson pitch 12 innings in a semipro game and lose it, 1-0, but he liked what he saw so much that he offered the 6-foot, 1-inch teen-ager a contract for $350 a month and a bonus of $100. Johnson accepted, took the long journey from Idaho to the nation's capital and joined a team that was in the throes of losing 102 of the 151 games it played that season.

But, for the next 21 years, throwing the fastest pitches in the big leagues, Johnson pitched winning baseball for a frequently losing team and did it with more virtuoso talent than anybody else. In his second season, he won 14 games and pitched six shutouts, three of them in a row in four days' time. On Friday, September 4, he gave six hits and beat the New York Highlanders, 3-0. On Saturday, he gave them four hits and won, 6-0. And, Sunday being a day of rest with no baseball in New York, he resumed the zeroes on Monday and this time pitched a two-hitter for a 4-0 victory.

In 1910, when he was 22 years old and pitching for a seventh-place team, he won 25 games and struck out 313 batters. It was the first of 12 strikeout titles he won during his career, which he closed in 1927 with 3,508 strikeouts, a record that stood for more than half a century. And, starting in 1910, he averaged 26 victories a year for the next decade for a team that averaged only 76 victories a year.

He eventually pitched in 802 major league games and won 416 of them, with 279 losses. And his life was almost as grinding as it had been back in the days when he was "discovered," digging holes in Idaho: The Senators were generally such a weak-hitting team that Johnson became involved in 1-0 games a total of 64 times. And he somehow won 38 of those.

He pitched one of those games on opening day in 1926, when he was 38 years old and starting his 20th season. It was a cold day in Washington, and Vice President Charles G. Dawes threw out the first ball. Bucky Harris, the "boy manager," who was still only 29 years old, received a floral piece for good luck. Johnson received a loving cup for two decades of prevailing over bad luck.

Then the great old righthander, pitching in the chill of April in the first game of a long season, went 15 innings, allowed five singles and one double, walked three batters and struck out 12 Philadelphia Athletics. He won it by the familiar score of 1-0.

By now, Johnson was the heir to Christy Mathewson as the classic pitcher in baseball. Mathewson, who pitched in the majors from 1900 through 1916, swept through 12 consecutive seasons during which he won 20 or more games a year. When Mathewson retired, he had 373 victories, a National League record that was matched in 1929 by Grover Cleveland Alexander, whose National League career ran on a somewhat parallel course to Johnson's American League career.

Alexander, like Johnson, was born in 1887 and came from a farm family in the West, or "Near West," anyway. He was one of 12 sons raised on a farm in Nebraska. And, like Johnson, he was working for the telephone company (as a lineman) when he started to pitch for pay.

While Alexander didn't reach the big leagues until 1911, he arrived with a clatter. Pitching for the fourth-place Philadelphia Phillies, the rookie righthander led the league with 28 victories, seven shutouts and 31 complete games, and he pitched four of his shutouts in consecutive starts.

Alexander went to France in World War I with the 89th Infantry Division, lost the hearing in one ear as a result of shelling and came home to resume his baseball career and also to struggle against epilepsy and later alcoholism. Despite a layoff of almost a year, he led the league in earned-run average in 1919; and did it again in 1920, when he also won 27 games. Including seasons both before and after the war, Alexander had the best earned-run average in the league for five straight years. And none of those ERAs was above 1.91.

It was ironic, but the most dramatic moment in his career came in 1926, the same season Walter Johnson opened by pitching his 15-inning shutout. Alexander, now 39 years old, was pitching for the St. Louis Cardinals in the World Series. And he made a remarkable revival by beating the powerful Yankees, 6-2, in the second game and then beating them again, 10-2, in the sixth game.

Alexander had absolutely no reason to suppose that he would work again in the Series, which was decided the next day in cold and damp Yankee Stadium. In fact, he watched from the bullpen bench while the Cardinals nursed a 3-2 lead.

But he was about to be jolted loose from his reverie and to be cast into a role that would be told and told again in story and film. But it really needed no embellishing because the scenario was dramatic enough.

With the Series on the line, the teams went to the bottom of the seventh inning of the seventh game with the Cardinals clinging to a one-run lead. The St. Louis pitcher, Jess Haines, had worn a blister on the index finger of his right hand, and he kept looking at it after every pitch. The sting was not soothed by the fact that he was about to pitch to the top of the Yankee batting order.

He began by yielding a single to Earle Combs, who moved to second base on a sacrifice bunt by Mark Koenig. The tying run was on second, the intimidating Ruth was at the plate. That was no mystery for Rogers Hornsby, the playing manager of the Cardinals. Four wide pitches later, Ruth was on first and Combs was still on second with one down.

Bob Meusel followed with an infield grounder, Ruth was forced at second and Combs moved to third. Next came Lou Gehrig, who had just completed his second full season in the big leagues with a .313 batting average, 16 home runs, 20 triples and 107 runs batted in. Gehrig, stocky and amiable and immovable, had taken over first base on June 2, 1925, when Wally Pipp went to Manager Miller Huggins and complained of a headache. And Gehrig, including a pinch-hitting appearance the day before, became a Yankee fixture for 2,130 consecutive games.

After Gehrig worked the count to 3-2 and drew a walk, the Yankees had the bases loaded with two down. Hornsby, who also played second base, trotted in from his position to the mound and waved to the bullpen. To the shock of the crowd of 38,093, out came old Grover Cleveland Alexander, who had pitched a complete game the day before and who had celebrated the achievement in full spirits the night before. Hornsby met Alexander as the veteran pitcher trudged across the outfield grass, stared into his eyes for a moment and handed him the ball.

The hitter was the aggressive rookie second baseman, Tony Lazzeri, who had knocked in 114 runs that season in the American League, second only to Babe Ruth and his 145. Alexander was weary, but he didn't seem worried. Lazzeri took a ball and a strike. Straining to pop the first pitch he liked, he lined the next pitch several feet foul outside third base. Then, with three runners leaning away, Lazzeri swung and missed for strike three.

It was such a storybook ending to the Yankee threat that many people remember it as a storybook ending to the World Series. But it wasn't. Alexander still had two tough innings to go. He retired the side in order in the eighth, then got Combs and Koenig in the ninth. Then, one out away from winning the Series, he went to 3-2 on Ruth, who watched a precisely placed pitch either hit or miss the outside corner for ball four and Ruth's 11th walk of the Series.

But fate wasn't abandoning old Pete Alexander; just teasing him. With the heavy-hitting Meusel at bat and Gehrig next, Ruth promptly took off for second base on an attempted steal. He was thrown out easily by Bob O'Farrell for the final out of the final game. It was, said Ed Barrow, the business manager of the Yankees, "the only dumb play I ever saw Ruth make."

It was also ironic, because Ruth got six hits in the seven games and four of them were home runs. He hit three of those in the same game, the fourth, and thereby touched off a cascade of prose that was remarkable in itself. Under a St. Louis dateline, James R. Harrison wrote in The New York Times:

"Contrary to reports, the king is not dead. Long live the king, for today he hit three home runs and smashed six World Series records as completely as his fellow Yankees smashed the Cardinals to tie the World Series at two victories apiece.

"After all, there is only one Ruth. He is alone and unique. Tonight he is securely perched on the throne again, and the crown does not rest uneasy on this royal head. For to his record of 59 homers in one season, he added today the achievement of three home runs in one World Series game."

Three paragraphs later, after describing this "bulky, swaggering figure," Harrison got down to specifics:

"Besides setting World Series records that may stand for all time, George Herman Ruth hit a baseball where only two other men had hit it—into the center-field bleachers of Sportsman's Park. It is 430 feet to the bleacher fence. The wall is about 20 feet high. Back of it stretches a deep bank of seats, and almost squarely in the middle of this bank Ruth crashed the third homer that made all history.

"It was not only one of his longest drives, but it was by all odds his best, for it automatically wiped four marks off the record book. It was, as noted above, the first time anybody had hit that many homers in a Series game. It made Ruth's number of homers for all Series games seven, beating by one the former record of 'Goose' Goslin. It made his total bases in one game 12, three more than Harry Hooper in 1915. His extra bases on long hits amounted to nine. Again three better than any other man had ever done.

"Besides those four marks, which were shattered by the one heroic blow, Ruth broke two more. He scored four runs, the most which any player has scored in a World Series game, beating a record of three set by Mike Donlin in 1905, which had been equaled often. Ruth also raised his own record of 18 extra bases achieved in World Series games to a grand total of 27."

Babe Ruth, barreling along in the right place at the right time, evoked more panting prose than anyone else in public life. But then, he played his role on the most visible stage in the largest city with the grandest flourishes. When he hit his 60th home run of the 1927 season on the next-to-last day, one headline in New York put it this way: "Ruth Crashes 60th To Set New Record. Babe Makes It a Real Field Day by Accounting for All Runs in 4-2 Victory." And the third "bank" of the headline saved the good stuff for last: "Zachary's Offering Converted Into Epochal Smash, Which Old Fan Catches."

The old fan was Joe Forner of 1937 First Avenue in Manhattan, who was said to be 40 years old and who had been "following baseball for 35, according to his own admission." And the ball he caught made history and also made waves in the language:

"Babe Ruth scaled the hitherto unattained heights yesterday," The Times reported. "Home run 60, a terrific smash off the southpaw pitching of Zachary, nestled in the Babe's favorite spot in the right-field bleachers, and before the roar had ceased, it was found that this drive not only had made home-run record history but also was the winning margin in a 4-2 victory over the Senators. This also was the Yanks' 109th triumph of the season."

But this was an era of style, and of excess style, and it never lacked performers with runaway style. And at times, understatement said it best, as the Associated Press suggested in a dispatch from Philadelphia on July 6, 1929, when it reported: "The Cardinals' losing streak was broken today." That was true, as far as it went. The real news was delayed: The Cardinals' losing streak was broken at *11 games* by the simple device of whaling the Phillies, 28-6. Now, that was style.

This was also an era of power hitting, the dramatic art form that suited the temper of the times, the clamor for action and pizzazz. But the dynamic success of the hitters of the day gave an even greater luster to the success of some of the pitchers of the day. And none achieved more than Lefty Grove did in three consecutive summers for the Philadelphia Athletics, who won 104 games, 102 games and 107 games, three American League pennants and two World Series from 1929 through 1931.

Robert Moses Grove was a 6-foot, 3-inch lefthander from Maryland who stopped going to school after the eighth grade and later got 50 cents a day working in the coal mines with his three brothers. He started playing baseball at 17, signed to pitch for Martinsburg in the Blue Ridge League at 20 and was promptly sold to the Baltimore Orioles of the International League. The boss in Baltimore was Jack Dunn, who had taken his power-hitting "Babe" to spring training six years earlier.

Grove liked Baltimore, and Baltimore liked Grove. In fact, he became a sizable gate attraction, earned a sizable salary ($7,500 a year) and stayed 4½ years. By then, he had a record of 109 victories and 36 defeats, and a ticket to Philadelphia. To get him, Connie Mack paid Dunn $100,000 in 10 installments.

By 1929, the Yankees were cooling off and the Athletics were soaring, and this is how Grove pitched that year (his fifth major league season): He won 20 games, lost six and led the league in winning percentage, earned-run average and strikeouts. The next year, Grove won 28 games, lost five and again led the league in percentage, earned-run average and strikeouts. He was so dominant in 1930 that he fashioned his earned-run average of 2.54 in a league that hit a collective .288 and had three entire teams and 33 regular players hitting over .300. The next closest earned-run average was 3.31 by Wes Ferrell of the Cleveland Indians.

The year after that, 1931, produced the *pièce de résistance*. Grove started 30 times, pitched 27 complete games and worked in relief 11 other times.

He won 31 games and lost four, and the scores of three of those losses were 2-1, 7-5 and 1-0. From June 8 through August 19, he won 16 straight. He struck out 175 batters overall, leading the league in that category for the seventh year in a row. And he once more led the league in earned-run average with 2.06.

When his 16-game winning streak was broken on August 23, he lost by 1-0 to the St. Louis Browns, who got three-hit pitching from Dick Coffman. The only run was scored off Grove in the third inning on a single and a misjudged fly ball that fell for a double. The Associated Press reported from St. Louis: "Grove, as usual, was good today, but Coffman was a little better."

Sooner or later, good pitching encountered good or even great hitting, and Babe Ruth was frequently the man holding the bat. In the 1932 World Series, after the Yankees had regained their ranking, at a time when the Depression was forcing teams like Philadelphia to sell stars to pay bills, Ruth took one swing that created perhaps more versions and legends than any other one that he took.

It was a somewhat characteristic assault on pitching by the heavy hitters on the Yankees, who won their third straight game over the Chicago Cubs, this time by 7-5. The game was played in Wrigley Field before 51,000 fans, a throng so big that it spilled outside the park and even jammed two temporary wooden bleachers that had been built there. One of the spectators was Franklin D. Roosevelt, the governor of New York and the Democratic candidate for President.

The Yankees weren't subtle. Ruth hit two home runs, Gehrig hit two and the Cubs never recovered. John Drebinger put it this way in The Times:

"Four home runs, two by the master hitter of them all, Babe Ruth, and the other pair by his almost equally proficient colleague, Columbia Lou Gehrig, advanced the New York Yankees to within one game of their third World Series sweep today."

Ruth was at his howling best as the star of the show. In the first inning, he nailed Charlie Root for a three-run home run. In the fourth, he tried to make a shoestring catch in left field, missed it and then tipped his cap to acknowledge the jeers of the crowd. And in the fifth, he went to bat with the score tied 4-4 and the fans roaring at him with joy, booing at him with passion.

"But it seems decidedly unhealthy for anyone to taunt the great man Ruth too much and very soon the crowd was to learn its lesson," John Drebinger wrote. "A single lemon rolled out to the plate as Ruth came up in the fifth, and in no mistaken motions the Babe notified the crowd that the nature of his retaliation would be a wallop right out of the confines of the park.

"Root pitched two balls and two strikes, while Ruth signaled with his fingers after each pitch to let the spectators know exactly how the situation stood. Then the mightiest blow of all fell.

"It was a tremendous smash that bore straight down the center of the field in an enormous arc, came down alongside the flagpole and disappeared behind the corner formed by the scoreboard and the end of the right-field bleachers."

So, Babe Ruth carried out his hilarious pantomime to the fullest degree and to that press-box witness, at least, there was no vagueness or mystery about his act: He was saying, in effect, "That's two strikes, but fasten your seat belts and watch this one."

Nine months later, on July 6, 1933, Ruth hit another famous home run, and he did it in Chicago again. But this time, the setting was Comiskey Park, where the first All-Star Game was played before 47,595 fans in the home of the White Sox. He went to bat in the third inning after a walk to Charlie Gehringer of the Detroit Tigers and hit a fastball from Bill Hallahan of the St. Louis Cardinals down the right-field line into the lower pavilion.

"That smash," Drebinger wrote, continuing his role as the great man's Boswell, "gave the team piloted by the venerable Connie Mack the victory by a score of 4-2. There was nothing the equally sagacious John J. McGraw could do about it.

"McGraw, coming out of retirement for this singular event, the first of its kind in the history of the two major leagues, threw practically all his available manpower into the fray. But there seemed to be no way whatever of effacing the effect of that Ruthian wallop."

McGraw and Mack, men commonly addressed as "Mr.," both dressed in business suits with white shirts and straw hats for this one, which was customary for Mack but not for McGraw. After the game, McGraw went to the American League's locker room and congratulated Mack.

"Ruth?" he asked rhetorically, as though sorting out the jarring memories across the years. "He was marvelous. That old boy certainly came through when they needed him."

★   ★   ★

Carl Owen Hubbell was born in 1903 in Missouri and was raised on a pecan farm in Oklahoma, and he grew into a tall and somewhat angular lefthander who perfected the pitch that came to be known as the screwball. It was a kind of reverse curveball: To a lefthanded batter, it broke in toward his body and not away. He perfected it well enough to win 253 games in the big leagues, all of them for the Giants from 1928 through 1943.

Hubbell dramatized the effects of the screwball with one memorable performance. On July 10, 1934, he went to the mound in the Polo Grounds in the second All-Star Game and was promptly tagged for a lead-off single by Charlie Gehringer. When Wally Berger juggled the ball in center field, Gehringer swept into second base. And, when Heinie Manush followed by drawing a walk, the American League had runners on first and second with nobody out and Babe Ruth coming to bat.

But Hubbell, throwing the screwball with fiendish precision, caught Ruth looking at strike three. Lou Gehrig swiped at strike three, while Gehringer and Manush pulled a double steal. But Hubbell then struck out Jimmie Foxx and the side was gone.

In the top of the second, he struck out Al Simmons and Joe Cronin, and now he had knocked off five of the renowned hitters of the day—in succession, and all on strikes. The streak was broken when Bill Dickey singled to left field, but Hubbell then struck out Lefty Gomez for his sixth strikeout in two innings.

One of the classic games that Hubbell won was pitched in the Polo Grounds on July 2, 1933, just four days before the inaugural All-Star Game. It was the first game of a doubleheader that was unusual in itself, because the Giants won both games over the Cardinals by scores of 1-0. But Hubbell's performance in the opener may have come closer to being a masterpiece than any other pitching performance of his time.

"The opener," wrote John Drebinger, "was a titanic pitching duel in which Hubbell gave one of the most astounding exhibitions of endurance and mound skill seen in many years as he survived the combined efforts of the elongated Tex Carleton and the veteran Jess Haines.

"Carleton, who stepped the first 16 innings for the Cards, gave no mean performance himself. As he had beaten the Giants in the opening game of the series on Thursday, it was not his turn to pitch. Yet he requested that he start, despite only two days of rest, and for 16 rounds kept the straining Terrymen away from the plate.

"But it was Hubbell who commanded the center of the stage. The tall, somber lefthander rose to his greatest heights, surpassing even his brilliant no-hit classic in 1929. He pitched perfect ball in 12 of the 18 innings."

Hubbell allowed six hits, never more than one in any inning. Two were doubles, the four others were infield singles. He struck out 12 batters, and walked *none*. The Giants made no errors, so nobody else reached base.

The second game wasn't too shabby, either. Roy Parmelee went to the mound after the Giants had won the first game in four hours and completed the shutout sweep by pitching New York to a four-hit victory, again by 1-0. He was opposed by the Cardinals' ace righthander, Dizzy Dean, who was just as heroic as Carleton: He was pitching on one day of rest, and had shut out the Giants in the second game of the series. Dean pitched five-hit ball this time, surrendered one run when Johnny Vergez hit a home run in the fourth inning, and lost.

Four weeks later, the Cardinals turned around and won a doubleheader from the Chicago Cubs, and Dean struck out 17 batters in the opener for a modern major league record. He was only 22 years old at the time, a one-time sharecropper from Arkansas, the perfectly cast traveling hillbilly who could mangle the language and pitch the baseball with the skill of a master. This was his second full season in the big leagues, he won 20 games, 30 the following year and then won 28 the year after that.

He also became the senior half of a celebrated brother act: Jay Hanna Dean and his kid brother, Paul Dee Dean. They were "Dizzy and Daffy," and they could pitch like no other brothers in sight. They showed it best on September 21, 1934, when they went to Ebbets Field and muzzled the Brooklyn Dodgers with absolute command. Dizzy pitched a three-hitter in the first game, and the Cardinals mauled the Dodgers, 13-0. It was his 27th victory of the season (against seven defeats), the most by any Cardinal pitcher since Cy Young won 26 back in 1899.

Then it was Paul's turn. With two down in the first inning, he walked Len Koenecke, but that was it. He retired the next 25 Dodgers and pitched a no-hitter, winning by 3-0 for his 18th victory of the season and the Dean boys' 45th. They were quick, too. It took Dizzy 1 hour, 54 minutes to whip through the opener, despite the 13 runs scored by the Cardinals; it took Daffy 1 hour, 38 minutes to whip through the finale.

The manager of the Dodgers then was Casey Stengel, who had watched both wipeouts from the solitary splendor of the third-base coaching box. After the Deans had ended their chores, he was walking toward the clubhouse and chanced to run into Dizzy, who had dressed into his civilian clothes after the first game to watch Paul in action.

"Wasn't that something?" Diz whooped at him. But Casey just snorted and continued walking down the runway leading to the Dodgers' locker room. Then, as the crowning indignity of a day of indignity, a heckler in the grandstand leaned out of the seats along the passageway and yelled:

"That's okay, Casey. You played a doubleheader today and didn't make one mistake."

"Yes," Stengel said, years later, thinking back to life in the third-base coaching box when the Dean boys reigned, "I didn't see a baserunner for 18 innings, so I *couldn't* make any mistakes."

Early in the next season, another phenomenon came on the scene, and the Dean brothers had nothing to do with that one: A major league game was played for the first time at night. The place was Cincinnati's Crosley Field, and the date was May 24, 1935. It was a curiosity during hard times, and it attracted a crowd of 20,422, the third largest of the season for the Reds.

People weren't certain how much light would be cast when the lights were switched on, and these lights were switched on with a flourish—from Washington, by President Roosevelt. But, creatively speaking, the lights were turned on by Leland Stanford MacPhail, the impresario of the Reds and a creative genius who as an Army colonel in World War I had once concocted and tried to execute a plan to capture the Kaiser.

Experimenting with night baseball in the big leagues was in some ways almost as risky, although it was well known in the minors. But this was the Depression, and both the major and minor leagues were straining to pay the bills. And nobody strained his imagination more than Larry MacPhail.

The Reds won the game over the Philadelphia Phillies, 2-1, and the Associated Press gave full scientific treatment to the matter of the lights, the question being: Could the players see the ball?

"The contest was errorless, depite the fact that it was the first under lights for practically all the players. The hurlers, Paul Derringer for the Reds and Joe Bowman for the Phils, performed in great style, the former allowing six hits and the visitor only four.

"Manager Jimmy Wilson of the Phils said the lights had nothing to do with the low hit total: 'Both pitchers just had all their stuff working, that's all. You can see the ball coming up to the plate just as well under those lights as you can in daytime.' "

Wilson added a postscript, however: "Night baseball is all right, if the fans want it, but I'd rather play in the daytime."

There were some shadows in the corners, and two long fly balls were dropped by Philadelphia outfielders. But both were scored as hits, perhaps in recognition of the new and high-risk business of catching a long fly ball at night.

MacPhail went on to great success as the guiding light of the Brooklyn Dodgers and later of the Yankees, although turbulence seemed to follow him hour by hour. In 1938, having advanced on the executive suite of the Dodgers, he introduced night baseball to New York after buying $72,000 worth of lighting equipment from the General Electric Co.—on the cuff.

Undaunted by the enormity of his own thinking, he then staged a carnival on the night of June 15, with the Dodgers playing his old team, the Reds, and with Jesse Owens, the Olympic sprinter, racing several ballplayers. Then, when the game finally started, the evening's entertainment soared far beyond MacPhail's expectations: Johnny Vander Meer, the Reds' 23-year-old lefthander, who had pitched a no-hit, no-run game four days earlier, pitched another.

Ladies Day was becoming a runaway success, too. It flowered most spectacularly, as might be expected, in Brooklyn, where two men were arrested one afternoon for trying to take advantage of the new promotional generosity by disguising themselves as women and getting by for just the tax. Another man brought suit against the Dodgers, alleging that he had been trampled in a Ladies Day rush. But in spite of diversions like these, Ladies Day began to interest wives in what was going on inside the fences of baseball parks. And MacPhail stoked this interest in 1939 when he imported Red Barber from Cincinnati and installed him behind the microphone in Ebbets Field just as the Dodgers were graduating from longtime losers to new winners.

Times were changing, the Great Depression was droning on, war was approaching. Babe Ruth left in May 1935, and left in the grand manner. Five days before playing his last major league game, he hit three mighty home runs in one game for the Boston Braves in Pittsburgh's Forbes Field, the third clearing the right-field grandstand, bouncing in the street and rolling into Schenley Park. It was his 714th and last home run.

One year later, in May 1936, Joe DiMaggio of San Francisco made his debut with the Yankees, and he did that in the grand manner, too. He was only 21 years old, but he played left field and batted third in a lineup that went like this: Frank Crosetti at shortstop, Red Rolfe at third base, DiMaggio in left, Gehrig at first, Bill Dickey the catcher, Ben Chapman in center, George Selkirk in right, Lazzeri at second and Lefty Gomez pitching four innings and Johnny Murphy pitching five. DiMaggio made his debut with two singles and a triple, and the Yankees crushed the Browns, 14-5.

At the baseball business meetings in Chicago that winter, Thomas Yawkey offered some unswerving clues to the changing of the guard. He estimated that he had spent more than $3.5 million since 1932, when he bought the Boston Red Sox, and he listed his chief expenditures like this:

$1 million to buy the Red Sox.
$1.5 million to rebuild Fenway Park.
$125,000 to the Philadelphia A's for Lefty Grove.
$250,000 to Washington for Manager Joe Cronin.
$35,000 to the New York Yankees for Lyn Lary.
$25,000 to Baltimore for Moose Solters.
$60,000 to the Yankees for Bill Werber and George Pipgras.
$55,000 to the St. Louis Browns for Rick Ferrell and Lloyd Brown.
$25,000 to the Browns for Carl Reynolds.
$25,000 to Cleveland for Wes Ferrell.
$350,000 to the A's for Jimmie Foxx, John Marcum, Roger Cramer and Eric McNair.
$100,000 "for miscellaneous but important deals."

"And yet," reported the Associated Press in listing the prices paid, "his great dream of a pennant for Boston has not been realized."

It was not going to be realized, either, until after World War II. But, in a time when baseball players were being sold for $25,000 and when none made $100,000, Tom Yawkey was trying to spend his way to baseball success in a pattern that would be repeated years later by another generation of spenders in an age of astronomical prices and pay.

One of the relics of the old order was the baseball barnstorming tour, and no teams toured longer or farther than the New York Giants and Cleveland Indians. They began traveling together in spring training in 1934 and, by the time they had been doing it for 50 years in 1984, they had played 492 games in more than 100 towns and cities in 27 states in intense heat, intense cold, high winds, dust storms and snowstorms.

They started their railroad caravan when Bill Terry, the manager of the Giants, got in touch with Alva Bradley, the president of the Indians, and asked if the Indians would be interested in going north with the Giants after the teams broke camp. Bradley said fine, and Terry worked out the itinerary.

They traveled in four Pullman cars, two for each club. Rookies slept in the upper berths, established players in the lowers. The train carried two dining cars, one for each team. In the evening, they were converted into lounge cars. And each club had its own baggage car.

When the train arrived in a town, it was pulled onto a siding, usually not too far from the ball park or maybe a hotel. For a while, the players even toted their own bags. They would often dress into game uniforms on the train, and then walk to the local ball park in their baseball gear. They were arriving in town like the circus in the springtime.

The idea was to barnstorm their way north and play in as many cities and even hamlets as possible, bringing the big leagues to the masses and bringing the masses to the big leagues. The Giants even warmed up for the first trip by stopping in Dothan, Ala., to play their Nashville farm club. Then they got back on the train and headed for New Orleans and the first of those 492 exhibition games against the Indians.

Nobody held back any resources, either. Carl Hubbell pitched for the Giants, and Thornton Lee for the Indians, who were managed by Walter Johnson. They drew a crowd of 7,000, and they played the game with two umpires, one of whom was Bill Klem.

Paul Richards, who was a third-string catcher for the Giants in 1934, remembered one thing in particular years later: "I really enjoyed watching the great Walter Johnson pitch batting practice. He could still throw it pretty good, even though 1927 was his last year with Washington. I guess he couldn't pitch much anymore because his leg was giving him a problem. But it was something just to see Walter Johnson out on the mound."

Three years later, in 1937, the new generation of strikeout pitchers appeared in the spring series: Bob Feller, the 18-year-old farm boy from Van Meter, Ia. In his first starting assignment with the Indians the year before, he struck out 15 St. Louis Browns. And the moment they laid eyes on him and his fastball, the Giants knew they were seeing someone special. They were right. Although he lost nearly four years from his baseball career while serving in the Navy during World War II, Feller compiled 266 lifetime victories for the Indians and achieved a winning percentage of .621. His fastball was once clocked at 98.6 miles an hour, and he developed a remarkably wicked curveball to go with all that heat.

By the time he was finished, he had pitched three no-hit games and 12 one-hit games.

Barnstorming, in the days before television, became the only way you could bring a national star like Feller to the railroad towns, and the Giants and Indians brought more stars to more towns than the other teams that also went barnstorming north. They played Tarboro and Hickory and Asheville in North Carolina; Selma, Sheffield and Claradega in Alabama; Greenwood and McComb in Mississippi; Kingsport in Tennessee, and Paducah in Kentucky. And one member of the traveling party once said:

"Bill Terry is finding towns to play in that are strange even to Rand McNally."

Nine of their games ended in ties, and one ended in a forfeit, as strange as that seems for an exhibition game. But it resulted from a certain heating-up of the springtime rivalry, which boiled over one day in April 1938 as they played in Longview, Tex.

In the second inning, the umpires ruled that any ball hit into the overflow crowd, whether it was caught or not, would be a ground-rule double. Not long after the ruling was issued, Moose Solters of the Indians hit a line drive into the crowd thronged on the grass in front of the fence in left field. Joe Moore of the Giants went diving into the crowd and came out with the ball, and somehow Solters was called out.

They went to the ninth inning, tied at four runs apiece, and now Solters was playing left field and Joe Moore hit one into the crowd in left field. Same players, roles reversed.

This time, Solters made the diving catch as the ball landed among the spectators. But, this time, the umpire ruled it a ground-rule double and waved Joe Moore into second base. Somewhat understandably, the usually mild manager of the Indians, Oscar Vitt, exploded into fury. He bearded the umpire, Claude Tobin, and demanded to know why the rule had suddenly been enforced against his team. Joe Moore stood firm at second base, Tobin stood firm on the grass. Then the fans broke loose from their corral in front of the fence and stormed across the rest of the outfield.

Vitt had one card left to play, and he played it: He ordered the Indians off the field and back to the train. Claude Tobin, with a sweep of the hand, played his card, too. He turned to the crowd, which was running berserk, swept his arm in a great arc and yelled: "This game is forfeited to the New York Giants. Final score, 9-0."

Bob Feller, who was 19 then, had pitched 2⅓ shutout innings in the game, and he was stunned to see how it all ended: The crowd swirling across the grass, the teams milling around in confusion, Vitt ranting in anger.

"Vitt was foolish in ordering us off the field," Feller told Gene Kirby years later, when they were reflecting on the barnstorming life. "We had a big crowd, and it was a beautiful day. The fans were really enjoying the game. We left the field, went to the hotel and changed, then got on the train and left town."

You could look it up

Joe DiMaggio arrived in the mid-to-late 1930s to take the baton from Lou Gehrig as the Yankees entered a new era under the approving eye of New York Mayor Fiorello LaGuardia.

CHAPTER 14

Eleanor Gehrig remembered what happened one day early in the 1938 baseball season when her husband reached 1,999 games in a row. She went to him just before he left home for Yankee Stadium, and said: "Lou, I've got an idea. Don't go to the stadium today. Tell them anything you want, but skip it."

"Skip it?" he said, sort of shocked. "You know I can't just skip it. They've got a ceremony planned and things like that, and Ruppert would be wild."

"So what?" she said. "Look, if you're worried about the streak, think how they'll remember a streak that stopped at 1,999 games in a row. That's a lot more remarkable than 2,000. That's a lot more memorable than 2,000. It'll make a terrific splash, much more than if you show up and go through the motions. 'Gehrig Stops At 1,999'—you can see the headlines now."

For a parting shot, Eleanor Gehrig fired this one: "All they'll do is hang a horseshoe of flowers around your neck."

But he went, leaving her with great pride and a great fear that somehow the streak was now in charge of the man. She may have been right. Six hours later, the door opened a crack and the Iron Man lurked across the threshold like a truant. He paused, opened the door wider and then stood there before her—a sheepish grin on his face, a huge horseshoe of flowers around his neck.

The streak lasted 130 more games and, by then, one of the intriguing questions in American life was Lou Gehrig's mysterious "slump." He batted only .295 in the summer of '38, and it was the first time since 1925 (his first full season in the majors) that he had slipped below the magic mark of .300. He hit 29 home runs, his smallest production in 10 summers. He knocked in 114 runs, and that was the fewest for him since 1926. One doctor surmised that he was suffering from a gall-bladder condition. His wife suspected a brain tumor. Other people voted for old age; at 35, Lou Gehrig was just past his peak.

Then, on May 2 the following year, Gehrig waited in the lobby of the Yankees' hotel in Detroit for Joe McCarthy, the manager, who was arriving from his home in Buffalo. They went to McCarthy's room, where Gehrig waited for the bellman to leave and then said: "I'm benching myself, Joe."

It was the first time since May 31, 1925, that the Yankees had played without Gehrig. It was the first time in nearly 14 years that they had carried on without the shy, stocky 6-footer who had become their Eagle scout and symbol of strength and stamina, the square from the Yorkville section of Manhattan who grew into Columbia Lou and who joined the Yankees as they were regrouping for new success after their three rousing World Series against McGraw's Giants.

In one game, he hit four home runs in Philadelphia and just missed hitting a fifth. One year, he led both big leagues in batting average, runs batted in and home runs, which is nice work if you can get it. Another year, he knocked in 174 runs; the next, 184. It's not clear how many times he went to bat with the bases loaded, but it is clear that he unloaded them 23 times.

Most of all, Gehrig was the American dream: The son of immigrant parents who worked to the point of laboring mightily but who brought up their son to be thrifty, honest and respectful. He played marbles at 181st Street and Fort Washington Avenue. He loafed away hours swimming with other kids in the Hudson River. He hitched sleigh rides, and got into snowball fights at Deep Grass Hill. He roasted stolen potatoes, "mickeys" to the neighborhood insiders, in vacant lots over trash fires. His mother took in laundry and later answered an ad for a cook-housekeeper in the Phi Delta Theta fraternity house at Columbia, where her son studied and hit memorable home runs and where her husband joined them as a handyman and janitor.

He was Larruping Lou, the poor kid who grew into the national hero and the national symbol of immovable strength. But now, he was a month and a half from his 36th birthday and suddenly showing signs of losing the strength, and the nation that had extolled him was worrying about him. In the World Series the year before, the Yankees had swept the Chicago Cubs in four games and became the first team in history to win three Series in a row. But Gehrig, the captain and anchor, who once hit .545 in a World Series and .529 in another, managed to hit .286 in this one: four hits in 14 times at bat, and all four were looping singles. After that, his salary was cut $3,000, and that was new for him, too.

The mystery ended seven weeks after he had removed himself from the lineup. Eleanor Gehrig, from their home in Larchmont, telephoned the Mayo Clinic and heard Dr. Charles Mayo say: "We think it's serious. We'll put him through the six-day tests, and hope to God that we're wrong."

They weren't. On June 19, Lou's birthday, Dr. Mayo telephoned her and said that Gehrig had maybe 2½ years to live.

To announce to the public that one of its baseball demigods had been stricken with a human and indeed mortal disease, the Mayo Clinic issued a brief but considerate statement that said:

"This is to certify that Mr. Lou Gehrig has been under examination at the Mayo Clinic from June 13 to June 19, inclusive. After a careful and complete examination, it was found that he is suffering from amyotrophic lateral sclerosis. This type of illness involves the motor pathways and cells of the central nervous system and, in lay terms, is known as a form of chronic poliomyelitis—infantile paralysis.

"The nature of this trouble makes it such that Mr. Gehrig will be unable to continue his active participation as a baseball player, inasmuch as it is advisable that he conserve his muscular energy. He could, however, continue in some executive capacity."

On July 4, the Yankees split a doubleheader with the Washington Senators in Yankee Stadium, but the main event came between the games, as John Drebinger reported in The Times under a headline that said: "61,808 Fans Roar Tribute To Gehrig."

"In perhaps as colorful and dramatic a pageant as ever was enacted on a baseball field," he wrote, "61,808 fans thundered a hail and farewell to Henry Lou Gehrig at the Yankee Stadium yesterday."

Babe Ruth was there, wrapping his burly arms around Gehrig. About a dozen other alumni of the 1927 Yankees and earlier teams were there, too: Bob Meusel from California, and Waite Hoyt, Wally Schang, Benny Bengough, Tony Lazzeri, Mark Koenig, Herb Pennock, Everett Scott and Wally Pipp, who sat out the one game in 1925 that became Gehrig's first start in his remarkable consecutive-game streak. The Seventh Regiment Band marched. Clark Griffith, the white-haired owner of the Senators and a Yankee himself in the days when they were the Highlanders, joined the procession. Mayor Fiorello H. LaGuardia gave the official salute, saying:

"You are the greatest prototype of good sportsmanship and citizenship. We're proud of you."

James A. Farley, the postmaster general and a frequent figure at Yankee games, gave the national salute, saying: "For generations to come, boys who play baseball will point with pride to your record."

The Yankees gave him a silver service. The Giants sent a fruit bowl and silver candlesticks. The Harry M. Stevens Co. presented a silver pitcher, and the Stevens employees added two silver platters. The stadium ushers and other workers gave him a fishing rod and tackle. A silver cup from the Yankee office staff; a scroll from the Old Timers Association of Denver; a scroll from Washington fans; a tobacco stand from the baseball writers, and a silver trophy from his teammates.

Then Gehrig walked to the microphone near home plate in his pinstriped uniform with the big No. 4 on the broad back of the shirt. Downtown, Tallulah Bankhead was sitting in her dressing room at the theater listening. Radio engineers sat in their control rooms listening. Sun-worshippers stretched on the beaches on the holiday afternoon, listening. And this is what they head from a generally silent man who had stepped to the plate nearly 10,000 times in the majors with a bat in his hands:

"Fans, for the past two weeks you have been reading about a bad break I got. Yet, today I consider myself the luckiest man on the face of the earth. I have been in ball parks for 17 years, and have never received anything but kindness and encouragement from you fans.

"Look at these grand men. Which of you wouldn't consider it the highlight of his career just to associate with them for even one day?

"Sure, I'm lucky. Who wouldn't consider it an honor to have known

Jacob Ruppert; also the builder of baseball's greatest empire, Ed Barrow; to have spent six years with that wonderful little fellow, Miller Huggins; then to have spent the next nine years with that outstanding leader, that smart student of psychology—the best manager in baseball today, Joe McCarthy?

"Sure, I'm lucky. When the New York Giants, a team you would give your right arm to beat, and vice versa, send you a gift—that's something. When everybody down to the groundskeepers and those boys in white coats remember you with trophies—that's something.

"When you have a wonderful mother-in-law who takes sides with you in squabbles against her own daughter—that's something. When you have a father and mother who work all their lives so that you can have an education and build your body—it's a blessing. When you have a wife who has been a tower of strength, and shown more courage than you dreamed existed—that's the finest I know.

"So, I close in saying that I might have had a tough break. But I have an awful lot to live for."

He lived two years. And, years later, when his wife looked back on the life she lived with his memories and his trophies but without the Iron Man of baseball, she said:

"Would I trade it all for 40 years of lesser joy and lesser tragedy? Not ever. Through the summers that have come and gone, there has been no comfort from the thought of basking as a professional widow; and there has been no comfort from the thought of another man, as in his case there could have been no thought of another woman.

"Loneliness, yes; even emptiness. But I had the answer, all right. I would not have traded two minutes of the joy and the grief with that man for two decades of anything with another."

★   ★   ★

On the day Lou Gehrig died in 1941, one of his former teammates, Joe DiMaggio, hit a single and double against the Cleveland Indians. That wasn't so unusual in itself, but it was part of a streak that had not yet reached great notice: He now had hit in 19 straight games. And he would keep hitting for six more weeks.

Joe DiMaggio was a kind of West Coast version of the American dream portrayed on the East Coast by Gehrig. His parents were also immigrants, they were poor, they raised nine children and they inscribed the birth certificate of this one Giuseppe Paolo DeMaggio Jr.

He was born in Martinez, Calif., on Nov. 25, 1914, but he was still an infant when the family moved into San Francisco not far from Fisherman's Wharf, where his father put out into the Pacific Ocean and made his living fishing. But Joe wasn't interested. He quit Galileo High School after one year, worked in a cannery and started playing semipro baseball.

When he was 17, he joined his older brother Vince on the San Francisco

Seals of the Pacific Coast League, made his debut at the close of the 1932 season, returned in 1933 for $250 a month, switched from shortstop to center field and hit in 61 straight games.

The streak began on May 28 and ran through July 25 before it was ended by Oakland's Ed Walsh, the son of the Chicago White Sox's Hall of Fame pitcher, on July 26. Walsh held DiMaggio hitless in five times at bat.

In his sixth season with the Yankees, DiMaggio started streaking again on May 15 with a single in four times at bat against the White Sox. The next day, he hit a triple and a home run. The day after that, a single. The day after that, they were celebrating "I Am An American Day" at Yankee Stadium, less than seven months before the attack on Pearl Harbor and only a month or so before Adolf Hitler turned his armies against Russia. Emotions and issues were building over the war in Europe, and over the role that might be played by "the arsenal of democracy." At the stadium in the Bronx, the Yankees marked "I Am An American Day" by blasting the St. Louis Browns, 12-2. DiMaggio went 3 for 3.

Streaks were nothing new for the tall, poker-faced center fielder, and his 61-game streak for the Seals gave the first clue. As a big-league rookie in 1936, he hit in 18 straight games. The next year, in 22 straight. In 1940, he hit in 23 straight. And in 1941, he hit safely in the final 19 games of spring training and kept hitting for eight games when the regular season began.

Five weeks into the '41 season, he had something going again. He got five hits in three games against the Browns (the series ended May 20), and three in two games against the Detroit Tigers. Then he got one hit each day during a three-game series against the Boston Red Sox, the hit in the final game coming against Lefty Grove, who beat the Yankees that day for his 296th major league victory.

Now the Yankees were in Washington, and DiMaggio was hurting with a swollen neck. In the opening game, he hit a home run and three singles. On May 30, he got a hit in each game of a doubleheader in Boston; on June 1, he hit in each game of a doubleheader in Cleveland. And in a series against the Browns later that week, he went 3 for 5 in the opening game and 4 for 8 in a doubleheader the next day, with three home runs and a double. He had hit in 24 straight games.

On June 17, he broke the Yankee club record of 29 games (shared by Roger Peckinpaugh and Earle Combs) with a bad-hop single that struck Luke Appling in the shoulder in the seventh inning. The next day, another scratch single that Appling knocked down, and the streak reached 31. In the evening, DiMaggio went to the Polo Grounds and was greeted tumultuously by the fans just before everybody watched Billy Conn outfight Joe Louis for 12 rounds. But, in the 13th, which was something like the bottom of the eighth inning, Conn got reckless with the heavyweight title in sight and Joe Louis knocked him out.

The next afternoon across the river in the home ball park, DiMaggio did some fancy hitting of his own: two singles and a home run in three times at bat against the White Sox. He is hot. The day after that, the Tigers were in town and he went 4 for 5, and the streak reached 33 games.

On June 26, they went to the eighth inning against the Browns and he had zeroes. But, in the eighth, he doubled with two out and the streak went to 38. Then, two days later, he faced Johnny Babich of the Philadelphia A's, who had beaten the Yankees five times the season before. Babich flexed his muscles for this one by promising that he would clip the Clipper's streak, but DiMaggio rifled a third-inning double—which, according to one newspaper account, kicked up dust in the pitcher's box—and the string was at 40 games.

The next day in Washington, in the first game of a doubleheader, they went to the sixth inning before he doubled off Dutch Leonard, and now he had tied George Sisler's 1922 streak of 41 games, the best in American League history. In the second half of the doubleheader, DiMaggio went to the seventh inning without a hit, then singled and broke Sisler's record.

The major league record of 44 straight games, set by Willie Keeler in 1897, was now in his gunsights. He took his shots in a doubleheader against Boston on July 1 before 52,832 fans in Yankee Stadium.

In the opener, he got a scratch single that raised a few eyebrows, but promptly settled any doubts by lining a clean single later in the game. Then the second game began, and DiMaggio singled in the first inning to match Keeler's record. One day later, he hit a home run in the fifth inning against the Red Sox, and Keeler's record was gone.

Four days later, the Yankees unveiled a plaque to Lou Gehrig before 60,948 fans; Joe went 4 for 5 in the first game of a doubleheader against the Athletics and 2 for 4 in the second game. He now had hit in 48 games in a row. On July 11, three days after the All-Star Game (in which DiMaggio contributed a double), he went 4 for 5 against his old victims, the Browns, and the streak reached 50. He also opened a hot streak within a hot streak: two hits the next day and three the day after that, giving him 9 for 14. And on July 16, the Yankees opened in Cleveland and he went 3 for 4 and the streak reached 56.

Now it was July 17, and the Yankees and the streak drew 67,468 persons into Municipal Stadium, the largest crowd at that point in history to see a night game in the big leagues. Three times, DiMaggio faced the veteran lefthander Al Smith. The first time, he smashed the ball down the third-base line, but Ken Keltner made a spectacular backhand stop and threw him out. The second time, he walked. The third time, he again hit a rocket behind third base; again, Keltner made an acrobatic stop and a long, hard throw for the out.

They went to the eighth inning, and now the Yankees loaded the bases with one down, and Al Smith was gone. He was replaced by 24-year-old righthander Jim Bagby Jr., whose father had pitched for the Indians 20 years earlier. Ball one and strike one, and then DiMaggio took his final cut of the game: A hard grounder to shortstop, where Lou Boudreau grabbed it and fired to Ray Mack at second, and on to Oscar Grimes at first for the double play.

The streak had started on May 15 and lasted through July 16, and during that time DiMaggio went to bat 223 times and got 91 hits for a .408 average: 56 singles, 16 doubles, four triples and 15 home runs. He drew 21 walks, was hit by pitched balls twice, scored 56 runs and knocked in 55. He hit in every game for two months, and struck out just seven times.

When the streak began, the Yankees were fourth in the American League. Three days later, they slipped to fifth. After the 56th and last game of DiMaggio's streak, they were first by six games. The Yanks won the pennant by 17 games over the Red Sox, and the World Series by four games to one over the Brooklyn Dodgers.

The day after Keltner stopped him with his glove and arm, DiMaggio started hitting again. No big deal. This time, he hit in 16 straight games.

★　　　★　　　★

His name was Charles Dillon Stengel, but because he had been born in Kansas City, Mo., he was the man from K.C.—*Casey*. But he also was called "Dutch," because his family was German; "the Professor," because of his Socratic manner of presiding over baseball dugouts, and "Doctor," because he had an uncertain memory for names and called everybody else "Doctor."

Branch Rickey, the "deacon" of major league baseball, called him "the perfect link between the team and the public."

It was a link Stengel started to establish in a place called Kankakee, Ill., in a league called the Northern Association in 1910, when he was a 19-year-old outfielder. That was four years before World War I, a decade before Babe Ruth became a Yankee, more than half a century before the first big-league game was played indoors. The league folded in July.

Stengel thereupon squirreled a couple of Kankakee uniforms into a suitcase and moved over to Shelbyville, Ky., in the Blue Grass League. The franchise collapsed.

He packed again and moved to Maysville, Ky., where a stream skirted the outfield grass, and one day he drifted back for a fly ball and caught it while standing in the stream. The link was taking shape.

For the next 55 years, Casey Stengel grew old, rich and famous while the United States moved from William Howard Taft to John F. Kennedy and beyond, with talking pictures, the automobile and the space program revolutionizing life, and baseball expanding as a multimillion-dollar business to the West Coast, the Deep South, Canada, Central America and even Japan. Casey had been transported to his early ball games in horse-drawn surreys, and he wound up a regular traveler from Los Angeles to New York in jetliners.

He was a player, coach or manager on 18 professional teams. He was traded four times as a lefthanded outfielder in the major leagues. He was dropped or relieved three times as a manager in the big leagues. He was even paid twice for *not* managing.

He retired at the age of 70, returned at 71, was rehired at 73 and 74. Then, as he was about to turn 75, he fell and broke his left hip somewhere between Toots Shor's restaurant in Manhattan and a house in Whitestone, Queens, and had to watch on television from a room in Roosevelt Hospital while 39,288 persons in Shea Stadium sang "Happy Birthday, Dear Casey, Happy Birthday to You."

One year to the day after the mishap, Stengel limped into the Hall of Fame at Cooperstown, N.Y., alongside Ted Williams, having run the course from Kankakee to Cooperstown as a national figure, an average player, a controversial coach, a second-division manager of dismal teams, a first-division manager of the Olympian Yankees and Branch Rickey's "perfect link."

Like Lou Gehrig and Joe DiMaggio, he was the son of immigrant parents. Like them, he started dirt-poor and followed his stars. And like them, he realized a kind of impossible dream as a celebrity, folk-hero and even legend.

Stengel was a turn-of-the-century athlete, country boy and Broadway character rolled into one. He drove a taxicab as a teen-ager in Kansas City; played football and basketball as well as baseball in high school; turned to semipro baseball in 1910 to earn money for dental school; consternated his laboratory instructors by attempting to practice dentistry lefthanded; was paid 25 cents for pumping the organ in St. Mark's Episcopal Church in Kansas City, $1 a day for pitching with the Kansas City Red Sox semipro club, $135 a month for playing the outfield with Kankakee and, 55 years later, $100,000 a year for managing the New York Mets until he limped off in 1965.

He earned all this to the accompaniment of theatrical antics and tricks both on and off the baseball field, until he was accused of carrying on in order to distract people from the less effectual performances of his teams. But even in his heyday as skipper of the lordly Yankees, he performed from a full repertoire of jokes, pantomime and anecdotes.

"He can talk all day and all night," John Lardner said, "on any kind of track, wet or dry."

"Every time two owners got together with a fountain pen," observed Quentin Reynolds, "Casey Stengel was being sold or bought."

"I never played with the Cubs, Cards or Reds," acknowledged Stengel. "I guess that was because the owners of those clubs didn't own no fountain pens."

When he was installed as a one-man triumvirate—president, manager and outfielder—for the Boston Braves' farm club at Worcester, Mass., in the

Eastern League in 1925, he fretted through his first assignment as an executive. He even played in 100 of the team's games, and the team finished in a virtual tie for third place. But at the close of the season, he executed a monumental front-office triple play to escape: As manager, he released Stengel the player. As president, he fired Stengel the manager. And as Stengel, he resigned as president.

He was widely considered a professional clown because of his style, mannerisms and language, and he enhanced the image as a professional player for 21 years and as a professional manager for 37. And comic relief seemed desirable during his first stretch as a manager in the majors starting in 1934 in Brooklyn and continuing in 1938 in Boston. He managed the Dodgers and Braves for a total of nine years, and his teams finished in fifth place twice, in sixth place twice and in seventh place five times. Then he went back to the minor leagues, where he managed Milwaukee to the American Association pennant in 1944. And, four years later, his Oakland club won 114 of its 188 games and swept to the pennant in the Pacific Coast League.

Only a few years earlier, The Sporting News conducted a poll of 151 newspaper writers on the subject of the "most" in major league managers. Leo Durocher, for example, was voted the most pugnacious. Connie Mack was voted the best-liked, Bill McKechnie the most studious. And Casey Stengel, who was not even managing in the major leagues that season, was declared the "funniest."

Consequently, it came as a distinct surprise and even shock when he was introduced in October 1948 as the new manager of the Yankees, the most rigidly unfunny and most persistently successful team in baseball. It was as though the State Department had borrowed Emmett Kelly from Ringling Brothers and introduced him as the government's new chief of protocol.

The Yankees did their unveiling on a cloudy, rainy day soon after the Cleveland Indians had won the World Series. The Indians, playing the season before home crowds that averaged nearly 40,000 a game, finished in a first-place tie with Boston, then beat the Red Sox in a one-game pennant playoff. Under the remarkably winning touch of their 31-year-old manager and shortstop, Lou Boudreau, they went on to defeat the Braves in six games in the World Series.

This was postwar America again, and Harry S. Truman was whistle-stopping across the country against Thomas E. Dewey, while George C. Marshall headed for the opening of the United Nations General Assembly meeting in Paris, saying the nation was "completely united" on foreign policy, though the presidential campaign suggested otherwise. And Great Britain at that hour was asking for a censure of the Soviet Union over Andrei Y. Vishinsky's disarmament proposals, charging that Vishinsky actually was obstructing disarmament.

The Alger Hiss-Whittaker Chambers controversy was embroiling the public. Stylists were reporting that Persian lamb collars on women's coats were about to make a solid appearance for the fall season. Ray Bolger had just opened in "Where's Charley?" at the St. James Theatre, and Brooks Atkinson noted that the dancer made "a mediocre show seem thoroughly enjoyable." Tony Pastor and his orchestra were holding the fort at the Paramount, with a new singing star, Vic Damone. It was Columbus Day. Yom Kippur began solemnly at sundown. And, at the 21 Club, Dan Topping stood before a cluster of microphones and introduced Casey Stengel onto the scene.

Stengel wasted no time living up to his reputation. With tape recorders, microphones and cameras all switched on from a common cue, he acknowledged the introduction and said: "I want first of all to thank Mr. Bob Topping for this opportunity."

That was all right, except that Mr. Dan Topping should have been thanked for this opportunity instead of his brother, Mr. Bob Topping, whose marital difficulties with Arlene Judge, the film actress, formerly Dan's wife, had put both Toppings in the headlines before Stengel arrived.

Cries of "Cut" and "Hold it" drowned out whatever else the Yankees' new manager had in mind for his opening remarks. But, although he continued to clown his way through life in baseball, he immediately aimed the Yankees in the direction of the most successful streak in history: Five straight pennants and five straight World Series championships. And, in 12 seasons as their master, the "Old Man" won 10 pennants and seven World Series.

From 1949, when they trailed the Red Sox by one game with two to go, through 1953, the Yankees won everything for five years. Then, in 1954, they won 103 games but ran second in the American League. For the next four years, they were first again. Nine pennants in 10 years.

Then, after winning the pennant but losing the World Series to Pittsburgh in seven games in 1960, Casey was retired or fired, but by no means was put into mothballs. Two years later, at the age of 71, he was hired as the first manager of the new National League team in town, the Mets, and found himself back in the cellar again. But it was there that he rose to his most eloquent heights as the master of "Stengelese."

It was a rambling sort of double-talk laced with ambiguous, assumed or unknown antecedents, a liberal use of "which" instead of "who" or "that," a roundabout narrative framed in great generalities and dangling modifiers, a lack of proper names for "that fella" or simply "the shortstop," plus flashes of incisiveness tacked onto the ends of sentences, like: "And, of course, they got Perranoski."

Strict followers of Stengelese always found a point at the end of the trail, often an hour later; between the layers of dangling participles and fused phrases, wisdom lurked. Sometimes the point was made rather quickly in a form of short Stengelese, most frequently to summarize a ball play-er's ability or quirks, or to define a situation starkly.

Of Jim Bunning, who had pitched successfully for both the Detroit Tigers of the American League and the Philadelphia Phillies of the National League, he said: "He must be good. He gets 'em out in both leagues."

Of Van Lingle Mungo, his impetuous pitcher with the Dodgers in the 1930s: "Mungo and I get along fine. I just tell him I won't stand for no nonsense—and then I duck."

Of Roger Maris, the sometimes-aloof power hitter of the Yankees: "That Maris. You'd tell him something and he'd stare at you for a week before answering."

Of Willie Mays, who played for the San Francisco Giants in windy Candlestick Park: "If a typhoon is blowing, he catches the ball."

Of baseball itself and the essence of the game: "You got to get 27 outs to win."

Of the logic of the double play: "It gives you two twenty-sevenths of a ball game."

But Stengel reached his full flowering as "the perfect link between the team and the public" when he was called to testify in the public arena. It was July 9, 1958, and the antitrust and monopoly subcommittee of the Judi-ciary Committee of the United States Senate was holding hearings in Wash-ington. It was considering H.R. 10378 and S. 4070: To limit the antitrust laws so as to exempt professional baseball, football, basketball and hockey. The chief witness was Charles Dillon Stengel, and the testimony went like this:

SEN. ESTES KEFAUVER. Mr. Stengel, you are the manager of the New York Yankees. Will you give us very briefly your background and your views about this legislation?

MR. STENGEL. Well, I started in professional ball in 1910. I have been in professional ball, I would say, for 48 years. I have been employed by numerous ball clubs in the majors and in the minor leagues.

I played as low as Class D ball, which was at Shelbyville, Ky., and also Class C ball and Class A ball, and I have advanced in baseball as a ball player.

I had many years that I was not so successful as a ball player, as it is a game of skill. And then I was no doubt discharged by baseball in which I had to go back to the minor leagues as a manager, and after being in the minor leagues as a manager, I became a major league manager in several cities and was discharged, we call it discharged because there is no question I had to leave. [Laughter.]

And I returned to the minor leagues at Milwaukee, Kansas City and Oakland, Calif., and then returned to the major leagues.

In the last 10 years, naturally, in major league baseball with the New York Yankees, the New York Yankees have had tremendous success and while I am not a ball player who does the work, I have no doubt worked for a ball club that is very capable in the office.

I have been up and down the ladder. I know there are some things in baseball 35 to 50 years ago that are better now than they were in those days. In those days, my goodness, you could not transfer a ball club in the minor leagues, Class D, Class C ball, Class A ball.

How could you transfer a ball club when you did not have a highway? How could you transfer a ball club when the railroads then would take you to a town you got off and then you had to wait and sit five hours to go to another ball club?

How could you run baseball then without night ball?

You had to have night ball to improve the proceeds, to pay larger salaries, and I went to work, the first year I received $135 a month.

I thought that was amazing. I had to put away enough money to go to dental college. I found out it was not better in dentistry. I stayed in baseball.

Any other questions you would like to ask me?

SEN. KEFAUVER. Mr. Stengel, are you prepared to answer particularly why baseball wants this bill passed?

MR. STENGEL. Well, I would have to say at the present time, I think that baseball has advanced in this respect for the player help. That is an amazing statement for me to make, because you can retire with an annuity at 50 and what organization in America allows you to retire at 50 and receive money?

Now, the second thing about baseball that I think is very interesting to the public or to all of us that it is the owner's fault if he does not improve his club, along with the officials in the ball club and the players.

Now, what causes that?

If I am going to go on the road and we are a traveling ball club and you know the cost of transportation now—we travel sometimes with three Pullman coaches, the New York Yankees, and I am just a salaried man and do not own stock in the New York Yankees, I found out that in traveling with the New York Yankees on the road and all, that it is the best, and we have broken records in Washington this year; we have broken them in every city but New York and we have lost two clubs that have gone out of the city of New York.

Of course, we have had some bad weather, I would say that they are mad at us in Chicago, we fill the parks.

They have come out to see good material. I will say they are mad at us in Kansas City, but we broke their attendance record.

Now, on the road we only get possibly 27 cents. I am not positive of these figures, as I am not an official.

If you go back 15 years or if I owned stock in the club, I would give them to you.

SEN. KEFAUVER. Mr. Stengel, I am not sure that I made my question clear. [Laughter.]

MR. STENGEL. Yes, sir. Well, that is all right. I am not sure I am going to answer yours perfectly, either. [Laughter.]

SEN. JOSEPH C. O'MAHONEY. How many minor leagues were there in baseball when you began?

MR. STENGEL. Well, there were not so many at that time because of this fact: Anybody to go into baseball at that time with the educational schools that we had were small, while you were probably thoroughly educated at school, you had to be—we had only small cities that you could put a team in and they would go defunct.

Why, I remember the first year I was at Kankakee, Ill., and a bank offered me $550 if I would let them have a little notice. I left there and took a uniform because they owed me two weeks' pay. But I either had to quit but I did not have enough money to go to dental college so I had to go with the manager down to Kentucky.

What happened there was if you by July, that was the big date. You did not play night ball and you did not play Sundays in half of the cities on account of a Sunday observance, so in those days when things were tough, and all of it was, I mean to say, why they just closed up July 4 and there you were sitting there in the depot.

You could go to work someplace else, but that was it.

So I got out of Kankakee, Ill., and I just go there for the visit now. [Laughter.]

SEN. JOHN A. CARROLL. The question Sen. Kefauver asked you was what, in your honest opinion, with your 48 years of experience, is the need for this legislation in view of the fact that baseball has not been subject to antitrust laws?

MR. STENGEL. No.

SEN. CARROLL. I had a conference with one of the attorneys representing not only baseball but all of the sports, and I listened to your explanation to Sen. Kefavuer. It seemed to me it had some clarity. I asked the attorney this question: What was the need for this legislation? I wonder if you would accept his definition. He said they didn't want to be subjected to the *ipse dixit* of the federal government because they would throw a lot of damage suits on the *ad damnum* clause. He said, in the first place, the Toolson case was *sui generis*, it was *de minimus non curat lex*.

Do you call that a clear expression?

MR. STENGEL. Well, you are going to get me there for about two hours.

SEN. KEFAUVER. Thank you, very much, Mr. Stengel. We appreciate your presence here.

Mr. Mickey Mantle, will you come around?

Mr. Mantle, do you have any observations with reference to the applicability of the antitrust laws to baseball?

MR. MANTLE. My views are just about the same as Casey's.

The venerable Casey Stengel, pictured while presiding over the 1953 opener in Yankee Stadium, became a flag-raising legend, winning 10 pennants in 12 seasons with the Yankees from 1949 through 1960.

We shall overcome

Jack Roosevelt Robinson signed with Branch Rickey and the Brooklyn Dodgers in 1947, crossing the color line into major league baseball.

CHAPTER 15

The first time Pee Wee Reese ever heard of Jackie Robinson was at the end of World War II when Reese was returning to the United States from the Pacific aboard a troopship.

"Somebody was reading one of the newspapers," Reese said, "and there was something about this black guy from UCLA who was going to get a shot with the Brooklyn Dodgers' farm club at Montreal. He could hit and field and run. I hadn't heard about him. I'd been away for three years in the war."

Before he went off to the war, Pee Wee Reese had been the shortstop for the Dodgers for the previous 2½ seasons. Now he was coming home to pick up the threads of his career. And somebody on board the troopship was telling him about Jackie Robinson, and Reese knew it was unusual because baseball's "color line" had forced black players to test their talent on the barnstorming teams of the Negro leagues.

"But," Reese remembered, "I didn't pay much attention until the guy said Robinson played shortstop."

Jack Roosevelt Robinson, the grandson of a slave, wasn't the only change in the world that was waiting for Pee Wee Reese and every other veteran coming home from the war. But he soon became the most significant one in the world of baseball, which had already been transformed along with everything else since Japanese planes struck Pearl Harbor on Sunday morning, December 7, 1941.

In baseball, the changes began even before America was jolted into the war. Earlier in 1941, the Selective Service System inducted the first "name" player in the big leagues: Hank Greenberg of the Detroit Tigers, one of the ranking power hitters in a generation of remarkable power hitters.

Greenberg was a tall and imposing New Yorker who was voted the Most Valuable Player in the American League in his third summer in the league. He was already one of the great run-producers in the business, and he knocked in 170 that season (1935). Two years later, he did even better. He got 200 hits, batted .337, whacked 40 home runs and knocked in 183 runs. And the year after that, he knocked in 146 runs and hit 58 home runs.

"But we had so many good first basemen who could hit in those days," Greenberg once said, "that I had trouble getting elected to the All-Star team. The year I batted in 170 runs, I had 100 by the time we got to the All-Star Game, and I still didn't make it. We always had guys like Lou Gehrig and Jimmie Foxx who put up terrific numbers, and Rudy York and Hal Trosky. Everywhere you looked, there were first basemen who hit with power."

Greenberg actually made the armed forces twice in the same year. He was drafted early in 1941, then was discharged two days before Pearl Harbor. But once the United States was involved, so was Greenberg: He enlisted, and spent the next 3½ years of his life in the Army Air Forces, much of it in the Pacific and even in China and Burma.

Joe DiMaggio missed three years because of military service, and so did Ted Williams, the hitting master of the Boston Red Sox, who became a Marine Corps pilot. And Bob Feller missed almost four entire seasons at the peak of his career. The depletion of the big leagues was deep, but President Roosevelt wrote in a letter to Commissioner Landis: "I honestly feel that it would be best for the country to keep baseball going. There will be fewer people unemployed and everybody will work longer hours and harder than ever before. And that means they ought to have a chance for recreation and for taking their minds off their work even more than before."

Baseball went to some extreme lengths to take people's minds off their work. The clubs filled their lineups with the very young and the very old, and in some cases with the lame and the halt. In one game, the Cincinnati Reds pitched a 15-year-old boy, Joe Nuxhall, the youngest person ever to appear in the major leagues. He pitched two-thirds of an inning against the St. Louis Cardinals, gave up two hits and five walks and did not pitch again in the majors until 1952. But when Nuxhall came back, he stayed a long time. He pitched in the majors for 15 seasons, winning 135 games and opening a career that led eventually to the broadcasting booth for the team he had joined as a teen-age pitcher.

The St. Louis Browns reached further than that: They shattered their long-standing record as a tail-end team and won their first pennant in 1944. Then, a year later, they joined the war effort by stationing a 28-year-old Pennsylvanian in the outfield despite the fact that he had lost his right arm in a childhood accident. He was Pete Gray, and he got into 77 games, went to bat 234 times, hit .218 and struck out only 11 times.

Will Harridge, the president of the American League, even issued special instructions to his umpires to guide them in ruling on whether Gray had actually caught the ball. He said that umpires should give credit to Gray for momentary catches. If he dropped the ball after starting to remove it from his glove, the catch would still be allowed. It was the same regulation applied by umpires in the Southern Association the year before, when Gray played with Memphis (and batted .333).

For the disbelieving, as well as for the umpires, it was explained this way: "After making a catch, Gray places the ball against his chest and moves his left hand to the stub of his right arm. In this motion, the ball rolls out of his glove and up his wrist as if it were a ball-bearing between the arm and the body. When the glove is tucked under the stub, Gray draws his arm back across his chest until the ball rolls back into his hand, ready for a throw."

But 15-year-old pitchers and one-armed outfielders weren't the only recruits. To replace Judge Landis, who had died on November 25, 1944, the 16 club owners went straight to Washington and conscripted a United States senator: Albert B. (Happy) Chandler, who also had served as governor of Kentucky. He was signed for seven years at $50,000 a year and, after demurring because of the war, he accepted the job on April 24, 1945, and said: "Now that the war with Germany is virtually over, I can conscientiously leave my other duties."

Not long after the war with Germany was over, the first overture with history in baseball was made by Branch Rickey, the president and general manager of the Dodgers. He sent an emissary, Clyde Sukeforth, to Chicago to carry a message to Jackie Robinson.

It was a message that would bring Robinson and generations of black athletes across the color line into the major leagues after years of riding the buses and beating the bushes in backwoods baseball, traveling from city to city and from coast to coast for short rations in hard times and never getting the chance to migrate to the big time and the big money. They were Satchel Paige and Josh Gibson and Cool Papa Bell, John Henry Lloyd, Buck Leonard, Martin Dihigo and Oscar Charleston, most of whom were too late, and Roy Campanella, Elston Howard, Monte Irvin, Willie Mays and Jackie Robinson, who were not.

Rickey and Robinson reached their crossroads from opposite ends of the spectrum. Rickey was born in Ohio in 1881, only five years after the National League was formed. He was raised by strict Methodist fundamentalists, studied at Ohio Wesleyan, played halfback in football and catcher in baseball, and knocked off high marks in Latin, Greek and history.

When he got to the major leagues in 1905, Rickey was living on borrowed time as a player: In a game two seasons later, while catching for the New York Highlanders, he set a red-faced record when the Washington Senators stole 13 bases against him. But he lived down that day of indiscretion once he became a manager, and particularly when he served as a general manager.

His first flash of creative genius came when he decided not to compete with the big bankrolls of baseball for minor league stars. Instead, working from the St. Louis Cardinals' front office, he began to develop his own players by building his own farm system, and he did it like a man opening supermarkets in towns across the country. It worked so well that the Cardinals won pennants in 1926, 1928, 1930 and 1931, and another in 1934. By the end of the 1930s, on the eve of the war, the Cardinals had more than 50 farm clubs and more than 800 young players under contract.

The empire was pretty much dissolved by Judge Landis, but the essence of the farm system remained as a monument to Rickey's vision. In the fall of 1942, Rickey left St. Louis and took charge of the Dodgers, who also had recently reversed years of losing and were now winning with charm and charisma. Then it was 1945, the war was over and he made the most sweeping move of all.

He sent Sukeforth to Chicago to see the Kansas City Monarchs play the Lincoln Giants in a Negro National League game in Comiskey Park. But the real target was Jack Robinson, and the message was: Branch Rickey wants to talk.

Robinson was then 26 years old, the youngest of five children in a poor sharecropping family from Cairo, Ga. His father left the family when Jackie was 6 months old, and after that it all hinged on his mother, Mallie Robinson, a strong-minded woman who soon moved her family to Pasadena, Calif. And it was there, at Pasadena Junior College, that Jackie made his debut as a star athlete headed toward some high but distant goal.

At UCLA, he grew into a superstar with towering credentials. In track, he was the broad-jump champion of the Pacific Coast Conference. In basketball, he was the leading scorer in the conference in 1940 and 1941. In football, he averaged 11.4 yards on 40 carries for the 1939 Bruins. And in baseball, he was a versatile head-first performer with great speed and fury.

Life took a strange turn in 1941 when he was playing small-time professional football for the Honolulu Bears. The season ended and he sailed for home—on December 5.

A few months later, he was going through Officers Candidate School. He came out with an Army commission and made it to first lieutenant before he was eventually discharged. But he chafed and even rebelled against the racial discrimination that separated blacks and whites under the same flag.

Pete Reiser of the Dodgers remembered a day in 1943 at Fort Riley, Kan., which had a baseball team staffed by major leaguers: "A Negro lieutenant came out for the ball team. An officer told him he couldn't play. 'You have to play with the colored team,' the officer said. But that was a joke. There was no colored team."

There were many "colored teams" on the outside, though, and Robinson was making $400 a month playing shortstop for one of them, the Monarchs, when Sukeforth brought him the message from Rickey in August 1945. Robinson had a sore shoulder at the time and wasn't in the lineup, so he accepted the invitation and took the train with Sukeforth to New York. When they got there, Sukeforth went to a hotel in Brooklyn, and Robinson went to the Theresa Hotel in Harlem. The next day, he was sitting across the desk from Branch Rickey.

Red Barber, the reasoned and renowned voice of the Dodgers, remembers that Rickey had confided in him several months earlier:

"I've put a team in the Negro leagues called the Brooklyn Brown Dodgers. They will play at Ebbets Field when the regular Dodgers are on the road. I've got my best scouts—Clyde Sukeforth, George Sisler, Wid Matthews, Andy High—combing the Negro leagues, studying the players in the Caribbean league, searching for the best Negro players. They think they are scouting for the Brown Dodgers. They don't know that what they are really searching for is the first black player I can put on the white Dodgers.

"I don't know who he is or where he is. All their reports funnel to me at my office. I study them, narrow them down. I'm doing that now. When the time is ripe for a decision on the one man, I'll make it. As I said, I don't know who he is or where he is. But he is coming."

It turned out to be Jackie Robinson who was coming, and Rickey looked beneath shaggy eyebrows across the desk and said to Jackie:

"I've sent for you because I'm interested in you as a candidate for the Brooklyn National League club. I think you can play in the major leagues. How do you feel about it?"

Before Robinson could answer, Rickey shot another question across the desk: "Do you think you can play for Montreal?"

Robinson said: "Yes." And then Rickey delivered the ultimate message: "I know you're a good ball player. My scouts have told me this. What I don't know is whether you have the guts. Have you got the guts to play the game no matter what happens?"

"But it's the box score that really counts," Robinson said. "That and that alone, isn't it?"

"It's all that ought to count," Rickey said. "But it isn't. Maybe one of these days it *will* be all that counts. That is one of the reasons I've got you here. If you're a good enough man, we can make this a start in the right direction. But let me tell you, it's going to take an awful lot of courage."

They talked for three hours. During that time, Rickey created scenarios for almost every situation, for every crisis that the first black player in the big leagues might face: hotels, restaurants, dining cars, stadiums, traveling in the Deep South. And finally, he created scenarios for games.

"Suppose a player comes down from first base," he said, "you are the shortstop, the player slides, spikes high, and cuts you on the leg. As you feel the blood running down your leg, the white player laughs in your face, and sneers, 'How do you like that, nigger boy?' "

"Mr. Rickey," Robinson replied, "are you looking for a Negro who is afraid to fight back?"

"Robinson," Rickey said with passion, "I'm looking for a ball player with guts enough not to fight back."

"You can't retaliate," Rickey said, driving the point home, time and again. "You can't answer a blow with a blow. You can't echo a curse with a curse. Can you do it? You will have to promise me that for your first three years in baseball, you will turn the other cheek. I know you are naturally combative. But for three years, you will have to do it the only way it can be done. Three years. Can you do it?"

"Mr. Rickey," Robinson said, "I've got to do it."

He did it. The following year, playing second base for the Dodgers' farm team in Montreal, he led the International League by hitting .349 and helped lead the team to the pennant and to the Junior World Series title over the champion from the American Association.

Then, in 1947, he went south with the Dodgers, where he was welcomed by Pee Wee Reese, who by now had heard plenty about him, and by some of the other stars of the team, like Reiser. But some of the other players, mainly Southerners led by Dixie Walker, did *not* want to play with Robinson and indicated so in strong terms. But the revolt was met head-on by Leo Durocher, the manager, who called a midnight meeting and told the team that it was he who would decide the lineup, and no one else. And Rickey went to each of the rebels and tried to reason with them, and apparently succeeded in most cases.

On April 10, 1947, Jackie Robinson was promoted to the Dodgers' roster. On April 15, he was playing first base on opening day against the Boston Braves at Ebbets Field. The deed was done.

But the ordeal was just beginning. One week later, the Philadelphia Phillies came to Ebbets Field and took their cue from their manager, Ben Chapman, the former Yankee outfielder, who was from Alabama. He promptly started to yell insults at Robinson, some of his players joined in and Robinson's vow of silence was tested under extreme pressure.

"Starting to the plate in the first inning," Robinson recalled later, "I could scarcely believe my ears. Almost as if it had been synchronized by some master conductor, hate poured forth from the Phillies' dugout.

" 'Hey, nigger, why don't you go back to the cotton field where you belong?'

" 'They're waiting for you in the jungles, black boy.'

" 'Hey, snowflake, which one of those white boys' wives are you dating tonight?'

" 'We don't want you here, nigger.' "

Robinson remembered the confrontation with great anger and anguish, and later wrote in his memoirs:

"For one wild and rage-crazed minute, I thought, 'To hell with Mr. Rickey's noble experiment. It's clear it won't succeed. I have made every effort to work hard, to get myself into shape. My best is not enough for them.' "

But Robinson struggled against his inclinations, which suggested a march on the Philadelphia dugout, and later hurt the Phils where it counted the most. In the bottom of the eighth inning, he singled, stole second, went to third when the catcher's throw carried into center field and scored on a single by Gene Hermanski. Final score: 1-0, Dodgers.

Six months later, Jackie Robinson ended his first season under fire with a .297 batting average, 12 home runs in 151 games and a league-leading 29 stolen bases. He also was voted Rookie of the Year in the major leagues, and the Dodgers won the pennant.

James (Cool Papa) Bell, the great outfielder who spent his entire career in the Negro leagues, just missed the revolution wrought by Robinson and later said:

"I played from 1922 through 1950, that's 29 seasons. Plus 21 winter seasons. That makes a total of 50 seasons."

He was asked if he ever got weary of it all, and replied: "I only got old."

★   ★   ★

It was the best of times, and the worst of times; mostly, it was the fastest changing of times.

Less than three months after Jackie Robinson broke into the majors, Bill Veeck signed Larry Doby for Cleveland and then signed Satchel Paige the next season, and Doby and Paige helped the Indians win the '48 pennant and World Series. In the same season, the Dodgers brought up Roy Campanella, a catcher who hit with power and who was voted the Most Valuable Player in the National League three times in his first seven full seasons. In fact, the new black players became stars so instantly that they were elected "most valuable" in the National League nine times during a stretch of 11 years, starting with Jackie Robinson in 1949: Campanella (three times), Don Newcombe of the Dodgers, Willie Mays of the Giants, Henry Aaron of the Milwaukee Braves and Ernie Banks of the Chicago Cubs (twice).

That wasn't all. During the same decade, the first postwar generation of young stars arrived, led by great new center fielders like Mays and Mickey Mantle, by Aaron and Roberto Clemente, by Whitey Ford and Sandy Koufax, and by Stan Musial, who won his first batting title before joining the Navy during the war and captured six more titles after the war. And by Ralph Kiner, who won or shared seven consecutive home run championships.

They were restless times and prosperous times. And, for both reasons, a group of players for the first time crossed an international border in a kind of gold rush touched off by sizable contracts to play in Mexico. Eighteen of them went, some stayed a year or two and then tried to return to the big leagues but found that the door had been closed behind them. It took some litigation and the threat of more to get them reinstated, which they were in the middle of 1949.

When they started jumping their contracts with major league clubs early in 1946, Commissioner Chandler offered them amnesty if they would jump back before the season opened. When opening day arrived on April 16, Chandler sat in Cincinnati watching the Reds play the Chicago Cubs and said the die was cast: "Those who did not return by opening day are now out. They can't even petition for a return to American organized baseball for five years."

In Mexico City, the colony of American self-exiles didn't seem to mind. Mickey Owen, the former catcher for the Dodgers, remembered that he had played in eight opening games in the National League, but said: "I'm perfectly happy here. My wife likes Mexico, and we moved into this super-modern apartment today and everything is dandy."

Owen was 30 at the time, and the Associated Press reported from Mexico City that he was scheduled "to make his debut with Veracruz on Thursday at mile-high Delta Park, where a well-hit ball takes off like a rabbit in the rarefied atmosphere."

Danny Gardella, who left the Giants "after a row with Manager Mel Ott," was still angry. When asked if he had any regrets on the day the season opened back home, he said with heat: "I assure you I'm just as happy as Ott and probably less confused."

Alex Carrasquel, the 33-year-old pitcher from Venezuela, who jumped from the Chicago White Sox, said: "I have no regrets—who would, leaving the White Sox?"

But the first crack in the facade was indicated by Luis Olmo, the 26-year-old Puerto Rican who might have won a regular job in the Dodgers' outfield if he had stayed in the National League. Now he was mostly sitting in his hotel room with his injured knee in a cast, and he conceded the point.

"Oh, I'm all right, and I like it here," Olmo said. "But you might say I'm just a trifle lonely. Who wouldn't be, in a hotel room, all alone?"

The most accomplished of the exiles was Max Lanier, the lefthander from North Carolina who had already pitched in three World Series for the Cardinals and who had won six straight games at the start of the 1946 season before he jumped.

"When I came to spring training in '46," Lanier said, "the Cardinals offered me a $500 raise that would bring me to $10,000. I didn't like it, but they said: 'Take it or go home.' I didn't have much choice, so I stayed. Later, I had a 6-and-0 record going for me when a recruiter from the Mexican League came to see me. They offered me $20,000 a year for five years plus a bonus of $35,000. So, I went.

"A lot of players were minor leaguers who felt this was a chance to play major league ball. Some were regulars like myself who just wanted to help themselves. Mickey Owen was the catcher and manager when I got there, and we had guys like Sal Maglie, Red Hayworth, George Hausmann, Danny Gardella and Jim Steiner. We'd all been brought there by Jorge Pasquel, who owned the ball clubs and watched the games from his private box behind home plate, where his meals were served on silver platters.

"The accommodations in Mexico City were first class, but they were primitive every place else. In Tampico, the fans had the habit of throwing firecrackers onto the field, and we had railroad tracks running through center field. They'd actually open the gates on both sides of the outfield to let the trains go through. In Puebla, they didn't have trains, but they did have goats grazing on the outfield grass before games.

"Veracruz was so hot that you didn't try to play doubleheaders there. During one game, one of the players was blinded by the sun and got hit by the ball. It was truly another world from the stadiums back north."

Three and a half years later, Max Lanier was back with the Cardinals, and he had some consoling memories through the years after he had retired to Florida and watched his son Hal grow into a big league player and manager.

"Stan Musial told me that he got a $5,000 raise right after I left the Cardinals," he said. "Enos Slaughter and Joe Garagiola both said they got $3,000 raises. And we might've influenced the most important change of all—the pension."

The pension was voted by the American and National Leagues on February 1, 1947, and it was revolutionary and also scant by the standards that exploded in the business a quarter of a century later. It provided that a player who worked five years in the big leagues would receive $50 a month for life when he reached age 50. For each additional year of service, the pension would grow by $10 a month until it reached the maximum for 10-year veterans: $100 a month.

The underwriter, the Equitable Life Assurance Society of the United States, calculated that it would take an annual pool of about $675,000 to keep the pension going. The fund would be raised by contributions from the players ($45.45 the first year, $90.90 the second year and on up to $454.75 in the 10th year); from the clubs ($250 for each player); from the total receipts of the All-Star Game, and from the radio broadcasting rights to the World Series ($150,000).

But if that seemed like a roaring contrast to the pension plans of later years, to say nothing of the relations of later years, an even greater contrast in roles and relations was suggested in The New York Times, which reported:

"Feeling in a surprisingly magnanimous mood, the club owners also adopted a rule which provides a minimum World Series players' pool of $250,000 whenever the receipts do not come up to that amount. Last fall, the players of the Cardinals and Red Sox shared in only $212,000, with the result that the individual players of the losing Boston club received less money than the umpires. Under the new arrangement, a player on a winning team will be guaranteed approximately $5,000."

That's right: The Red Sox got less than the umpires, $2,140 a man, the smallest Series share in almost 30 years.

During an era of change, this was a year of gyrating change, the year Jackie Robinson made his debut, the year the players' pension appeared, the year Happy Chandler suspended Leo Durocher as manager of the Dodgers for the entire season. Durocher got the ax after a furious feud that embroiled Durocher and Rickey on one side against Larry MacPhail, the former boss of the Dodgers who now was running the Yankees.

The Dodgers and Yankees, who met in the World Series that fall, were also fined $2,000 apiece "because their officials engaged in a public controversy damaging to baseball." Charlie Dressen, who had left his job as a coach with the Dodgers to become a coach with the Yankees, was suspended 30 days because he had switched sides despite a "verbal agreement" to stay with the Dodgers. And, for the judicial *pièce de résistance*, Chandler fined Durocher's ghost-writer, Harold Parrott, the traveling secetary of the Dodgers. As far as anybody knew, it was the first time a ghost-writer had been disciplined in baseball. Parrott, a former baseball writer for the Brooklyn Eagle, was fined $500 because he had written "derogatory statements" in Durocher's column in the Eagle.

No wonder the World Series became a grudge match of historic dimensions. The Dodgers made a memorable comeback in the fourth game after Bill Bevens had pitched within one out of a no-hitter for the Yankees. But, with two down in the ninth and two Dodgers on base after walks, Cookie Lavagetto pinch-hit a double off the right-field wall, both runners crossed the plate and the Dodgers won, 3-2—on one hit.

The Yankees revived the next day and again took the lead in the Series. But the Dodgers once more made the melodramatic comeback and tied the match by winning the sixth game, 8-6, before a record crowd of 74,065 in Yankee Stadium.

There were 38 players in Game 6, none more famous than Joe DiMaggio, none more anonymous than Al Gionfriddo, who became famous on one play in the sixth inning with the Dodgers leading, 8-5.

"With two on," John Drebinger wrote, "DiMaggio sent a tremendous smash in the direction of the left-field bullpen, only to see Gionfriddo rob Jolting Joe of his greatest moment.

"Dashing almost blindly to the spot where he thought the ball would land and turning around at the last moment, the 25-year-old gardener, who had been merely tossed as an 'extra' into the deal that shipped Kirby Higbe to the Pirates earlier this year, leaned far over the bullpen railing and, with his gloved hand, collared the ball.

"It was a breathtaking catch for the third out of the inning. It stunned the proud Bombers and jarred even the usually imperturbable DiMaggio. Taking his position in center field with the start of the next inning, he was still walking inconsolably in circles, doubtless wondering whether he could believe his senses."

There were a couple of consolations. The Yankees finally squelched the Dodgers and their tricks and their heroics, and won the Series by taking the seventh game, 5-2. And one month later, DiMaggio was voted the American League's Most Valuable Player for the third (and last) time, and the election was even closer than the World Series. He got 202 points in the balloting by a committee of 24 baseball writers; Ted Williams of the Red Sox got 201. Williams had won the award the year before, but this was the third time he had missed winning it with exceptional credentials, which reinforced his feeling that popularity with the press counted in the polls.

In 1941, Williams went into the final day of the season with a batting average of .39955. The Red Sox were playing a doubleheader in Philadelphia against the Athletics, and in the first game he attacked the .400 mark and roared past it by getting three singles and his 37th home run. He could have sat out the second game and rested on his laurels, but he had no qualms about going for it, and he did. In the second game, he hit a double and single in three times up, went 6 for 8 on the day and rang down the curtain with a season's average of .4057 (.406). DiMaggio, who had hit in his 56 straight games that summer, was voted the league's Most Valuable Player.

In 1942, Williams once more won the batting title, but once more failed to be elected the Most Valuable Player. Second baseman Joe Gordon of the Yankees won that one. Gordon hit .322 with 18 home runs and knocked in 103 runs. Williams hit .356 with 36 home runs and knocked in 137 runs.

Now it was 1947, and Williams again was No. 2. He batted a cool .343 that season (again, best in the league), hit 32 home runs and knocked in 114 runs for the Red Sox, who finished third in the league. DiMaggio batted .315, hit 20 home runs and knocked in 97 runs for the Yankees, who won it all.

The bottom line apparently was that Williams was rated the best hitter of his time; DiMaggio, the best all-round player of his time. They were a pair of originals. DiMaggio, born in 1914, played a total of 13 big-league seasons, batted .325 and hit 361 home runs. He went into the Army when he was 28 and at the peak of his career, and missed three full seasons. Williams, born in 1918, wore a Boston uniform in 19 seasons, batted .344 and hit 521 home runs. He was phenomenal for sustained performance: Twice, he went on active military duty; twice, he returned and resumed his career. He missed three years in World War II in his mid-20s, then was recalled during the Korean War and missed most of two more seasons.

DiMaggio's final season was 1951, which also was Mickey Mantle's first season with the Yankees. But the most electrifying performance of that year, and maybe of any year, was given by Bobby Thomson of the Giants. He went to bat in the bottom of the ninth inning of the third and final playoff game for the National League pennant, with the Dodgers two outs from beating back a sensational homestretch challenge by their arch-rivals.

The challenge started on August 12, when the Giants were trailing Brooklyn by 13 games. (The day before, they had fallen 13½ games back when they lost a single game and the Dodgers won the opener of a double-header.) To add to the drama, they were managed by Leo Durocher, late of the Dodgers. Then, in one of the great stretch runs in history, the Giants won 16 straight and 37 of their last 44 regular-season games, caught the Dodgers at the wire and now had two outs to go before wasting all that storybook drama.

The Giants went into the ninth inning losing, 4-1, with Don Newcombe firing a four-hitter for Brooklyn. The crowd of 34,320 included several members of the Yankees, who had already won the American League pennant

Jackie Robinson (right), the man who shattered baseball's color barrier, meets his American League counterpart, Larry Doby, who was signed by Bill Veeck and the Cleveland Indians three months after Robinson's debut with the Dodgers in 1947.

and were waiting to see who would make it in the National. They included Yogi Berra, who made a commuter's command decision as the Giants went to bat in the bottom of the ninth: Head for home.

So, Yogi was heading for the exit when Alvin Dark opened the final inning by banking a hard single off the Gold Glove of Gil Hodges at first base. Don Mueller singled to right. Monte Irvin popped out, but Whitey Lockman rammed a double to left, Dark scored and Mueller raced to third, slid into the bag, severely injured his ankle and had to be carried off the field on a stretcher.

Now, the Giants had runners on second and third and trailed by two. Charlie Dressen, the manager of the Dodgers, decided that Newcombe had exhausted himself after pitching nearly 15 innings in the final two games of the regular season and 8⅓ innings in this one. He called to his bullpen for Ralph Branca, and then made another decision: First base was open, but they would pitch to Thomson and take their chances, rather than walk him and pitch to the rookie Willie Mays with the bases loaded.

Hodges crouched wide of first base. Jackie Robinson crouched wide of second base. Billy Cox guarded third, and Pee Wee Reese coiled to cover everything else. The regular catcher, Campanella, was out with an injury; his place was taken by Rube Walker, who signaled for the fastball.

Branca, who wore No. 13 on his uniform by choice, fired the fastball and Thomson took it. Strike one. Then he threw another fastball, inside and probably not a strike. But this time, Thomson took his rip. He lined the ball to left field, where it carried to the wall at the 315-foot marker, cleared the barrier and disappeared into the crowd in the lower grandstand for three runs and the pennant.

"The *next pitch*," Rube Walker said years later, wincing at the memory, "would have been the breaking ball."

"I never saw it," Yogi Berra said, wincing at his own waywardness at the moment of history. "But I heard it on the car radio. I left in the ninth—I wanted to beat the crowd."

Frontiers

16

Curt Flood, the man who dared challenge baseball's "reserve clause" in 1970, enters the United States Courthouse in New York with Marvin Miller, the man who later would revolutionize the business.

CHAPTER 16

The Edward W. Bok prize for distinguished service to the city of Philadelphia was awarded each year to artists, scientists, educators and philanthropists—until 1929, when it was bestowed on Connie Mack, the owner and manager of the local American League baseball team. Mr. Mack was honored for bringing the Athletics to the pinnacle of public success—first place. And he deserved a prize for that. The Athletics had not finished in first place since 1914, after which they achieved one of the most startling changes of fortune in baseball history: For the next seven years, they relentlessly held last place.

All this was brought to memory on October 18, 1950, when Mr. Mack again made banner headlines in Philadelphia and other cities. He was retiring after 50 years as the longest-running show in the business. He was born in 1862, just six months before the Battle of Gettysburg. He started playing ball as a catcher in 1880. He helped organize the American League in 1901. And now, after 67 years in professional baseball and precisely 50 as the manager of the Athletics, the team's *only* manager, he was retiring at the age of 87. No wonder they gave him the Bok Award in 1929.

On the day he stepped down, he stood tall and erect and elegant in dark suit and white shirt, and said: "It's a pleasure for me to be here today. I'm retiring from baseball, and this is the way I'm retiring—as manager of the baseball club. I'm not quitting because I'm too old, but because I think the people want me to."

When the longest-running show in town closes, things are happening. And they were happening in baseball after World War II with whirling changes of fortune, with new stars and new stadiums and new cities and even new frontiers. In the next generation, the world of the old game was made new.

April 1951: Mickey Mantle, the switch-hitting 19-year-old outfielder from Commerce, Okla., played his first game for Casey Stengel's Yankees. They played Washington in the Senators' home opener, which turned out to be an April 20 doubleheader after rain had postponed a single game scheduled four days earlier. President Truman, a lefthander wearing an infielder's glove on his right hand, threw out the first ball. Allie Reynolds caught it on the bounce. The Yankees lost both games.

May 1951: Willie Mays, the 20-year-old outfielder from Birmingham, Ala., played his first game for the Giants. The manager, Leo Durocher, had seen him play only once, but Willie had been hitting .477 for 35 games at Minneapolis and the Giants' trumpeted his debut by announcing: "No minor league player in a generation has created so great a stir." Tommy Heath, the manager at Minneapolis, advised Durocher on the telephone to keep

Mays in center field because it was the only position Willie had played and he could "cover it like a tent."

July 1951: Bob Feller pitched the third no-hitter of his career, and became the first pitcher in modern times to do it. Larry Corcoran and Cy Young pitched three in the primeval era, Corcoran throwing his no-hitters in the 1880s and Young pitching no-hit games in 1897, then in 1904 and again in 1908. Feller pitched one on opening day in 1940 against the Chicago White Sox, another in 1946 against the Yankees and this one against the Detroit Tigers. He won the first two by scores of 1-0, and this one by 2-1. It was his 11th victory of the season against two losses, and the 219th of his career, more than any other pitcher still active in the big leagues.

September 1951: Bill Klem, the Old Arbitrator, died in Miami at the age of 77. He was a National League umpire for 37 years, he called them in 18 World Series and he called them with more self-proclaimed command than any umpire who ever lived. He once got into a vicious argument with John McGraw after the Giants lost a tight one to the Cubs on a ball that struck the scoreboard right where the foul line would have extended—if it had been painted up the scoreboard. Klem called it fair and a home run. McGraw angrily ordered his park superintendent to check the scoreboard, where he found a dent about one inch on the "fair" side of the projected line. "Naturally it was fair," Klem roared back at McGraw. "I never missed one in my life."

September 1951: Ford C. Frick, the president of the National League, was elected commissioner of baseball to succeed Happy Chandler, who was denied re-election after six tempestuous years and many tempestuous decisions that cost him the votes he needed for re-election.

March 1953: The Boston Braves announced that they were moving to Milwaukee, which had a population of 871,047 in its metropolitan area and a "potential" of 1,500,000 Braves fans within a radius of 100 miles. In Boston the year before, the Braves played to a total audience of 281,278. Lou Perini, the construction man who owned the Braves, said it first: "I definitely feel that since the advent of television, Boston has become a one-team city."

Still, he needed a unanimous vote to switch cities, and The New York Times reported that he got it this way:

"One negative ballot would have brought rejection, but once Walter O'Malley of the Dodgers had moved for approval of the Braves' transfer and Horace Stoneham of the Giants had seconded the motion, every hand, including Perini's, went up in approval in the open vote."

The switch was the first in the big leagues in 50 years, but it was just the beginning. Six months later, the baseball map underwent its second change of the year when the American League unanimously approved the transfer of the St. Louis Browns to Baltimore.

The ringmaster of the Browns was Bill Veeck, the craggy and curly-haired former Marine who had dazzled them in Cleveland when he presented orchids to the ladies, hired baby-sitters for their children and fielded a smashing team that won the World Series in 1948 and drew a record attendance of 2,620,627. But in St. Louis, even the tricks didn't work—the midget pinch-hitter, the grandstand managers who voted on tactics during games (infield in, infield back, walk him, pitch to him). The Browns played out the string before 297,238 persons and headed for Baltimore and a new and soaring life as the Orioles.

But baseball geography, now being changed, was about to be revolutionized. And the revolution was staged by the man who had "moved for approval" of the Braves' switch from Boston and by the man who seconded the motion: Walter O'Malley and Horace Stoneham. Four and a half years after their motion carried, they combined on a blockbuster: The Dodgers left Brooklyn and crossed the continent to Los Angeles, the Giants left New York and also made it coast-to-coast to San Francisco.

When Stoneham announced on August 19, 1957, that the Giants were leaving the Polo Grounds, he said: "It's a tough wrench." Asked why they were going, he said: "Lack of attendance. We're sorry to disappoint the kids of New York, but we didn't see many of their parents out there at the Polo Grounds in recent years."

When O'Malley announced on October 8 that the Dodgers were indeed leaving Ebbets Field, as people had surmised, a rousing World Series was in full tilt between the Yankees and the Milwaukee Braves, one of those little ironies of history. The announcement was made because the deal had been confirmed the night before in Los Angeles: The City Council voted to put into law the city's agreement with the Dodgers (four of the 14 councilmen voted against it), and the statute was then signed by Mayor Norris Poulson, who had been courting the Dodgers for months.

Warren Giles, the president of the National League, tried to cast the best light on things when he said in a statement: "The National League has again demonstrated it is a professional organization. The transfer of the Giants and the Dodgers means that two more great municipalities are to have major league baseball without depriving another city of that privilege."

That was one way of putting it, but not the essential way. It was true that baseball was pushing its big-league frontiers from the Atlantic to the Pacific. But it was also true that New York was losing its two pioneering teams, and now ostensibly belonged to the phenomenally successful and thriving Yankees.

"In deserting Brooklyn for Los Angeles," The Times noted, "the Dodgers will leave an aching void in the Borough of Churches. Few baseball clubs have had greater identity with, and greater impact on, their communities than the Dodgers have had on Brooklyn.

"Brooklyn basically has always been the city's dormitory, and for 60-odd years its major league ball club has been its principal claim to public attention. It is peculiarly expressive of the Dodger fan's fierce devotion that he could scream from the Ebbets Field stands—and mean it—'Ya bums, ya,' without surrendering one iota of loyalty."

The Yankees had New York for their own for four years, and then the National League got back into town with a new team, the Mets, who soon seemed to be ancestral cousins of the Dodgers in their zany time. The league also extended its frontiers into the Southwest, adding Houston and growing to 10 clubs as the majors reached into Texas for the first time. The two expansion franchises opened business in 1962, but the American League beat them to the map-changing punch in 1961 by adding the Minneapolis-St. Paul area and Los Angeles.

There was no holding the ranks now. In 1969, the National League threw another blockbuster when it crossed the Canadian border and added Montreal, and then reached diagonally across the continent and added San Diego. The American League, meanwhile, placed expansion teams in Seattle and Kansas City (where the new team replaced the Athletics, who had leapfrogged from Philadelphia to Kansas City to Oakland).

One year later, the Seattle club moved to Milwaukee, which had been vacated in 1966 by the Braves, who took yet another history-making turn by switching to Atlanta and bringing the big leagues to the Deep South for the first time. Then, in 1972, the Washington Senators (formed as an expansion team when the old Washington club left for Minnesota in '61) moved to Texas and pitched camp in Arlington. And, in 1977, the American League expanded for the third time by adding Toronto and Seattle (again), and now it had 14 clubs while the National League had 12.

The most remarkable of all these new baseball teams was probably the New York Mets, at least in terms of going from rags to riches. They sprang from the soil in 1962 with no hope of success, but with Casey Stengel blowing the horn with nonstop fury, and inviting everybody: "Yes, sir, come see my amazin' Mets, which in some cases have played only semipro ball."

The Mets responded nobly. They were scheduled to open play on April 10, 1962, in St. Louis, but the game was rained out. And that was probably their finest hour. The next night it didn't rain, and they regretted it. Stan Musial, who was 41 and the nearest thing in age to Stengel on either team, went 3 for 3 for the Cardinals, who pounded the Mets, 11-4. Roger Craig, the first starting pitcher for the New York club, committed a balk that contributed to St. Louis' two-run first inning, and a whole new concept in losing ball games was unfolding.

The Mets, in fact, lost the first nine games they played, and Stengel began to wonder. "This sets up the possibility," he said, "of losing 162 games, which would probably be a record in the National League, at least."

Well, they didn't lose 162, but they did lose 120 that year and 111 the next year and 109 the year after that. In their first seven summers, they finished in last place five times and next-to-last twice. But then, in one spectacular and unthinkable leap forward, in the summer of 1969 when men first walked on the moon, the men of the Mets rose from ninth place to first. And, as the clowns and ragamuffins of the business, 100-to-1 longshots manned by a few veterans seemingly miscast and by a cluster of young pitchers supposedly mismatched, they strong-armed their way to 100 victories, won the pennant and then wiped out the highly favored Baltimore Orioles in five games in the World Series.

The way they got there was stunning enough. They were trailing the Chicago Cubs by 9½ games on August 13, then won 38 of their next 49 games and captured the Eastern Division championship of the National League by eight games. It was the first year that the major leagues split themselves into Eastern and Western Divisions, with playoffs in each league to decide the pennant. But the Mets defied format along with everything else, and roared.

Tom Seaver, their third-year pitching star, won 25 games, including 10 straight at the end of the season, and was not beaten after August 5. Left-hander Jerry Koosman, pitching his second full season in the majors, won 17 games, including eight out of nine at the end, and was not beaten in the last month of the season.

Frank Sullivan, the humorist and bard of Saratoga Springs, was moved to rhapsody, to wit:

> Heroic kids! Embattled youth!
> The town regards you with feelings couth
> Come to our arms, you beamish boys
> The while we greet you with joyful noise
> As, filled with festive joie de vivre
> We drink to the prowess of Tom Seaver.

Joe DiMaggio, the old Yankee, who had thrown out the first ball of the last Series game, said: "I never saw anything like it."

"I never saw any team play the way this team played," said Yogi Berra, who saw it all from the Mets' first-base coaching box after 18 years as a Yankee.

"It was the greatest collective victory by any team in sports," said Tom Seaver.

"It was a colossal thing that they did," said Gil Hodges, the old Dodger who now was manager of the Mets. "These young men showed that you can realize the most impossible dream of all."

★   ★   ★

Judge Irving Ben Cooper called the case to trial at 10 o'clock in the morning on May 19, 1970, in the United States Courthouse on Foley Square in lower Manhattan. On the docket, it was listed as: "70 Civil 202: Curtis C. Flood, plaintiff, vs. Bowie K. Kuhn, individually and as commissioner of baseball, et al, defendants."

The *et al*, it developed, included all the brass and all the corporations of the superstructure of the major leagues. And the legal minds going to bat for such a lineup seemed just as imposing.

For Curt Flood, the 32-year-old outfielder who was challenging the entire *modus operandi* of the national pastime on that morning in May: The firm of Paul, Weiss, Goldberg, Rifkind, Wharton & Garrison, Esqs., of 345 Park Avenue, plus Allan H. Zerman of Clayton, Mo. The team was headed by Arthur J. Goldberg, former Secretary of Labor, former ambassador to the United Nations, former justice of the United States Supreme Court.

For Bowie Kuhn, himself a Wall Street lawyer, and only 15 months into his job as commissioner of baseball, the team was built around Donovan Leisure Newton & Irvine, Esqs., of 2 Wall Street, plus Arnold & Porter, Esqs., of Washington, D.C.

For Joe Cronin, the old shortstop, now the president of the American League: Baker, Hostetler & Patterson, Esqs., of Cleveland. And "for all defendants except Bowie K. Kuhn," the legal talent was supplied by Willkie Farr & Gallagher, Esqs., of 1 Chase Manhattan Plaza, New York, which took care of the defense of *et al*.

In the face of this staggering array of legal brains, Judge Cooper lost none of his own flair as he took the bench to umpire the long-awaited challenge to the business of baseball and, by extension, of most professional sports. The defendant New York Yankees were preparing to play the defendant Baltimore Orioles uptown that night, and the defendant St. Louis Cardinals, who had touched off the whole thing by trading Flood to the defendant Philadelphia Phillies, were due in the Astrodome to play the defendant Houston Astros.

But, for everybody else in the business, this was the whole ball game right here in Irving Ben Cooper's courtroom.

Judge Cooper: Call the first witness.

Mr. Goldberg: Mr. Curtis Flood, Your Honor. What is your occupation, Mr. Flood?

Mr. Flood: I am a professional baseball player. I play center field.

Q.—And when did you begin to play baseball?

A.—I started at age 9, of course, and I played Little League ball, sandlot ball, American Legion ball right into high school.

Q.—When did you graduate from high school?

A.—In 1968—1958, excuse me.

Q.—When did you first begin to play professional baseball?

A.—That was in 1958.

Q.—And how old were you when you signed your professional baseball contract, the first that you signed?

A.—I was 18.

Q.—And with whom did you sign your first contract?

A.—I signed with the Cincinnati Reds.

Q.—Now, you were presented with a contract at that time for signature? Did you read it?

A.—Well, not really. I knew very little about contracts and the provisions of them.

Q.—What salary did you sign for?

A.—It was $4,000.

Q.—Did that result from negotiation with the Cincinnati Redlegs?

A.—Well, not really. There was a bonus rule at the time where if you received more than $4,000 there was sort of a penalty involved. You would have to stay on the roster of the parent club for at least one year. I forget the exact years. And $4,000 was the limit that I could sign for.

Q.—Now will you tell His Honor, Judge Cooper, your experience in your first year of professional baseball?

A.—Well, of course, I was with the Reds at the time, and they sent my contract on an option to High Point, N.C., where I played a full season—this was Class B—with the High Point club—in the Carolina League.

Q.—And when you were sent down to the High Point team, were you consulted about that transfer to this Class B team?

A.—No, sir, I was not.

Q.—Will you tell His Honor and others, the counsel, what type of year did you have in baseball terms?

A.—Well, I think I had a very good year. I hit .340, I led the league in everything except home runs that year. I think I hit 30 home runs that year as well.

Q.—That isn't bad, is it?

A.—That is a very good year.

Q.—Now, would you explain your living accommodations in High Point. How did you live, where did you live, how did you conduct your business activity in baseball during the year?

A.—Well, this is very difficult. Back in those days, they were just integrating all the high schools in Carolina and it was particularly bad being a black ball player in Carolina. Of course, we lived separately. We were housed and we ate separately. We would go on a road trip and there would be times when we would stop, oh, halfway, for dinner, we would get off the bus and, of course, the white fellows would get off the bus and go into a restaurant and eat a nice meal, and we would have to go around to the back and get our meals there.

Mr. Flood: [at the end of the 1957 season] I talked to the general manager of the Reds and he asked me if I wanted to go to South America and learn to play the infield, and of course when they ask you to do something like that you are inclined to do it; and I did exactly that. I went to Venezuela to learn how to play the infield and, of course, this is where I learned my trade.

Mr. Goldberg: What kind of infielder were you?

A.—Terrible.

Q.—That is what you learned from your experience in playing in Venezuela?

A.—That I was an outfielder, yes.

Q.—Now, what happened to you then after you had the Venezuelan experience with respect to the future of your professional baseball career? Did you get notice as to what your future career and disposition would be?

A.—Well, of course, I was down there learning how to play the infield for the Reds and I received a telegram stating that I had been traded to the St. Louis Cardinals, and this was rather a surprising thing; after all, I had gone all the way to South America to learn how to play the infield for them, and to find out you are traded is rather shocking.

Q.—Were you consulted?

A.—No, sir.

Q.—And how much were you paid in 1958 (with the Cardinals)?

A.—I undoubtedly made the minimum salary then, which was approximately seven thousand.

Q.—[in 1959, 1960 and 1961] you made between $7,000 and $15,000 during those years? Do you recall the circumstances under which your salary was fixed?

A.—I would go into the general manager's office knowing full well I couldn't play anyplace else in the world and "negotiate" for a better contract. Well, we would negotiate across his desk. I would state my statistics— that I hit a certain amount and I had so many RBIs, I had "X" amount of home runs, and I thought this merited a raise in salary.

Mark F. Hughes [of defense counsel]: The record indicates that in 1961 Mr. Flood's salary was $12,500 with a bonus of $1,000 for signing his contract; in 1962 his salary was $16,000; in 1963 his salary was $17,000; in 1964, $23,000; 1965, $35,000; 1966, $45,000; 1967, $50,000; 1968, $72,000; 1969, $90,000.

Q.—Are you prepared to sign a contract with Philadelphia for $90,000 to play?

A.—No, I'm not.

Q.—Are you ready and eager to play baseball now?

A.—Yes.

Q.—With whom do you want to play?

A.—The team that makes me the best offer.

★　　　★　　　★

The issue in the trial was the "reserve clause" in baseball contracts, which reserved the player's services to his team from one year to the next until he was traded or released, or retired. And the issue was argued forcefully by two men who had just come into public prominence as the chief spokesmen and strategists for the club owners and the players and who would remain the chief movers for the next 15 years of historic change in baseball and all professional sports.

The owners' man was Bowie K. Kuhn, a tall and scrubbed Princeton graduate whose New York law firm had represented the National League for more than 30 years. Kuhn was elected commissioner of baseball early in 1969 when the two leagues remained deadlocked over Michael Burke, the stylish and even dashing president of the Yankees, and Charles (Chub) Feeney, the engaging vice president of the Giants and a longtime baseball man as a member of the Stoneham family.

Baseball needed a new commissioner because the club owners had evidently made a gigantic mistake when Ford Frick retired at the end of 1965 after 14 years in the job. To replace him, the owners looked for a man who could lead them through the complex and difficult years that seemed to be looming, and preferably a man with Washington connections and clout who could protect the game against any fundamental legal changes by Congress. They were right about the complex years to come, but wrong about Congress: The fundamental changes were imposed by the federal courts. And they were exceedingly wrong about the man they picked to guide them.

He was a retired Air Force lieutenant general, William Dole Eckert, who had no previous ties with baseball and very little knowledge about it. He tried hard to learn the job, but was so shy of the target that people suspected he had been elected in a case of mistaken identity. Whatever the source of the confusion, he was dismissed after three years and was paid for all seven of his term, and was eventually succeeded by Kuhn.

The players' man was Marvin Miller, an economist with the United Steelworkers union who had been picked as executive director of the Major League Baseball Players' Association at about the same time. He was razor-sharp in debate and far-seeing in range with a piercing view of what the players needed and a clear sense of how to get it.

They met face to face in the Curt Flood trial, and Miller got right to the point when he testified.

Mr. Miller: Paragraph 10 (a) of the Uniform Player's Contract is the one commonly referred to as the reserve clause. It actually is an option clause rather than a reserve clause. It provides that the club may tender a contract to the player on or before January 15th.

It provides that if there is no agreement between the player and his club by March first next succeeding that January 15th, then the club may unilaterally renew last year's contract simply by advisng the player with a notice in writing within 10 days of March first. The club may place any salary figure it pleases in that contract renewal, except that it may not cut the player's salary by more than 20 percent below the prior year.

Now, there is another rule which states that a player will not be allowed to play in a regular championship season unless he has signed a contract for the current year. This means literally that a player not in agreement with the terms offered him receives a notice within 10 days of

March first advising him that he is again under contract under a one-year renewal and if he wants to play he must put his signature to that document, which in effect gives another renewal right for the following year to the club to do the same thing.

So that into perpetuity, as long as the club is interested in exercising this option, the player has no say whatsoever in terms of what conditions he plays under, always bearing in mind he has the one alternative: He may decide to find a different way to make a living.

Mr. Kuhn (testifying on the competition faced by baseball as a business): Baseball competes with a host of activities in the entertainment field. To enumerate some of these, it competes to a degree with other professional sports, notably professional hockey, professional basketball, professional football and to some extent professional soccer.

It competes, however, outside of the sports field with a great many other types of activity, such as horse racing, both flat and harness; the movie industry; all forms of outdoor recreation, which of course are at their peak during the warm months when baseball is played. This would be golf and tennis and camping and fishing, and the use of automobiles. The vast expansion of our highway systems and our automobile supply has put America on the roads, and not necessarily to ball parks.

★　　　★　　　★

Ten weeks after the trial, Judge Cooper issued his decision. He noted that Jackie Robinson had testified that he favored modification but not elimination of the reserve clause and that Hank Greenberg had predicted chaos if the system were changed abruptly, and he recalled that baseball had been granted an exemption from the antitrust laws half a century earlier by Justice Oliver Wendell Holmes, no less. And he concluded:

"Existing and, as we see it, controlling law renders unnecessary any determination as to the fairness or reasonableness of this reserve system. We are bound by the law as we find it and by our obligation to 'call it as we see it.'"

Curt Flood, asserting his own obligation to call it as we see it, appealed to the higher courts. But on June 19, 1972, the Supreme Court by a 5-to-3 vote affirmed that baseball (and only baseball) remained exempt from the antitrust laws. But it conceded that the exemption was an "aberration," and suggested that Congress resolve the "anomaly."

But, before Congress resolved anything, somebody else did. And, in fact, the temper of the times gave the baseball club owners little comfort despite their apparent victory over Curt Flood. Only two months before the Supreme Court's ruling, the players staged a 13-day strike, the first general strike in baseball history. It delayed the start of the season and wiped out 86 games, and that happened 18 months after the umpires had refused to work the opening games of the 1970 playoffs. Times were changing.

In March 1973, another strike was narrowly averted when the owners agreed to submit salary disputes to arbitration. They also agreed that any player with 10 years of seniority, the last five with the same team, could not be traded without his consent. Later in the year, Ron Santo of the Chicago Cubs vetoed a trade to the California Angels. Times were definitely changing.

In 1975, the deluge. Two established pitchers, Andy Messersmith of the Los Angeles Dodgers and Dave McNally of the Montreal Expos, refused to sign their contracts. Both were renewed under the reserve clause by their teams. The Expos gave McNally a $10,000 raise that brought his contract to $125,000, and he pitched until June 8, when he quit and went home to Billings, Mont. The Dodgers gave Messersmith a $25,000 raise and renewed his contract at $115,000, and he pitched the entire season. He won 19 games, lost 14 and then made baseball history after the season ended.

McNally did not intend to be a pioneer in toppling the legal foundations of baseball contracts. He said after he had gone home to become a partner in an automoblie agency: "It got to the point where I almost was stealing money. I was being paid quite a bit. I knew what my job was supposed to be, but I wasn't even coming close to doing it."

But on October 7, Messersmith did become a pioneer. On his behalf, the Players Association filed a grievance contending that his "renewal year" had been completed and that he therefore no longer had any relationship with the Dodgers and was "free to negotiate with any of the 24 clubs with respect to his services for 1976." Two days later, a companion grievance was filed for McNally.

"I gave it a lot of thought," Messersmith said. "I am not a martyr, but I think it had to be done. I didn't do it necessarily for myself because I'm making a lot of money. I don't want everyone to think, 'Well, here's a guy in involuntary servitude at $115,000 a year.' That's a lot of bull and I know it."

The baseball clubs quickly replied that the grievances were not the sort that could be submitted to arbitration, and added: "It is our position that both players remain properly reserved by their respective clubs." And Ewing Kauffman, owner of the Kansas City Royals, filed a lawsuit a few days later asking for an injunction. He said that he had paid more than $6 million for his club, and added: "Should the reserve system become the subject of arbitration, the investment I have made could be substantially jeopardized."

"They're trying to screw the players," Marvin Miller said. "The Basic Agreement provides for rapid adjudication of all grievances, but they're trying to cancel the arbitration hearings until they get a final and unappealable decision in the courts. That would take years."

The day of decision was December 23, 1975, and the man of decision was Peter Seitz, a 70-year-old lawyer with 40 years in the arbitration business. He ruled that the two players were free, and said: "I'm not a new

Abraham Lincoln freeing the slaves. I wasn't striking a blow at the reserve clause. This decision does not destroy baseball. My own feeling is that the problems of the reserve system ought to be worked out by the parties in collective bargaining."

Six weeks later, Federal Judge John W. Oliver in Kansas City upheld Seitz, and his authority to arbitrate the issue, and even said in a footnote that he had "discharged his duties with the highest sense of fidelity, intelligence and responsibility." The reserve clause was shot down.

Ironically, Seitz by then was no longer the baseball arbitrator. As soon as his ruling had been issued, he was "terminated" as the arbitrator by the club owners. Then, reflecting on his own fate, the man who toppled the system said:

"Every arbitrator is terminated. It's part of the professional mortality. It's expected because somebody wins and somebody loses. But I've never been terminated this way—two minutes after I signed the order, I'm gone."

★   ★   ★

Ten years later, Mike Schmidt of the Philadelphia Phillies, Jim Rice of the Boston Red Sox, Eddie Murray of the Baltimore Orioles and George Foster of the New York Mets were making more than $2 million a year. Three dozen other players were making between $1 million and $2 million. And the *average* salary in the big leagues had climbed past $300,000.

Players and their agents aimed for "the big contract" with such success that one big contract competed with every other for creative rewards. Omar Moreno at one point was guaranteed $214.29 every time he went to bat, and it was merely a bonus within his five-year, $3.5 million contract. Bob Horner of the Atlanta Braves, a home run hitter with a waistline as well as a $5.1 million, four-year contract, was guaranteed $7,692.31 on each of the 13 Fridays the team played at home—if he weighed in at 215 pounds or less. Ozzie Smith of the St. Louis Cardinals, an acrobatic shortstop with a generally weak bat, signed in 1983 for three years at $3.6 million plus a free membership in the stadium club restaurant. And, early in 1985, he signed again for $2 million a year, which made the club membership somewhat moot.

Jim Rice signed a four-year extension with the Red Sox early in 1985, and it was so complicated that nobody knew for sure how much it was worth. For four years, either $8.6 million or $9.8 million, depending on how interest rates and other variables were computed.

It started with a signing bonus of $3.2 million (of which $1.85 million was deferred without interest, to be paid from 1990 to 1999 at $185,000 a year). It provided annual salaries of $1.5 million in 1986, and then raises of $100,000 a year for the next three years. And, if the Red Sox wanted to keep him in 1990, they would have to pay him $2.3 million. Along the way, incentives: $250,000 if he was voted the league's Most Valuable Player; $200,000 if he finished *second* in the voting; $100,000 if he was voted "most valuable" in the league's Championship Series or in the World Series, and $25,000 if he was voted to the All-Star team, which, for a man of the ability to command such a contract, seemed like a foregone conclusion in the first place.

When salary disputes were submitted to arbitration, they weren't in this class, of course, but they were no longer in the lower class, either. Fernando Valenzuela, the Mexican pitching prodigy of the Dodgers, became the first player to win $1 million from an arbitrator (who made $475 a day for hearing cases). Tim Raines of the Expos then won $1.2 million from the arbitrator in 1985 after turning down the club's offer of $1 million. Raines' lawyer pointed out that Raines got on base about 40 percent of the time, stole nearly nine bases every 10 times he tried and scored almost 20 percent of his team's runs. The arbitrator agreed.

But everything was going up, along with the price of talent. Attendance in the 24-team major leagues was 29,789,913 in 1975, the year Peter Seitz freed the serfs. In 1985, the 26 big-league clubs totaled 46,838,819.

The price of a ball club reached a record when Nelson Doubleday's publishing company bought the Mets in 1980 for $21.1 million from the family of Joan Whitney Payson. Three years later, John Fetzer sold the Detroit Tigers to Tom Monaghan for close to $50 million. And that was only 10 years after Monaghan had started selling pizza in a little shop in Michigan.

The value of television time shot up, too, when the clubs negotiated a six-year deal with the American Broadcasting Company and the National Broadcasting Company. It was worth a total of $1.125 billion for air rights from 1984 through 1989. For the teams, it meant a significant jump in TV revenue. The year before the new contract was signed, each team got $1.9 million from the TV pool; under the new contract, each team figured to average $7 million a year.

Construction also had been booming for a quarter of a century as teams switched cities and cities built stadiums. It was a boom that began in 1960 when San Francisco paid $15 million to build Candlestick Park, a rugged, remote and wind-swept ball park that grew old fast. Two years later, the Los Angeles Dodgers, who played their first four West Coast seasons in the Memorial Coliseum, paid $15 million for Dodger Stadium, and struck gold.

The National League added Shea Stadium in New York in 1964, the Astrodome in Houston in 1965 (with the first roof in the big leagues), Atlanta Stadium in 1966 and Busch Memorial Stadium in St. Louis the same year, San Diego-Jack Murphy Stadium in 1969, Riverfront Stadium in Cincinnati and Three Rivers Stadium in Pittsburgh in 1970 and Veterans Stadium in Philadelphia in 1971. The American League, meanwhile, was adding Metropolitan Stadium in Bloomington, Minn. (and replaced it 21 years later with the Hubert H. Humphrey Metrodome in Minneapolis), and then opened Robert F. Kennedy Stadium in Washington in 1962, Anaheim Stadium in

California in 1966, the Oakland-Alameda County Coliseum in 1968 and Kansas City's Royals Stadium in 1973.

Even after that spasm of about a dozen years, new ball parks were appearing. The Montreal Expos moved out of quaint little Jarry Park and into Olympic Stadium (site of the 1976 Olympic Games) in 1977, and the Seattle Mariners arrived on the scene in '77 with a roof over their heads inside the Kingdome.

The only thing wrong with the astronomical economics of baseball, the club owners said in 1985, was that it raised everything to record levels—including losses.

For Exhibit A, they offered the season of 1981, when the players went on strike for 50 days and the industry suffered its longest shutdown. The central issue was the free-agent system—specifically, how to compensate teams that lost players as free agents, and how to compensate them without inhibiting the movement of free agents. Before the issue was settled, 712 games were canceled, the 650 players lost $28 million in pay (Dave Winfield of the Yankees lost $7,770 a day) and the 26 teams dropped $116 million in revenue, although they collected about $50 million in strike insurance.

For Exhibit B, they submitted a list of financial reverses to the players during the next round of labor disputes in 1985, when the players went on strike for two days. The owners said that the clubs had lost $92,094,948 in 1982, the year after the long strike, and that the teams had lost $66.6 million in 1983. And, in fact, they went on, they collectively showed a profit only once in nine years: $4,586 in 1978.

They did not have to remind the players that the new economics had prompted the owners to search for new solutions and even new problem-solvers, and that the most dramatic result of that was the end of Bowie Kuhn's reign as commissioner. His re-election to a third seven-year term had been blocked by a minority of five National League owners on November 1, 1982, and baseball operated in a kind of twilight zone for nearly two years while Kuhn fought to stay, then agreed to stay when no successor emerged and finally agreed not to stay when the search committee produced Peter V. Ueberroth, who had just demonstrated his flair for economics as president of the Los Angeles Olympic Organizing Committee.

The 1984 Olympic Games became a business *tour de force*, returned high profit where past Olympics had returned mostly deficits and political anger and propelled Ueberroth onto the national scene as the sixth commissioner of baseball. And Ueberroth seemed perfectly cast for the role of business redeemer, even if his association with baseball seemed slight: He graduated from San Jose State University with a degree in business, he started a small travel agency with captial of $5,000 and one employee and he developed it into a giant, the second largest travel business in North America with 1,500 employees and $300 million in annual revenues. Like the country boy who wants to grow up to hit home runs in the big leagues,

Ueberroth in his way cut a slice of the American dream, too.

He also reflected the public's passion for business, and the club owners' desperation for better business, just as Bowie Kuhn in 1969 had reflected their apparent need for legal and political power. And when Ueberroth took over the office on October 1, 1984, he found that baseball was reflecting all sorts of public passion, good and bad, the need for dramatic entertainment, the drive for big bucks.

He also found that baseball was reflecting the curse of cocaine in life, and acknowledged that the danger was acute. Four members of the 1983 Kansas City Royals already had served time in federal prison after an investigation into drug trafficking in the Kansas City area: Willie Wilson, Willie Aikens, Jerry Martin and Vida Blue. They also were suspended for part of the 1984 season by Kuhn (who kept Blue out the entire season), and Steve Howe of the Los Angeles Dodgers was suspended for all of '84 after several lapses caused by the use of drugs.

Then, in the summer of 1985, many more players were named in a federal court trial in Pittsburgh, and the lid was blown off, so to speak. Nineteen players were named in testimony, including several stars, and seven of them appeared as witnesses under grants of immunity in the trial of a Philadelphia caterer who was sentenced to four to 12 years in federal prison for selling cocaine to players.

Some sadly lurid details were added outside court by some of the players, including Tim Raines, who remembered that in the past he sometimes had slid into third base head-first on his chest—to keep from breaking the vial of cocaine he had stashed in his pants pocket before the game or between innings.

★   ★   ★

Life may imitate art, or maybe art imitates life. But, to most of those 46,000,000 or so persons who pay their way into major league ball parks each year, and to the hundreds of millions who watch games in Mexico, Latin America, Japan, Italy and other countries each year, with a World Series and a Caribbean World Series and a Japan Series—to all of those, baseball absolutely has little to do with new concrete stadiums, new financial losses or even new commissioners. But it has everything to do with players on the field, with glove and bat and helmet, "between the lines," as they say. It has everything to do with performers and performances.

It is Vic Wertz whaling the ball in the 1954 World Series, and Willie Mays chasing the ball and catching it 460 feet from home plate in the Polo Grounds, a feat that John Drebinger called "one of his most amazing catches" and that he described this way in The New York Times: "Traveling on the wings of the wind, Willie caught the ball directly in front of the green boarding facing the right-center bleachers and with his back still to the diamond."

It is Don Larsen pitching to 27 Brooklyn batters in Game 5 of the 1956 Series, and getting them all out. The Yankees got only five hits off Sal Maglie, but one of them was a home run by Mickey Mantle, and they won the game, 2-0. It was the first perfect game in 34 years in the big leagues, and the first ever in the World Series, and it was pitched by a 27-year-old fun-loving righthander who had distinguished himself in spring training by wrapping his car around a tree just before dawn. "The only thing he fears," Jimmie Dykes said, "is sleep."

To the crowds, baseball is a wiry little lefthander named Harvey Haddix who did even better than that. On May 26, 1959, he pitched perfect ball for the Pittsburgh Pirates for 12 innings—he retired 36 Milwaukee Braves in a row, including Eddie Mathews four times and Henry Aaron four times. Then, in the 13th inning of the scoreless game, Felix Mantilla was safe on a low throw by Don Hoak, the Pirates' third baseman. Mathews bunted him to second, and Aaron was walked intentionally. Up came Joe Adcock, and United Press International reported:

"Then Adcock connected. The hit barely cleared the right-center-field fence, and the big first baseman hesitated a moment before starting around the bases. Then two boys crawled under the barricade and snatched the ball.

"Adcock at first was credited with a home run, and the final score was announced as 3-0. But then he was declared out for passing Aaron between second and third base, and his home run became a double. The jubilant Aaron, who had cut across the diamond without touching third, was sent back by his mates to touch third and then home."

The umpires said the true score was 2-0, and that's baseball, too—passing the next guy between second and third, or cutting across the infield. Actually, a later ruling made the score *1-0:* Since the home run was nullified, only the number of runs sufficient to win the game were allowed. And that's baseball, too.

It is also 39-year-old Stan Musial appearing in his 19th All-Star Game, and pinch-hitting a home run. And it is Bill Mazeroski ending a titanic struggle with a ninth-inning home run that won the 1960 World Series for the Pittsburgh Pirates over the Yankees, who hit .338 and scored 55 runs while the Pirates hit .256 and scored 27 runs in the seven games.

It is the Yankees' Roger Maris hitting his 61st home run in the 162nd and final game of the 1961 season. He hit it in Yankee Stadium in his second time at bat against Tracy Stallard of Boston, and it was the only run scored in the game. Sticklers, including Commissioner Frick, noted that Babe Ruth hit his 60 home runs in a 154-game season in 1927. But, incredibly, they went to the plate almost the same number of times, walks and all: 698 for Maris, 692 for Ruth.

It is Sandy Koufax pitching no-hit games in four consecutive years, and striking out 300 or more batters three times in four seasons, and winning 97 games in four virtuoso years with consecutive earned-run averages of 1.88, then 1.74, then 2.04 and 1.73. He pitched the Dodgers to three pennants in four years, then retired in 1966 at the age of 31 with arthritis in his left elbow.

It is the San Francisco Giants taking the field with three outfielders named Alou: the brothers Felipe, Matty and Jesus. And Tom Seaver striking out 19 San Diego Padres one afternoon in 1970, including the last 10 Padre batters in the game. And Johnny Bench, Pete Rose, Tony Perez, Joe Morgan, George Foster and the Big Red Machine, the team that won four National League pennants in the 1970s. And Reggie Jackson, Joe Rudi, Sal Bando, Vida Blue and the rest of the sassy but superior Oakland A's, the team that won three straight World Series in the '70s.

It is Roberto Clemente getting his 3,000th hit in his final start of the 1972 season, then kissing his wife Vera goodbye at the San Juan airport on New Year's Eve with a plane-load of relief supplies for the earthquake-torn people of Nicaragua, and disappearing into the ocean with the plane shortly after takeoff. He was 38 years old.

To the crowds, baseball is Henry Aaron hitting the 714th home run of his big-league career in the opening game of the 1974 season and then, in his third game, hitting the 715th and breaking the record set by Ruth—and skyrockets arched over Atlanta Stadium as the 40-year-old man from Mobile, who once played for the Indianapolis Clowns of the old Negro leagues, ran around the bases in the rain and touched home plate for the 2,064th time in a major league career that had begun 20 years earlier.

The game is the modern wave of 300-game winners: Warren Spahn, Early Wynn, Steve Carlton, Gaylord Perry, Tom Seaver and Phil Niekro. And Niekro was 46 years old when he made it on the final day of the 1985 season. Of course, Hoyt Wilhelm pitched in the majors until he was almost 49, and Satchal Paige came back one more time and winged it for three scoreless innings when he was 59.

It is the modern wave of 3,000-hit men: Henry Aaron, Stan Musial, Carl Yastrzemski, Willie Mays, Lou Brock, Al Kaline, Roberto Clemente, Rod Carew—and Pete Rose. And the highly select and absolutely exclusive club of the 4,000-hit men: Peter Edward Rose, who caught Cobb on September 8, 1985, at Chicago's Wrigley Field and passed him on the night of September 11 in Cincinnati's Riverfront Stadium. He was 44 years old now, and the playing manager of the Reds, and a throng of 47,237 stood and roared at Riverfront as he went to bat in the first inning against Eric Show of the San Diego Padres, crouched in his lefthanded stance with his red helmet gleaming and his eyes fixed on Show, and on the count of two balls and one strike he lined a single into left-center. Hit No. 4,192. And he got it on a field about 10 miles from the sandlots where he had started playing baseball as a boy.

After the game, Pete Rose went back to home plate for a celebration that included a phone call from the White House that was carried to the crowd on the stadium's public-address system. This was not just a sign of the times but a symbol of the times, the way Dwight Gooden became the national symbol of the strikeout in 1984 as a rookie with the Mets at 19. This was the presidential telephone call, made at once to the nation's hero by the nation's leader to reflect the nation's mood. And Ronald Reagan told Pete Rose that he had set "the most enduring record in sports history."

"Thank you, Mr. President, for taking time from your busy schedule," Rose replied. "And you missed a good ball game."

About seven weeks later, the White House was calling again, and Ronald Reagan was reflecting the nation's mood again. The 82nd World Series had just ended, and it was enough to give the nation's mood a good jolt: The Kansas City Royals, down by three games to one to the Toronto Blue Jays in the American League playoff, had come back to win the pennant. And, down by three games to one to the favored St. Louis Cardinals, they had come from far back to win the World Series.

Not only that, but the Cardinals, who had come within three outs of winning the Series the night before, got blown out of the final game by 11-0 in a surge of sulking and bitterness.

Whitey Herzog, the manager of the Cardinals, who had been thrown out of the game by the home-plate umpire at the depth of the arguing, dressed into his street clothes and subsided after the game had been ended and the show had been lost. The White House was on the line, congratulating the winners and consoling the losers. And Herzog got right to the point.

"I'm sorry we didn't put on a better show," the manager of the Cardinals told the President of the United States. "We kind of stunk up the joint tonight."

Then he thanked the President for calling and hung up the phone. And Whitey Herzog, often crusty and sometimes curt and not easily impressed by anything, suddenly seemed amazed that the national mood had reached into his locker room after the main event of the national pastime.

"It's not every day you get beat, 11 to nothing," he said, marveling at it all, "and can talk to the President of the United States."

The 4,200-hit man, Pete Rose, is the ultimate baseball player. . . . Young Dwight Gooden gives a vision of things to come.

EPILOGUE

When Connie Mack was 11 years old in 1873, he worked 12 hours a day in a cotton mill, and he observed later: "It didn't seem so bad. Besides, we got an hour for lunch."

When he grew to his full height of 6 feet, 1 inch and to his full weight of 150 pounds, he rather resembled a dignified ostrich in a high stiff collar. By then, he was the manager of the Milwaukee baseball team, it was the decade of the Nineties and he was still working 12 hours a day.

"I signed players," he remembered, "made the trades, arranged our railroad transportation, found hotels for the players and paid all the bills."

Half a century later, by now the owner and manager of the Philadelphia Athletics, Mack was still paying all the bills—out of his own pocket. Even after his 1931 team won 107 of its 152 games, he discovered that the one-man operation in sports was growing risky. Two years later, the Depression convinced him.

"We didn't have a man under $10,000 on the payroll," he said, "and we operated in an industrial city where the Depression hit hard."

It hit hard, all right. The country lost 5,000 banks, 12,000,000 jobs and $50,000,000,000 in stocks. So Mack, who had just spent $700,000 renovating his ball park, started to peddle talent to pay the bills. Baseball, you might say, was his agony and his ecstasy.

Ronald Wesley Taylor, who was born when Connie Mack was about to turn 75 years old, worked his way through the minor leagues like an itinerant with stops at Daytona Beach, Fargo-Moorhead, Minot, Reading, Salt Lake City and Jacksonville before reaching St. Louis by way of Cleveland. He helped the Cardinals win the 1964 World Series as a relief pitcher, was traded to Houston a year later and was written off by the Astros a year and a half after that.

"They sent me a minor league contract for $10,000," Taylor remembered. "They promised me more if I made the team. I was going on 30 and had a bad back.

"The next spring, I was at Cocoa Beach for spring training and one day the phone rang. It was Bing Devine, my old boss in St. Louis, who now was running the New York Mets. 'How do you feel?' he asked. And I said, 'Great. Buy me.'

"He did buy me—for Jacksonville. Ten thousand dollars, and fifteen if I made the team. And the Mets were a last-place team. But I couldn't give up on myself. I needed that one more year, that fifth year in the big leagues, to qualify for my *pension*."

Taylor, who already had a degree in electrical engineering, gave his baseball career one more shot. Two years later, he was making twice the money, the Mets won the pennant and World Series and he collected $18,338 as his winning share.

Now, Taylor doesn't exactly need the pension. He went to medical school in his 30s, spent some of his baseball money for a new career as a doctor and eventually became the team physician of the Toronto Blue Jays.

"Kipling said your life is determined by the flip of a coin," he reflected. "That was *my* flip of the coin."

Baseball can be all things to all people. A job, a career, a life's work, an opportunity or an expense. Maybe a pension. Probably a flip of the coin. It is also a business, and some people think it is a big business. It is stadiums and bond issues to some cities, and political issues to others, and grievances to some players and fortunes to others.

But it is essentially an *image*—a man with a ball and a man with a bat. Whatever else it is depends on the magic and the mystery of that image, and of that moment when the man with the ball faces the man with the bat. And the moment has rarely been captured so tellingly as it was by an editorial writer on the St. Louis Post-Dispatch after the death of a famous American on August 16, 1948. He didn't use the famous American's name in the editorial, but he certainly caught the image:

BAMBINO

There he stood, a great tall inverted pyramid at the plate. At the top were two of the broadest, most powerful shoulders the bleachers had ever seen. His slender legs hugged each other and his feet came together like the dot of an exclamation point. He was not fussy. No nervous swinging of the bat. No uneasy kicking of his shoes. No bending over. No straightening up. Just a deliberate getting set. Maybe a little motion at the wrists—that and a death watch on the man on the mound.

Then the first pitch. Low and outside. Everybody tense except the inverted pyramid. Another pitch—low and away. Were they going to walk him? With two on and the winning run at bat, a walk was the play.

Then a third pitch. The pyramid gathers himself, steps into the ball and swings—all in one motion. Before the crack of the blow reaches ears in the stands, the ball is lofting away on wings. It rises right of second, arches higher and higher over right field and drops into a sea of upraised hands for another home run. The Babe is jogging around the bags, two runs scoring ahead of him.

Another game won for the New York Yankees, another game nearer the American League pennant and still another World Series. Jogging on, around second, up to third as the din rises, now spikes down on the plate and home again—home for all time.